TEXAS
LOUD, PROUD, AND BRASH

TEXAS
LOUD, PROUD, AND BRASH

HOW TEN MAVERICKS CREATED THE TWENTIETH-CENTURY LONE STAR STATE

RUSTY WILLIAMS

TWODOT®

ESSEX, CONNECTICUT
HELENA, MONTANA

A · TWODOT® · BOOK

An imprint of Globe Pequot, the trade division of
The Rowman & Littlefield Publishing Group, Inc.
4501 Forbes Blvd., Ste. 200
Lanham, MD 20706
www.rowman.com

Distributed by NATIONAL BOOK NETWORK

Cover image credits (clockwise, left to right): Tom Hickman (UTSA Special Collections); Babe Didrikson Zaharias (AP Images); Boyce House (Courtesy, Fort Worth Star-Telegram Collection, Special Collections, The University of Texas at Arlington Libraries); Sam Baugh (Photo courtesy of Southwest Collection/Special Collections Library, Texas Tech University, Lubbock, Texas. Institutional Research and Information Management collection - box 7 folder 18, U 278.1.); Glenn McCarthy (MSS-0067–658, Houston Public Library); Enid Justin (Fang family San Francisco Examiner Photograph Archive Negative Files, BANC PIC 2006.029—NEG box 668c, sleeve 095355DD_05, © The Regents of the University of California, The Bancroft Library, University of California, Berkeley)

British Library Cataloguing in Publication Information available

Library of Congress Cataloging-in-Publication Data

Names: Williams, Rusty, 1948- author.
Title: Texas loud, proud, and brash : how ten mavericks created the twentieth-century Lone Star State / Rusty Williams.
Description: Essex, Connecticut : TwoDot, [2023] | Includes bibliographical references.
Identifiers: LCCN 2023003342 (print) | LCCN 2023003343 (ebook) | ISBN 9781493064397 (paperback) | ISBN 9781493064403 (epub)
Subjects: LCSH: Texas—Biography. | LCGFT: Biographies.
Classification: LCC F385 .W57 2023 (print) | LCC F385 (ebook) | DDC 976.40630922—dc23/eng/20230327
LC record available at https://lccn.loc.gov/2023003342
LC ebook record available at https://lccn.loc.gov/2023003343

♾️™ The paper used in this publication meets the minimum requirements of American National Standard for Information Sciences—Permanence of Paper for Printed Library Materials, ANSI/NISO Z39.48-1992.

CONTENTS

Introduction: From Old Texas to New Texas vii

CHAPTER 1: Boyce House 1

CHAPTER 2: Tom Hickman 15

CHAPTER 3: Mildred "Babe" Didrikson 37

CHAPTER 4: Bob Thornton and Amon Carter. 57

CHAPTER 5: Sam Baugh. 81

CHAPTER 6: Stanley Marcus. 99

CHAPTER 7: Enid Justin 117

CHAPTER 8: Audie Murphy 135

CHAPTER 9: Glenn McCarthy. 151

Notes. 165

Bibliography 183

Index. 189

About the Author 195

INTRODUCTION

FROM OLD TEXAS TO NEW TEXAS

IN 1921, A YOUNG MAN FROM A PRIVILEGED DALLAS HOUSEHOLD WAS accepted for admission to Amherst College in Massachusetts. He arrived on campus with bespoke suits, custom Lewin shirts, and a selection of Sulka neckties, all chosen to fit in among classmates at a sophisticated Eastern school. Even so, the Texas boy was greeted as a curiosity by other freshmen on campus.

"My classmates had only the most vague idea where Texas was located and what life was like on the 'frontier,'" the young man recalled. "They were extremely disappointed when I told them my family was transported by automobile and not horses, that I had never been on a ranch, and had never seen a genuine cowboy or an Indian."

When it came to knowing about Texas, he said, "much the same state of ignorance characterized most Americans in the second decade of the twentieth century."[1]

In the 1920s you could ask any non-Texan to describe the Lone Star State, and you'd hear about cattle, cowboys, and cactus, all scattered over an endless prairie where simple folk lived in frontier towns, tied their horses to hitching posts, and strolled along board sidewalks to the general store. This was the Old Texas.

If you asked the same question in 1950, however, most non-Texans would describe a far different place: a Texas that was insufferably loud, unbearably proud, boastful, brash, and ready to throw down (with firearms, if need be). Texas retained its heritage of frontier tenacity and cowboy individuality, but by mid-twentieth century Texans were considered overconfident, overassertive, overdressed, football crazy, land crazy, oil rich, and too big for their own britches.

It's this less-than-complimentary impression of the Lone Star State that percolated into American popular culture and persists well into this century, and most Texans revel in it. The New Texas we recognize today burst forth in just twenty-five years, a mere ticktock on the time line of Texas history. But why? And why at that particular time?

Unfathomable oil riches discovered in Texas—particularly the 1917 West Texas oil booms around Eastland County—forced residents of the other forty-seven states to give the Lone Star State a second glance. Meanwhile, old-timers were beginning to tell their stories of early Texas, and those tales were beginning to make their way into print and into the hands of non-Texas readers. (Scholar J. Frank Dobie's *Legends of Texas* and *Folk Songs of the South* earned respectable reviews in such prestigious national magazines as *Saturday Review of Literature*.)[2]

The history of New Texas, the Texas we know today—loud, proud, and brash—begins in the 1920s, when a horned frog wakes from its thirty-one-year nap in a courthouse cornerstone and flabbergasts the nation. Over the following twenty-five years, ten cheeky Texans—with their words, actions, and accomplishments—came to define the New Texas of the twenty-first century.

What follows are the stories of those ten largely unsung men and women responsible for the Texas that outsiders love, hate, and (secretly) envy today.

First off, however, it's necessary to understand how Texans worship their history, folklore, and myths, and what happens when they get the three mixed up.

From the earliest times, myth and folklore have wafted through Texas's history like a cooling breeze off the Gulf of Mexico. The Texas creation stories, the determined frontiersmen, and the hearty cowboys are not so much a "history history" as a "myth history" that paints Texans as a people set apart, willing to fight and die for independence, and blessed with plenty of good land and the determination to make it productive.

Journalist-author John Steinbeck understood: "Texas has its own private history based on, but not limited by, facts."[3]

Texas's myth history was built from additions to and omissions from the full historical record (often for political expediency, propaganda, economic, or racial reasons). Some of it came from (or was reinforced by) non-Texans; some came from Texans who couldn't resist telling a good story.[4]

For example, the story that the earliest colonists declared their independence from Mexico in 1835 due to a burning desire for freedom from oppression overlooks the fact that much of the dispute between Mexico and its colonists involved the importation of slaves, which the Mexican constitution prohibited, and the payment of export taxes, which Mexico required. The last stand at the Alamo makes a stirring story of determined patriotism, but defense of the Alamo was contrary to the orders of General Sam Houston, who could've made better use of the troops than martyrdom in a foreordained massacre.[5]

The Republic of Texas is remembered as a proud, independent nation. For the ten years of its existence, however, it was wading in quicksand, unable to protect its own borders and citizens, and teetering on the brink of bankruptcy. Texas joined the Confederate states in 1861 not as an act of regional unity but largely to maintain slavery, according to the state legislature in its own "Declaration of Causes."[6]

Texas resisted invasion by federal troops during the Civil War and suffered only minimal battle damage. The state paid mightily for seceding, however. Along with the ten other Confederate states, Texas endured years of federal occupation, economic and social upheaval, political turmoil, and lawlessness before readmission to the United States.

The mythmaking continued after the Civil War as Texas began shedding its "Southernness." While the severely damaged states of the South rebuilt after the Civil War, an unscathed Texas was building new settlements, towns, courthouses, banks, schools, gins, sawmills, and gristmills. Texas's agricultural economy thrived. Galveston, San Antonio, Houston, Dallas, and Jefferson were becoming urban centers for banking, trade, and manufacturing. New settlers, many from other Southern states, flooded Texas, drawn by the promise of a fresh start and huge plots of new land. Foreign immigrants—Germans, French, Czechs, Irish, and others—arrived by the boatload. Rail lines were beginning to knit a network across the state.

Livestock production also served to boost the economy. The first large-scale cattle drives from Texas northward to rail connections began in 1866, with two hundred thousand head of scraggly, free-range long-horn cattle. In 1871 alone, cowboys drove almost a million cattle north over well-worn trails for shipment to the East.

Texans pushed westward into the frontier lands, anxious to nurture their livestock or till their acreage. But the frontier was still a dangerous place, where civilization pushed back against savagery. "Wild barbarians infested Texas," one resident wrote, "its frontiers subject to all the horrors of savage warfare." Armed and mounted Comanche Indians were a danger to settlers on the western plains of the state, despite the efforts of Texas Rangers and federal troops. A major hunt-and-destroy campaign by U.S. troops in 1874 marked a first step in the eventual removal of the plains Indians from the frontier.[7]

Initially, it fell to others to propagate the Texas myth history. Even before the first Indian was marched off to the reservation and the first large cattle drive crossed the Red River, non-Texans were describing and defining the Lone Star State as "The New American Frontier."

Texas was still a "faraway" state in 1900, a great distance south of the ten largest U.S. cities of the time. It was too big and too distant, perhaps, for many of the Eastern writers, editors, authors, and speakers to fully explore and understand it. At first, they could describe the state only by its numbers. "Its length is one-half that of our country from north to south," one writer told his readers. "Its width is equal to one-third the distance across the widest part of the country. Texas has an area of 265,780 square miles, or about one-twelfth that of the entire United States."[8]

But those outsiders who visited the Lone Star State recognized Texas as a unique place and Texans as distinctive people. "No other section of the United States is advancing so rapidly in population, agriculture, railroad construction, and maritime commerce," wrote columnist Charles

H. Harvey in *Munsey's Magazine*. "[Texas] will be the Empire State of the Future."

A noted social science professor used the healthy physique of Texans to illustrate his point about the benefits of some racial characteristics. "Texans have become proverbial for stature," he said at the annual meeting of his professional group. "To the wilderness go—not the brainiest, noblest, or highest bred—but certainly the strongest and most enterprising." In other words: big and successful.[9]

Georgia native Lee C. Harby set out across the state in 1890 to describe "Texan Types and Contrasts" to readers of *Harper's* magazine. She found the true character of Texas on the frontier: "specimens of those strong, brave early settlers who live literally with their lives in their hands, establishing themselves far beyond the outposts of civilization."[10]

And cowboys: Mrs. Harby discovered the cowboy "on the vast grazing grounds of the West" and wrote adoringly of his taciturn masculinity. "He is ever a picturesque figure whether in groups or dismounted and standing alone on the great prairie. His Winchester and lariat are slung from the pommel of his saddle." Her cowboys are "fearless," "generous," and "exceedingly chivalrous to all women."

Other visitors to Texas discovered the literary possibilities of the hardy pioneers and the solitary riders of the range. William Sidney Porter—better known as O. Henry—lived in the Lone Star State for fourteen years, coming to know the wry young ranch hands, beribboned women, and dogged law enforcers who would populate many of his stories. *Heart of the West*, his collection of fourteen mostly Texas short stories, became a national best seller. "The stories provide crisply focused little snapshots of Texas in the 1880s taken by someone who was there," a critic wrote. Dime novel and pulp magazine publishers adopted the frontier—often the Texas frontier—and found eager audiences for their stories.[11]

It wasn't only magazines and books portraying frontier Texas at the turn of the twentieth century. Cowboys, settlers, and the loneliness of the open prairies were fertile subjects for playwrights and songsmiths. One of the most popular stage plays of the 1890s was *A Texas Steer*, a farce by Charles Hoyt. The play's hero is Maverick Brander, a Texas cattle king with the best of intentions who is elected to Congress. "'Home on the Range' is almost more a hymn than a song," writes Texas history author Stephen Harrigan. "It's a great song, even a candidate for the greatest American song." "My Heart's Tonight in Texas (By the Silvery Rio Grande)" was a hit song in music halls and vaudeville houses in the 1900s, just one of scores of Texas-themed songs from that decade alone.[12]

"Texans have two pasts—one made in Texas, one made in Hollywood," writes author Don Graham in *Cowboys and Cadillacs: How Hollywood Looks at Texas*. It is likely that more people in the world have seen movies about Texas than have seen or read about the state. That would certainly be true during the first three decades of the twentieth century.[13]

From the earliest days of fictional narratives on film, moviemakers embraced the settler, the cowboy, and the rugged scenery of Texas to tell their stories. Often ignoring historical reality and a realistic landscape, early movies about Texas placed ordinary melodramas beneath a Texas-themed proscenium, implying that the story was set in a unique place and about a distinctive people. Moviegoers watched the same stock characters—the good cowboy, his sweetheart, livestock rustlers, murderous Indians, cattle, and plenty of horses—in not-actually-in-Texas settings in movie after movie after movie about Texas and the West.[14]

Non-Texans—the article writers, storytellers, playwrights, songwriters, and moviemakers—defined Texas to the rest of the country during the decades surrounding the turn of the twentieth century. These non-Texans discovered the Texas cowboy and made of him the archetypical Westerner: hard working, individualistic, self-reliant, fair minded, and restless. In their stories, songs, and movies, the out-of-staters painted Texas's history and frontier days with the mythology of America's westward movement: discovery, exploration, brutal hardship, dominion over the landscape and all that dwelled there, and eventual peaceful settlement.

Soon it was Texans' turn to tell their own versions of the early days.

Texas was booming in the final decades of the nineteenth century, its people driven by a shared recall of providential successes. As the nineteenth century flowed into the twentieth, Texans were shrugging off the collapse of the Confederate nation, the odium of federal occupation, and the restraints of Reconstruction. They began to downplay their Southern roots and fashion for themselves a uniquely Texan persona, a version of the myth history that would come to be known as "Texas exceptionalism."[15]

Most academics describe Texas exceptionalism as a perception that Texas differs from other states because of its unique origins, historical evolution, and individualistic people. The early Texans—Anglo farmers and businesspeople—carved out a productive community within a harsh province of Mexico, fought a war for independence against an oppressive Mexican regime, shed blood in the heroic defense of the Alamo, defeated the Mexican army at San Jacinto, and formed a republic that earned recognition by major foreign powers. "This history fostered a people who considered themselves capable of doing anything," according to John E. Dean in his *How Myth Became History*. Latter-day Texans began to consider themselves "an exceptional population imbued with a fierce sense of nationalism and local pride," a people destined for progress and triumph. This self-confidence allowed nineteenth-century Texans to push back a hostile Indian population, cultivate millions of acres of highly productive farmland, feed the nation with its livestock, and build large cities and efficient centers of commerce.

Lone Star humorist Boyce House said, "A man with ten acres of cotton is too busy to write poetry." Texas had packed a lot of history into the seventy-five years following the Alamo, and Texans themselves had had little time to contemplate it or talk about it.

As they aged into the new century, the old settlers began to look back at all that had been accomplished, so much of it hard won. At informal gatherings, aging pioneers would tell how their instinct, nerve, and luck had served them while navigating Texas's natural and historical hazards. Some credited the hand of Providence; others became the heroes of their own stories.

The Texas Folklore Society, chartered in 1909, began to collect, preserve, and publish these tall tales, along with Texas customs, traditions, and songs. With *The Cow Country* and some of his later works, J. Frank Dobie massaged those folk tales and diaries into a half dozen popular books about Old Texas. Other Lone Star writers wove the Old Texas stories into their novels. Philip Stevenson's *The Edge of the Nest* and Dorothy Scarborough's *The Wind* found national audiences in the late 1920s.

(Hollywood snatched up rights to *The Wind* for a major motion picture starring Lillian Gish.)

"No one reading the reviews for the last few years can have failed to be impressed by the passion for Western Americana which has possessed eastern publishing houses," wrote book editor Carey MacWilliams in the *Saturday Review of Literature* in 1930. "Texas really led the way in the development of a regional point of view."[16]

In the main, this "regional point of view" was still a vision of Old Texas: six-shooters, bonnets, cattle stampedes, marauding Indians, and one-room schoolhouses. They were often tales of exceptional men and women who bent the land to their own purposes by clearing, building, fighting, and farming.

Myth making triumphed over history: little wonder that Amherst College classmates of the young man from Dallas "had only the most vague idea where Texas was located and what life was like on the 'frontier.'"

By the 1920s, Texas was long past its frontier history. San Antonio, Houston, Dallas, and Fort Worth were becoming major cities engaged in trade across the nation. Smaller towns boasted thriving commercial centers, good schools, parks, and recreation facilities. In 1920, for the first time, the U.S. Census reported that the state's population was more urban than rural.

Yet even as non-Texans still thought of the Lone Star State as a place of cattle, cowboys, and cactus; black gold was changing the character of the state, and a new type of Texan was stepping up to create a myth history more suited to modern times. Every Texan today contributes in some manner to the state's reputation as a place that's too loud, overly proud, and brash to a fault. But between 1925 and 1950, the ten Texans on the following pages introduced the New Texas to the rest of the country.

The ten mavericks include: a new breed of Texas lawman who uses a tommy gun, a windup phonograph, and a sense of humor to halt a border war. A store owner's son who turns the world's eyes to the natural beauty inherent in Texas women. The typist at a Dallas insurance company who becomes a national sensation overnight when she dons a tank top and a pair of running shorts. Two civic leaders whose bitter rivalry plays out in front of seven million Texas visitors.

The words, actions, and accomplishments of these individuals and others helped change the national perception of Texas during a particularly significant twenty-five years. The quarter century from 1925 to 1950 saw the birth of America's era of mass communications. Demographic, economic, and political changes were opening doors to new technologies, new means and methods of mass communication. The period was marked by huge increases in the number, spread, and circulation of newspapers. Commercial radio—banned by the U.S. government during WWI—was bringing news, music, and sports into living rooms across the country soon after the manufacture of radio receivers ramped up in the 1920s. Even as the Depression rocked the economy in the 1930s, motion pictures (along with the requisite newsreel and cartoon) drew ninety million people a week into theaters. Technical advances allowed mass circulation magazines to feature colorful images and vivid news photography on their pages.

These ten mavericks were in the right place and the right time to benefit from the new technologies and conditions, where words and images could be shared with vast swaths of the U.S. population simultaneously on paper, celluloid, or over the airwaves. The words, actions, and accomplishments of these ten were amplified by the new mass media, introducing to non-Texans a Lone Star State that was far more than the Alamo, cattle, cactus, and cowboys.

It all begins with a gawky, thirty-two-year-old, small-town West Texas newspaper editor who hears a rumor about a bizarre Texas creature.

CHAPTER I

BOYCE HOUSE

THE RESURRECTED TEXAS HORNED FROG

THERE'S AN OLD POEM OF UNCERTAIN ORIGIN CALLED "HELL IN TEXAS," widely circulated when a saloon owner in San Antonio printed hundreds of thousands of copies and gave them away to visitors in the late nineteenth century. The poem describes how the Devil was given title to the land just north of the Rio Grande and commenced turning it into Hell.

> So the trade was closed and the deed was given
> And the Lord went back to his home in Heaven—
> And the Devil had everything he needed
> To make a good Hell, and sure succeeded.

The Devil turns this wasted land into an overflow Hell by sowing it with rattlesnakes, scorpions, ants, mosquitoes, and other noxious critters.

> He tied up thorns on all of the trees,
> And mixed the sand with millions of fleas;
> He scattered tarantulas over the roads,
> Put needles on cactus and horns on toads.

On September 20, 1928, hundreds of newspaper front pages across the country featured a story with some variation of this headline: "Texas Horned Frog Found Alive!" The story of Old Rip, the resurrected horned frog from West Texas, gave the rest of the world a glimmer of the strangeness of Texas and the pride of Texans, with a little bit of science thrown into the mix. During a decade of flagpole sitters, marathon dances, and bunion derbies, Old Rip became a national sensation, eventually traveling to the White House for an audience with President Coolidge and proving the legend that, in Texas anyway, there really were toads with horns.[1]

The man who documented Old Rip's life—and who some say invented him—was Boyce House, a gangly thirty-two-year-old newspaper editor in Eastland, Texas. In later years, Boyce House would become a syndicated columnist, best-selling author, radio personality, and sought-after speaker on all topics Texas. *Life* magazine called him "Texas's number one booster." *Saturday Evening Post* named him "Mr. Texas." The *New York Times* referred to him as "the world's leading authority on Texas humor."

Boyce House was a man whose words—written and spoken—would bring Texas to the rest of the nation. And he wasn't even a native Texan.

Boyce didn't lay an eye on Texas until he was ten years old. He was born in 1896 in an out-of-the-way farming and timbering town in a far corner of Arkansas.

At the time of Boyce's birth, his father was attempting to start a newspaper but couldn't make a living with it. That came as no surprise to his wife or in-laws. Boyce's father could sweet-talk water out of a well, but he had trouble holding onto the bucket. He was a dabbler at professional jobs, and it was becoming apparent to both him and his wife that he was, as gossipy in-laws termed it, an "inconsistent provider."[2]

The House family's financial uncertainties were exacerbated by Boyce's poor health; while still a toddler he contracted a chronic, life-threatening bronchial disease that gave recurring shortness of breath and fevers, a whistling sound with every breath, and blood in his sputum. At the time there were a few home remedies but no cure. Symptoms could recur time and again into adulthood.

Boyce's attendance at school was erratic due to the recurring illness, but he was diligent about completing any lesson the school superintendent sent home for him. And he was a voracious reader. Library books, passed-along magazines, seed catalogs—he devoured them all. Unable to participate in the neighborhood play or ball games, Boyce was often the designated scorekeeper, sitting in the stands and recording every play.

Despite the domestic uncertainty, Boyce was a likable, cheerful, and *very* well-read kid. Unfortunately, most youngsters with his medical condition didn't live to see their teens. In January 1906, his father desperate for another new start and his mother hoping that a change to a drier climate might prolong her son's life, Boyce's family boarded a train for Brownwood, Texas.

Boyce seemed to thrive in the drier Texas climate, but the House family grocery store in Brownwood faltered and failed in its first six months.[3]

For Boyce's mother, it was the last straw. She and Boyce's two sisters left Brownwood to stay with her family in Mississippi while Boyce's father traded what was left of the grocery store inventory for a covered wagon and two horses. The out-of-luck father and his ten-year-old son would travel across Texas, looking for work and living out of the wagon bed.[4]

Boyce usually drove the wagon to wherever they might find work or a load to haul while his father slept in back. For most of a year their horses plodded through much of South, Central, and West Texas, once as far as El Paso and a corner of New Mexico. The ten-year-old boy fell in love with Texas from the wagon bench. He was captivated by the strange plants and animals, the limitless horizons, the drastic weather changes, and the speech of the locals.

Somehow father and son found enough work to feed themselves and the horses. Boyce flourished while living outdoors. His breathing problems disappeared, he became tanned and fit, and he grew confident dealing with adults in his father's stead. Boyce's father, on the other hand, grew sicklier and less connected every day. He lay on bedding in the back of the wagon, occasionally seized with a fit of deep, watery coughing followed by hours of shortness of breath. Each night Boyce would be the one to gather firewood, build the campfire, slice the bacon, prepare the potatoes, onions, and coffee, and afterward clean the tin plates and the steel knives and forks.

His father was dying, but Boyce kept the wagon rolling: New Braunfels, San Marcos, up crowded Congress Avenue in Austin, Round Rock, and finally to Taylor, where his father's spirit left the wagon, and their travel together ended.[5]

In January 1908 Boyce buried his father, sold the livestock and wagon, and bought a train ticket to join his mother and sisters in Mississippi.

Boyce wouldn't return to Texas for twelve years. He and his sisters moved to Memphis when his mother found work there. Boyce tested well enough to enter the local high school with youngsters his age. On graduating, he was confronted with the necessity of earning his own way. "Since I was not strong enough for manual labor and not trained for any particular calling," Boyce wrote, "I decided to turn to newspaper work."[6]

Boyce talked his way into a job as cub reporter on the *Memphis Commercial Appeal*. Obituaries, boat landings, hotel arrivals, and other miscellaneous editorial debris were the province of the newspaper cub reporter. Boyce was more than diligent, he was prolific (once he learned to type), writing clear, clean two-paragraph stories. He became known in the newsroom as "a good hand," the ultimate compliment from an editor.[7]

In time, he was assigned to cover the Memphis police beat. The young man saw the city's dark underside for the first time—the beatings, stabbings, murders, and lesser human tragedies—and became a friend of the burly beat cops when he overlooked their petty graft. "I was nineteen, stood five feet, ten inches, but weighed only a few pounds above a hundred," he recalled.

After four years at the newspaper, Boyce's health deserted him. His boyhood bronchial infection returned, leaving him gasping for breath and choking on his sputum. He couldn't work, and a physician advised that he should leave the region—the ground was too damp, the air too humid. You need a dry climate, the grim doctor insisted.

So, twenty-three-year-old Boyce House quit his job, bought a ticket, and boarded a train for his return to Texas.

Boyce arrived in Eastland in 1921, thin as a fiddle string and looking like death warmed over. Eastland's *Daily Oil Belt News* was the county's largest newspaper in a town that was popping like water on a hot skillet. Four years earlier, on October 17, 1917, a local wildcatter's throw-of-the-dice oil well in Eastland County blew in from 3,431 feet below ground, setting off an oil boom bigger than any that Texas—or the world, for that matter—had ever seen. Overnight, the sleepy little town of Ranger, population five hundred in 1915, became a city of thirty thousand. Nearby Ranger and the surrounding area were spiked with tall wooden derricks. At night, the countryside for miles around was illuminated by gas flares more numerous and far brighter than the stars in the sky. Every three days a million dollars' worth of liquid gold flowed from the gushers.[8]

The first major oil discovery in the United States outside Pennsylvania was in 1901 with a well named Spindletop near the Gulf Coast of Texas. Oil and petroleum products were replacing whale oil for lighting and used increasingly for mechanical lubrication. Overextraction and limited demand soon caused the Gulf Coast oilfields to become less profitable.

By the time of the West Texas oil discoveries in 1917, the United States needed vast amounts of oil for automobiles, heating, lighting, construction equipment, and war machines. With Eastland County at the center, the West Texas oil finds quickly produced more wealth than the California Gold Rush and the Colorado silver mines combined.

Though no one knew it at the time (and technology didn't exist then to extract oil from the deep pools if they had), West Texas sat atop a vast ocean of oil that's still producing today. Eastland County sits at the far eastern edge—the shallow edge—of the Permian Basin. Some oil was so close to the surface there, Boyce wrote with tongue in cheek, that some fields had to post signs saying, "Men with Peglegs Keep Out!"

The town of Eastland, the county seat and home of the *Daily Oil Belt News*, was doing—literally—a land-office business at the courthouse as landmen arrived to file claims, successful wildcatters formed oil production companies, and attorneys came to litigate real estate and royalty contracts. Eastland's hotels were awash with promoters, speculators, equipment salesmen, the newly rich, bootleggers, gamblers, and the party girls who entertained them all. Cafés and lunch counters sprang up, some operating beneath canvas tents when downtown real estate couldn't keep up with the demand.

As editor of the *Daily Oil Belt News*, Boyce was feeding on the most sumptuous buffet of stories a newsman could imagine. He enjoyed the process of collecting news, and he was practiced at churning out stories—lots of stories—as fast as the linotype operator could set them. He worked eighteen hours a day, six days a week. The young man who had come to Texas for his health was soon having the time of his life.[9]

He came to Eastland determined to write about the romance of oil and would eventually write three books and dozens of magazine articles about Texas oilmen and oil boomtowns. Boyce had ample opportunity to discover the greed, anger, fear, blood, murder, and all the strange things men do when made delirious by the smell of the golden grease. (In 1939, MGM Studios hired Boyce as script and technical adviser for the movie *Boom Town*, with Clark Gable and Spencer Tracy. Old-time oil men would say that the opening scenes of the movie provided the best re-creation of a frantic boomtown of any movie ever made.[10]

In Eastland, the young newspaperman wrote stories of Cinderella-like changes in fortune—thrifty farmers who suddenly earned thousands of dollars a month in oil royalties. And there was the unemployed schoolteacher who, when told he'd be charged twenty-five cents for a glass of milk at a café, stalked out, promising to start his own dairy. True to his word, the teacher bought some cows and brought them to town, where he was offered such a large profit that he sold the herd. With the proceeds he went into the oil business and made a fortune.[11]

Not all gushers brought happiness, especially when the gusher behaved unexpectedly. Once, a well came in with a big flow, and a local man who had a percentage quit his job and went out on the town to celebrate. When he sobered up, he found that the flow had stopped. Even when fitted with a pump, the well would produce only a dollar or two a day. The man was forced to ask his boss for his old job back, and he spent the rest of the boom times at manual labor.[12]

Boyce gave every story its own bit of such poignancy, drama, or humor such that his writing earned a reputation not only in Eastland

County, but with editors of newspapers across the region. Two stories, in particular, captured an audience far beyond the borders of Texas.

Friday morning, December 23, 1927, the sidewalks of the Eastland County town of Cisco were crowded with decorations, smiling adults, and squealing children. A tall Santa Claus, wearing a smiling mask and a lumpy fur-trimmed red coat, strolled down Main Street toward the center of town. Children ran to the familiar figure in the red suit and bearded mask to tell him their last-minute Christmas wishes.[13]

Santa peeled the clinging children off him as he walked into the lobby of Cisco's First National Bank. Unnoticed, three men in civilian clothing followed him. Once inside, Santa and his three helpers went into action, pulling pistols, commanding customers to put up their hands. Then they turned their weapons to the head cashier. Santa pulled a sack from under his costume and ordered the cashier to open the safe.

One customer managed to slip out a back door and run down an alley to the nearby police station shouting, "Help! The bank is being held up." With their bag full of cash and bonds, Santa rounded up the bank customers (including two girls, ages ten and twelve, who had followed him into the bank) and herded them toward the alley door as human shields.

Meanwhile, alerted by the escaped customer's shouts and the sound of gunfire, everyone nearby who had a gun (and that was most every man and a few women) dropped their packages and drew their sidearms. Cisco's history as a rough-and-tumble boomtown was not far in the past; many citizens still carried weapons on their persons or in their autos and weren't shy about using them to maintain law and order. Several of the human shields were able to break away or simply sit down and refuse to move. Santa Claus picked up the two girls, one under each arm, and with his three elves ran to a getaway car, trading shots with additional law enforcement, a hardware merchant, a printer, and at least a dozen others.

As the bandits roared away down Main Street, they were ripped by gunfire. More than two hundred shots had been fired in just a few short minutes, six citizens lay wounded, and two fatally injured lawmen were bleeding out in the alley. The robbers still held the two little girls as hostages. Townspeople rushed to their cars to follow the bandits.

The bank robbers weren't making much of a getaway. Santa and his three elves were all suffering bullet wounds; one elf had a head wound that was obviously mortal. Worse still, the getaway car was almost out of gas. (The robbers had neglected to fill it before the robbery.) They tried to hijack another car, but the driver ran away with the ignition key. Losing a few minutes trying to start the car and hearing gunshots from the cars pursuing them, they moved back to the original auto, leaving the dying elf behind. In their rush, they also left the bag of loot—$12,000 cash and $15,000 in bonds. Santa Claus, his two remaining helpers, and the two little girls raced out of town in a crippled car just ahead of the civilian posse.[14]

Someone in Cisco phoned the county sheriff's office in Eastland about the robbery and wild escape. Sheriff John Hart and his deputies piled into cars and sped toward Cisco, hoping to cut off the bandits. Alerted by the sheriff, Boyce dictated a hurried bulletin to the Associated Press office in Dallas, then drove off after the sheriff.

The three remaining robbers drove their car deep into a thicket of cactus, mesquite, and scrub oak. There they abandoned the auto, and the two girls and ran until the thicket swallowed them up.

The manhunt continued into Friday night, through Christmas Day, and into the following week. Hungry, tired, and wounded, the Santa Claus Bank Robbers (as they became known) dodged the posses that chased them on foot, with bloodhounds, on horseback, and in autos. Two Texas Rangers, Captain Tom Hickman and "Lone Wolf" Gonzaullas, arrived in town, commandeered an airplane, and searched from the air.

Boyce followed the pursuit over the fields, hills, and canyons all week, writing his stories by hand, sending them back to his Eastland office to be distributed nationally on the newswire, and always hoping to score an interview with Santa Claus himself. Editors across the country sent telegraphs, asking for more copy about the robbers and the manhunt.

The brutal shootout, the cruelty of taking two little girls hostage, the running gun battle on Cisco's streets, the dogged pursuit through Texas scrubland, and the sheer effrontery of dressing as Santa Claus to commit this deadly crime filled front pages every day for a week. Boyce's newspaper coverage primed the rest of the nation for another gang of killer bandits six years later when Bonnie and Clyde swept over the landscape of Texas and the Midwest.[15]

The three robbers, wounded and beaten by their time on the run, were captured alive fewer than fifteen miles from the site of their crime. One was sentenced to die in the electric chair; another was given life in prison. Boyce never got his chance to interview Santa Claus; the robber who had worn the Santa suit eventually was dragged from the Eastland County jail and lynched from a telephone pole by furious citizens.

A century later, the Santa Claus Bank Robbery is still remembered and reenacted. It is the subject of musical plays and books, and Boyce House is the reporter most often credited with telling the story to Texas and the nation.[16]

A routine conversation with an old-timer gave Boyce the story of his career, a feature story that was recognized by newsroom professionals as the biggest feature story of the year. It began as he was gathering information about a new county courthouse planned for Eastland.

Sometime in early 1928, Boyce was chatting with Ernest Wood, a courthouse regular. "Did you ever hear of the West Texas tradition that a horned frog can live a hundred years without food or water?" Wood asked. "Well, we'll soon know whether the tradition is true."[17]

Ernest Wood went on to tell Boyce how, in 1897, he and his son managed to slip a Texas horned frog into the cornerstone of the old Eastland courthouse, along with the various documents, newspapers, and Bible intended to be there. The stone was sealed with a tin cap to keep the contents safe, and the cornerstone was mortared onto the foundation.

Thirty-one years later that courthouse was proving too small for the increasing judicial needs of Eastland County, and it was condemned to make way for a larger building. Demolition would begin in a few days. In less than a month, Wood, Boyce, Eastland County residents, and (as it turned out) the rest of the world would learn whether a Texas horned frog could indeed hibernate for thirty-one years.

The Texas horned frog is more lizard than frog. In the twentieth century, this harmless little creature could be found by the thousands in the more arid parts of Texas and by the dozens in many urban gardens, but it is much rarer today. The lizard wears spiky horns on its head and can spit foul blood from its eyes, both characteristics used as a last-ditch defense against predators, though it mostly prefers to flatten itself out to about the shape and color of a chocolate chip cookie and play possum. Since Texas's settlement, youngsters have found the horned frog to be an ideal pet. It is docile, easily handled, and loves to be scratched.[18]

Boyce's "does-the-frog-still-live?" story appeared in the *Eastland Telegraph*, and he made sure the story went out on the newswires. The uncommon combination of uncanny creature and West Texas folklore was considered especially newsworthy, and his story earned headlines nationwide. "Hundreds of letters and clippings of stories which have been received in Eastland are conclusive proof that the story has been widely circulated," one newspaper reported.[19]

Some editors treated the story with a chuckle. Other newspapers, such as the *Washington* (DC) *Evening Star*, surveyed scientists for the likelihood of the frog's survival, finding that few thought it was possible. A geology instructor and student of reptile life at Southern Methodist University, on the other hand, declared that it could happen.[20]

"Thus, all and sundry—including the scientists—were placed on notice," Boyce said. "When destruction of the courthouse got underway, dispatches were sent out, telling of the progress toward the cornerstone."[21]

The cornerstone opening ceremony would be held shortly before noon on February 17, 1928, and Boyce was becoming increasingly nervous. He was "not wishing to face the gibes of my friends in the crowd for all the ballyhoo our paper had given."[22]

On the morning of the cornerstone opening, thousands of spectators packed Eastland's courthouse square. The crowd included reporters from around the state and wire service reporters. An eight-foot section of untouched courthouse wall—including the still-sealed cornerstone itself—stood upright amid the construction remains.[23]

By Boyce's later telling, three men—a pastor, an oil producer, and a county judge—stood by the cornerstone waiting for a worker to strike the final hammer blows that would expose the contents. When the worker finally freed the stone and lifted the tin lid, Reverend F. E. Singleton pointed his finger toward the still-hidden cavity and shouted, "There's the frog!" The crowd exploded with cheers, then quieted to learn whether the frog still lived.

Oilman Gene Day reached into the cavity, withdrew the gray, motionless horned toad, and displayed his body to the crowd. Cheers at first, then a disappointed groan at the apparently lifeless reptile.

Day handed the frog to Judge Ed S. Prichard, who grasped it by a hind leg and brought it near his face for a closer inspection. At that moment, the frog's other back leg began to twitch, then all legs wriggled, and its body swelled with a gasp of air.

The cheers of the crowd were deafening. Spectators rushed toward the frog and might have crushed it, Boyce said, except for a city motorcycle officer who pushed through the crowd, grabbed the horned toad, placed it in a small box he happened to be carrying, and roared off on his cycle to the edge of town.

The horned frog—dubbed "Old Rip," after the Dutchman who slept for twenty years—spent his first few days of liberation in a drugstore show window while more than twenty thousand people filed past him for a close look.

Within hours of opening the cornerstone, citizens of Eastland and their hibernating horned frog were front-page news in newspapers from coast to coast. New York: "Toad Alive after 31 Years in Texas Cornerstone." Chicago: "Buried Thirty Years." Los Angeles: "Thirty-Year Toad Siesta Supported."[24]

Suddenly, everyone wanted to see a Texas horned toad. Eastland welcomed visitors and tourists in numbers not seen since the height of the boom years; zoos fortunate enough to have a horned frog on display reported thousands of visitors. The curator of the Philadelphia Zoo sent urgent telegrams to every source he knew in Texas trying to secure specimens; a Texas promoter responded with an offer for twenty-five authentic Texas horned toads for five dollars each, and the Philly zookeeper was happy to pay the price.[25]

Marketers saw the value of the Old Rip brand, too. Within weeks, grocers were stocking Old Rip coffee ("Wake Up!"), and smokers were puffing on Old Rip cigarettes ("For the Rugged Smoker"). A candy manufacturer rushed out an Old Rip chocolate bar ("Look for the bar with the horned frog"). Advertising clip art included drawings of horned frogs and variations on the headline, "Don't Wait 31 Years for This Deal!" An entrepreneur in Coleman shipped horned toads by the hundreds to a metal plating company in Chicago. The frogs were bronzed like baby shoes, and the entrepreneur reported that he "found ready sales for hat pins, watch charms, and stick pins at good prices."[26]

Everyone wanted in on Old Rip's fame. Andrew J. Volstead, father of the Prohibition Act, was asked for his opinion. "Thirty-one years without a drink!" he exclaimed. "I think that toad should be heartily commended."[27]

After some debate, Eastland County authorities awarded custody of the miracle frog to Will Wood, the now-grown boy who had been playing with the frog when it was placed in the cornerstone thirty-one years before. Will kept Old Rip in a glass bowl in his home, trotting him out to show any eager tourist who might drop by. On warm days, Will placed the bowl outdoors near the kitchen door. He applied to an Eastland insurance company for a $100,000 life insurance policy on the frog.[28]

In May 1928, Will agreed to accompany a trade delegation from Eastland to Washington, DC, to lobby Texas Senator E. B. Mayfield for more water resource funding. The delegation would bring a horned toad for every senator; Will would bring Old Rip. During the visit to Mayfield's office, the senator became so enthusiastic about his famous reptile constituent that he phoned the White House. Within minutes, Will and Old Rip were out of the Capitol, into a taxi, and on their way to meet President Calvin Coolidge.[29]

A reporter accompanied Will and Old Rip into the president's office. "Mr. Wood took [the horned toad] out of the bowl and pointed out its various features with his hands," the reporter wrote. Old Rip and the president stared at one another for a full minute. "The president gave several gentle pokes with his eyeglasses, evidently to satisfy himself that the horned toad was actually alive." Silent Cal Coolidge said only, "Most extraordinary." The horned frog said nothing.[30]

No one was more surprised than Boyce about how his story had taken off. "The Eastland frog became the most famous animal since the serpent in the Garden of Eden," he said. "Mark Twain's renowned jumping frog became an also-ran. In newspaper space, Old Rip's total was exceeded only by Lindbergh for a like span of time."

Oil brought Eastland's first boom; a resurrected horned frog sparked another.

That summer, Eastland enjoyed a tourist season rivaling any in the town's history. Hundreds of families a day pulled off the state highway and came into the city, determined to see the nation's most famous horned frog. Some of the visitors ate in the diner, had their autos serviced at the gas station, shopped for Old Rip souvenirs in the stores, and stayed overnight at the tourist court. And every one of them would line up at the window of Foster's drugstore to see the famous Old Rip resting comfortably on a bed of leaves in his glass bowl.

But booms never last.

As the summer tourist season slacked off, Will Wood returned Old Rip and the glass bowl to his home, where the horned frog could bask in a particularly sunny spot on the Wood's back porch. On a January morning, just eleven months after Old Rip had left his cornerstone, Will Wood awoke to find that an unexpected Texas norther had swept through at night, frosting the windowpanes. Wood raced to the bowl on the back porch to find Old Rip frozen solid and irrecoverably dead.

Boyce learned of the tragedy that afternoon and prepared an obituary to run in the *Telegraph*: "Rip is dead. The body of the world-famous horned toad was found today, his head protruding above the carefully guarded leaves and sand in which he had been hibernating since his emergence from the cornerstone of the Eastland County courthouse months ago. Preparations were being made this morning for the body to lie in state at the Barrow Undertaking parlors in order that people who wish to see him again may view his body."[31]

The wire services picked up the news and spread it across the country. "There was no inquest after discovery of the body today," the *Washington Post* said in a solemn report on its front page. "Details concerning disposition of the body have not been announced."[32]

Other newspapers speculated on where Old Rip would be interred. "The owner of the *iguanidae* said today that at least three resting places have been suggested for the remains," the *Los Angeles Times* reported. Some thought Old Rip should spend his hereafter in Washington at the Smithsonian Institution; Texas Christian University, whose mascot was a horned frog, put in a bid.[33]

In the end, an Eastland mortuary embalmed Old Rip, and his remains were placed in a glass case in the new Eastland County courthouse, just a few feet from where he spent most of his long life. He is still there today, visited daily by schoolchildren and tourists.

Old Rip, the resurrected horned frog, remains the subject of occasional newspaper and magazine articles today. A few writers and readers suspect that Boyce pulled the old switcheroo, using sleight of hand to substitute a fresh-from-the-landscape horned frog for the powdery remains of the original. After all, they say, look at how the town benefited from all those visitors and all that publicity.

Boyce always denied it. With a twinkle and a sly grin, the young newspaperman would point out that several thousand eyewitnesses saw a preacher pull a live horned frog out of a sealed cornerstone. "Why, I've seen men go to the electric chair on less evidence than that."

The stories of Old Rip and the Santa Claus bank robbers might not have gained national currency a decade earlier. National newswires such as the Associated Press and United Press were affordable only to the larger metropolitan media. By the mid-1920s, many smaller daily newspapers could boast wire service tickers in their newsrooms.

In a full-page article, *Editor & Publisher*, the weekly news magazine of the journalism profession, recognized Boyce's coverage of the Old Rip story. "A young newspaperman in West Texas developed and put over the greatest feature news stories of 1928," the magazine wrote. "Boyce House of Eastland, Texas, is the man who started Rip, the Texas horned frog, on the road to fame."[34]

Every newspaper publisher in the country read the article and noted the name of the talented young editor from the jerkwater Texas oil town. Among those publishers was Amon G. Carter, a Fort Worth man determined to make his newspaper the largest daily in the Southwest.

CHAPTER 2

TOM HICKMAN

TEXAS RANGERS HOLD THE BRIDGE

THE RED RIVER IS A BORDER RIVER. FOR MUCH OF ITS 1,300-MILE length, the river flows east-southeast, marking the border between Texas and Oklahoma before turning southward, cutting off a corner of Arkansas on its way to the Mississippi.

Mostly, the river is a slow-moving, shallow stream with rivulets braided over the red clay streambed. At other times the river can become a mile-wide torrent.

News of Texas statehood spread quickly in 1846, attracting throngs of settlers eager to claim their share of the rich farmland south of the Red River. Many of the immigrants moving west took the Texas Road, a wagon route that crossed Indian Territory from its northeast corner near Joplin, Missouri, southwestward to the Red River. There, on the north riverbank, the settlers came to a disheartening halt before they could enter Texas.

Even when the flow is barely a trickle, the Red River is difficult to ford with wheeled or four-legged transport. The loose sand of the riverbed can sink a loaded wagon to the axles or break the legs of livestock caught in it. Immigrants could search up and down the riverbank for a better crossing (and there were few dependable ones) or wait for more water in hopes that they could float their wagons and swim the livestock across into Texas—a risky gamble.

Frank Colbert, an entrepreneurial citizen of the Chickasaw Nation, saw an opportunity. In 1850, Colbert asked the Chickasaw government and the Texas legislature for a franchise to build a toll ferry across the Red River. Both governments granted his exclusivity for three miles up and down the river.

Colbert's first ferry was a tippy wooden raft barely large enough to accommodate a single wagon and the men who poled the boat through the river's current. Soon he built larger ferry flatboats capable of carrying a fully loaded freight wagon and its harnessed team. By the mid-1870s, Colbert was ferrying as many as two hundred wagons a day across the Red River.[1]

Business was good, and the ferryman began planning to build a toll bridge. Once again, Colbert obtained exclusive franchises from the Chickasaw and Texas legislatures, and the U.S. Congress passed a bill granting him the right to build "a transit or wagon bridge" over the Red River. The law also made it unlawful "for any person or persons to construct a bridge or to establish a ferry over Red River within three miles of the present location of Colbert's Ferry."[2]

Colbert's bridge didn't last long, broken and swept away by a powerful flood. The second bridge met the same fate. And the third. Unable to afford to continue building (and losing) bridges, he chartered a corporation—the Red River Bridge Company—and invited some of the area's most influential businessmen as investors.[3]

By 1891, bridge-building technology was beginning to catch up with the challenges of the Red River. In 1890, the new bridge company began construction of a $50,000 iron-and-steel wagon bridge. Flooding delayed construction, but the new(est) wagon bridge opened in September 1891.[4]

Within a month, more than 250 paying customers were crossing the company's bridge every day: caravans of manufactured goods moving from Denison north to Durant and into the increasingly populous Indian Territory; wagons full of household goods; carts packed with crates of fresh produce, milk, or eggs; carriages of well-dressed families out for excursions; buggies and pushcarts; livestock and lone riders. It was the busiest crossing point on the Red River, and everyone who traversed it paid a toll to Colbert's Red River Bridge Company.

In 1913 the Red River Bridge Company announced plans to build a wider, stronger bridge to replace the older one. This time, the company would build its new toll bridge for the modern motor coaches and motor carriages.[5]

Toll bridges spanning intrastate and interstate waterways played an important role in the development of Texas and Oklahoma. Entrepreneurs such as Frank Colbert risked their own money to build ferries and bridges, recouping their investment through the collection of tolls. The system worked well when little public money was available to invest in highway infrastructure.

Through the 1920s, as the public began to press for better roads, the states and the federal government increasingly funded the construction of roads and bridges that were free for all to use. Why, motorists asked, should I have to stop my trip along a free roadway and pay the toll taker for a service my state should be supplying? The highway departments of Texas and the new state of Oklahoma began buying up old toll bridges (or bypassing them) to build modern new free bridges.

In 1929, Texas and Oklahoma passed legislation allowing them to build free bridges across the Red River connecting the two states. The chairman of the Texas Highway Commission, Ross S. Sterling, announced that the first free bridge would be built at the site of the old Colbert's Ferry crossing, just a half mile upstream from the Red River Bridge Company's toll bridge.

The Red River Bridge Company was not about to see its profitable bridge become worthless, bypassed by a new free bridge. Months of angry negotiations, lawsuits, and secret meetings between the Texas Highway Commission and the Red River Bridge Company failed to reach an agreement, even as construction began on the free bridge. In the autumn of 1930, however, the bridge company quietly withdrew its lawsuits and claims, and bridge construction continued unhindered.

Almost simultaneously, Ross Sterling announced his candidacy for governor of Texas. His platform rested on his success at bringing free roads and bridges to the citizens of Texas.

With an election victory in his pocket, Sterling was inaugurated governor in January 1931, even as the steel girders of the free bridge were being erected. When the highway department announced that the bridge would open on July 4, North Texans and southern Oklahomans were ecstatic. Lower crop prices, bank failures, padlocked businesses, vanishing jobs, and other effects of the Depression had begun to hammer the area. "No longer will the citizen of the Sooner State be required to dig deep into his pocket before he will be allowed to pay a friendly call to his neighbor on the Texas side," the local newspaper exulted. "No longer will it be necessary for the friendly Texan to halt himself and his flivver when he reaches the shores of this beloved and historic old river."[6]

Area communities planned a July 4 celebration to coincide with the opening of the new bridge. Suddenly, all planning came to a halt. A federal judge in Houston had issued a restraining order against Governor Sterling and the state of Texas, prohibiting them from opening the bridge until a hearing could be held. The judge was holding Governor Sterling personally responsible for keeping the bridge closed. Nine days before the scheduled opening, the community was forced to cancel its celebration—caravans, christening, speeches, the terrapin race, watermelon park, and street dance.

Newspapers quickly discovered that Sterling, when chairman of the state highway department, entered into a secret contract, committing the state to buy the bridge to boost his election chances. The contract required Texas to pay the owners of the toll bridge up to $140,000 *before* the new bridge opened. Now governor, Sterling was balking at the payment.

The bridge company knew that if the free bridge were to open without payment, its toll bridge would be worthless, and any contract leverage would be lost. They wanted Sterling and Texas to honor the contract. They sought the injunction to force Texas to pay what Sterling had promised, holding the free bridge hostage until he did.[7]

Sterling tried to bluff it through. "There is nothing to be done now regarding the contracts," he said, "but when the new free bridge is put in operation it will then be up to [the bridge company] to call for a settlement and state its claims." If Sterling failed to honor the contract later, the bridge company couldn't sue the state to collect.

When the Texas attorney general ruled that payment on Sterling's unauthorized contract would be illegal, the governor asked the Grayson

County sheriff to put sawhorses and oil lamps on each end of the pristine bridge and hire a guard to redirect traffic. It was his only choice; the judge was holding him personally responsible for enforcing the closing.

Area farmers, tradespeople, businessmen, and town residents were stunned. A new free bridge offered hope and some measure of economic freedom from daily payments to the toll taker. A free bridge meant that mills, gins, and shops on both sides of the river would be more competitive. It meant that a family's visit to a sick relative on the other side of the river wouldn't cost a half-day's wage.

The legal issues were little more than legal gobbledygook to most folks, but there was nothing they could do. The new bridge's untouched concrete roadway and silvery girders overhead gleamed white in the moonlight, and people began gathering on the bridge at night. They came to stroll, meet old friends, and ask, "When?"

But one man wouldn't be satisfied to wait it out. Oklahoma Governor William H. "Alfalfa Bill" Murray was a skilled constitutional lawyer, a savvy politician, a zealous populist, and a scientific farmer. (He earned his nickname for his fervent advocacy for alfalfa as the most efficient crop to farm in Oklahoma's clime.) Murray had his hands full with other crises brought about by the Depression in Oklahoma. But he had his eye on the Red River bridge issue, expecting the Texas governor to break the legal logjam, pay what he owed, and open the new bridge that Oklahoma had helped pay for.

A hearing in federal court on July 10 provided no solution. The judge ruled that the new bridge would remain closed until Texas settled up with the toll bridge owners. He warned that allowing (or not preventing) travel over the new free bridge by the public would result in serious consequences to the individuals involved.[8]

People living near the bridge crossing on both sides of the river were dismayed by the decision. It appeared that their free bridge wasn't going to open soon, and angry voices began to be heard among the evening visitors to the barricaded span.

Oklahoma was not a party to the injunction, however. Governor Murray called a small group of Oklahoma Highway Department officials into his office for a quiet chat.

One afternoon the following week, four men in a dark sedan pulled up to the Oklahoma end of the bridge and removed the sawhorse barricade. They drove to the Texas end and confronted the old guard.[9]

"I'm with the Oklahoma Highway Department," the leader of the group told the watchman. "We're here under the orders of Governor William H. Murray to open our bridge." He handed over a copy of Governor Murray's order, telling the guard he could walk away if he chose not to resist.

The stunned guard wisely retreated from his post. By the time he reported to the sheriff, Texans and Oklahomans were zipping across their new free bridge at the rate of seven hundred cars an hour.[10]

The Red River Bridge War was on.

Governor Sterling heard of Governor Murray's action that evening, and he was livid. The report described the scene at the bridge: cars driving from one end to the other, flashing lights, honking horns, and shouting, "Hurrah for Alfalfa Bill!" Sterling's first inclination was to call out the Texas National Guard, and he reached his adjutant general by phone at a hotel in Fort Worth to give the order.

Adjutant General William W. "Bill" Sterling (no relation to the governor) was a former Texas Ranger. Sterling told the governor, "You just need a few Texas Rangers."

Bill Sterling and Ranger Captain Tom Hickman left at midnight for the bridge. By sunup, the two lawmen, armed with Colt six-shooters, had cleared the road of all traffic and rebuilt and reinforced the barricades.

The two Rangers rescued from a ditch the hand-painted sign that the Oklahomans earlier had tossed aside. "WARNING!" was written across the sign in six-inch letters. "This bridge is closed by order of district judge of the eastern dist. of Texas on the suit of the Red River Bridge Co. of Texas & its receivers." They nailed the sign to the barricade, effectively stopping any auto from passing.

The Texas Rangers would keep the bridge closed, no matter what Oklahoma dared to throw at them.

The Texas Rangers date their beginning to before the Republic of Texas. In 1823 empresario Stephen F. Austin hired the first ten experienced frontiersmen to "range" the mesquite and pear thickets between San Antonio and Galveston Bay to protect his fledgling colony from Indian predation. Later, lacking any other local law enforcement, presidents of the Republic of Texas hired men with similar experience to keep the peace.

The rest of the nation's first glimpse of the Texas Rangers came during the Mexican War. Texas had only recently become a state and was facing border incursions by Mexico on its southern boundary. President James K. Polk ordered General Zachary Taylor and two thousand U.S. troops to the border. Mexico's government was uncertain of U.S. military plans; still embarrassed over their nation's loss of Texas a decade earlier, they responded by sending their own troops to the border. The inevitable shooting war broke out in April 1846.

General Taylor and his officers knew little of Mexico or Mexicans. He asked the Texas governor for the "loan" of Texas Rangers to serve as scouts and a behind-the-lines light cavalry. The Rangers, along with another three hundred or so rugged volunteers, met General Taylor near Matamoros, Mexico. The Texans turned out to be as handy as shirt pockets.

The Rangers were noted for their tracking and stealth as well as their willingness to engage the enemy when necessary. The Mexicans referred to them as *Los Diablos Tejanos*, those Texas Devils, due to their indiscriminate killing. [11]

Scruffy and insubordinate as they were, the Texas Rangers came out of the Mexican War as a symbol of the North American public's fascination with Texas and the American West. Soldiers' letters home, journalists, and battlefront dispatches reported only the heroism of the rough-and-ready Texas fighting men. "The Texas Rangers have been earning a high place in the hearts of the people of the United States," according to a story shared in many newspapers. [12]

As Texas's population swelled after the Civil War, settlers pressed the western boundaries of the new state. Comanche Indians pressed back, often by burning ranches, stealing livestock, scalping settlers, and kidnapping white children. The governor's Texas Rangers—extremely hard, experienced fighting men—were assigned to protect settlers by chasing

Indians and killing them when they could. By 1874, the Indians of Texas were near the end of their string, and war leader Quanah Parker led his band of Comanches onto a reservation in 1875.[13]

The Rangers were heroes to early Texas residents and legends throughout the West, but the Bandit Wars of 1915–1920 blackened their reputation. The massacre of fifteen villagers—including two teenagers—in a Mexican community on the U.S. side of the border rated a legislative inquiry.[14]

The legislators and the public demanded changes, especially in hiring practices, and the guilty Rangers were fired. They were replaced by experienced law enforcers untainted by thuggery.

That's when Thomas Rufus Hickman was appointed a Texas Ranger. "They changed the Ranger force, raised the pay to sixty dollars a month and tried to get a better bunch of men," Tom Hickman said. "And I got in on that better bunch."[15]

Tom Hickman was no Hollywood Texas Ranger, though he was an enthusiastic cowboy. He was well dressed in a fashionable necktie and a suit tailored to his six-foot frame. He wore a tipped-back fedora instead of a wide-brimmed Stetson. Except for his unsettling dead-man grin, some might have mistaken him for the president of a local chamber of commerce or the greeter at an Elks Club open house.

Hickman had a smile as broad as a jack-o'-lantern. For seven outlaws (to date), that smile was the last thing on earth they would ever see. A .45 Colt revolver was hidden in the cut of his suit coat.

Tom Hickman was born in 1886 on a cattle ranch in northwest Cooke County. The Hickman family didn't exactly ride to town two to a mule. Their 2,300-acre Hickman ranch supported cowboys, hands, and house help. With plenty of livestock on the ranch and people on hand to teach the boss's son, Tom soon became an accomplished rider, a crack marksman, and an experienced cowboy. He graduated in 1907 from the Gainesville Business College but decided he'd rather ride and shoot than cipher. Hickman rode north into Oklahoma to tour with the Miller Brothers 101 Ranch Show (where he began lifelong friendships with movie cowboy Tom Mix and rope twirler Will Rogers.)

When the wild west show ran its course, Hickman returned to Gainesville. There, he found that he had a knack for law enforcement and worked as a fire marshal and a deputy constable. Hickman could use his smile and personality to persuade a drunk to follow him to the jail for an overnight stay or to convince a criminal to surrender his weapon. In a pinch, however, he could always shoot the miscreant between the eyes. "But I always tried to talk my way out of a situation," he said, "instead of having to shoot my way out."[16]

Hickman became a Texas Ranger in 1919. The 1920s had its share of cattle rustlers, fence cutters, train robbers, Mexican bandits, and desperadoes, but the decade also saw new types of criminals and crimes of the type that transcended the capabilities of jurisdictional law enforcement. Hickman found himself increasingly involved with car thieves, oil patch claim jumpers, casino operators, bootleggers, and serial bank robbers. His easygoing manner and competence with these new types of crimes and criminals won him a promotion to captain after just three years.

Captain Hickman and the Rangers who reported to him were assigned to North Texas, where robbers were picking off country banks at the rate of two or three a day. Hickman wasn't afraid to employ new technologies to catch the robbers. When a gang led by a man in a Santa Claus suit hit the bank in Cisco and shot two lawmen, Hickman procured an airplane to scout the fugitives from the air. He loved being on horseback, but it was a fast automobile that helped him cover the large territory.

Sometimes, though, it was the old tried-and-true that got the best results. Tipped that a gang would hold up the bank in Clarksville, Hickman, another Ranger, and a constable waited nearby while two men drove up to the bank and hurried inside. When the pair exited the bank wearing masks and holding a suitcase, Hickman and his stakeout team opened fire. The robbers got off a few shots, but they ended up on the short end of their encounter with Hickman's lawmen: they lay dead on the sidewalk. The dead men were later found to be responsible for a string of robberies across North Texas during the previous months.[17]

Except for dozens of locals who drove to the closed Red River bridge to see real Texas Rangers, the first day was uneventful. A young reporter from the *Denison Herald* was one of the visitors. The local newspaper was besieged by telephone calls from many north Texas and southern Oklahoma newspapers wanting facts about the incident, he said. "Calls also came from eastern and Midwestern points."[18]

Newspapers from New York and Chicago picked up the story from the wire services of the Oklahoma governor's "seizure" of an interstate bridge and of Texas Rangers dispatched to "recapture" it. They were considering sending reporters to Denison. A newsreel company already was arranging to get bridge footage.

Governor Murray had spent much of the previous evening phoning editors of Texas newspapers. He knew from experience that newsmen are like good farm dogs: feed them well, and they'll hunt for you.

To the *Denison Herald*, Murray explained why he sent highway department men to tear down the barricades. "We have a right to cross a state boundary under United States laws. When we cross a bridge and find an obstruction, we have the right to tear it out of the way."[19]

The *Sherman Democrat* was next. The reporter asked why Murray chose to open the free bridge. "I assumed that the Texas government wanted the Denison bridge opened, otherwise it wouldn't have been so foolish as to create an expense to complete the highway, then close it."[20]

Murray's call to the *Austin Statesman* was intended to twist Governor Sterling's tail in the Texas capital city. "Oklahoma owns half of that bridge lengthwise," Murray said. "A bridge that just goes to the middle of the stream is no bridge at all. Since your governor doesn't want it open, he has the power to keep his side closed."[21]

It appears we'll be here for a while, Bill Sterling told the reporter.

Hickman called in two more Rangers before Sterling left to return to his Austin office. That night, Hickman still wasn't sure if this open-ended bridge assignment would involve "mostly waitin' or mostly shootin.'" To cover both contingencies, he and Rangers Kirby and Huddleston unrolled tents and prepared to spend the night next to the bridge but not before assigning shifts to ensure that at least one Ranger would remain awake all night.

Just before sunup the grinding mechanical sounds of heavy equipment moving on the Oklahoma side of the river woke the Rangers and put them on alert. Hickman took his pistol and walked to the other end of the bridge. An Oklahoma Highway Department worker met him on the Oklahoma side and explained that they weren't touching the free bridge. Oklahoma's governor had sent in bulldozers to rip up the Oklahoma approach roads to the toll bridge.

With the free bridge closed and approach roads to the toll bridge torn up, travelers were left with a low water crossing of the riverbed five miles upstream or an obsolete wagon bridge a mile downstream. Neither was suitable for safe crossings by trucks, buses, or even heavy autos. By noon, travel between the two states on this part of the river effectively ended.

Governor Murray's action to pressure Governor Sterling had the intended result. Newspaper editors on both sides of the river ran editorials urging the Texas governor to open the new bridge and restore trade. Mayors and city officials wired the governor to tell him of the effects a prolonged closure would have on their already Depression-stricken towns. Reporters representing newspapers from all over the state appeared at the bridge, and the Ranger encampment was their first stop.

Unlike most lawmen, Hickman was open when talking to the press. He related how he'd been called out to close the bridge and secure it. His Rangers would keep the new bridge closed as long as the governor of Texas ordered. What if Governor Murray himself showed up to open it? Well, Hickman said with a wide grin, I suppose we'll arrest him and frisk him for weapons. Reporters were pretty sure he was serious.[22]

Sunday, July 19, dawned with clear skies after an overnight rain; the morning promised a cooler day, not the blast-furnace heat more typical of July. It was the bridge, not the weather, that was the primary topic of conversation when people gathered for church that morning. The end of cross-river access would start to pinch on Monday, they knew, when shoppers couldn't get to stores and farmers couldn't get crops, eggs, or milk to market or to the freight depot in Denison. There would be no more tourist trade for the diners, gas stations, or campgrounds; no collecting a paycheck from a cross-river employer. People were becoming frightened and needed to find comfort with others.

That afternoon five hundred visitors from Oklahoma and Texas—some still in church clothes, some in overalls or homemade dresses—came to the river. With no motorists on the span, the Rangers allowed them to walk out on the bridge and be with other families. More out-of-town reporters, stringers from the national wire services, and a magazine writer or two arrived to interview the locals. Spirits rose when word passed through the crowd that Governor Sterling was assembling a group in Austin that afternoon to settle the mess, possibly working out a settlement right that minute.[23]

The cooler weather and news from Austin turned the families gathered there more hopeful, even festive. Several farmers sold watermelons to the crowd, sparking impromptu picnics. The Rangers added to the buoyant atmosphere at the bridge by staging a shooting demonstration. With rifles and six-guns, they plugged away at bottles—set on a board and allowed to float down the river or thrown into the air—in a mock competition. (Later, *Time* reported that Ranger Bob Goss split playing cards held edge-on, and Hickman hip-shot eighteen out of twenty matches at fifty feet. The report was certainly exaggerated, perhaps by Hickman himself.)[24]

As a finale to the demonstration, Hickman retrieved a war surplus Thompson submachine gun. He stood on the riverbank, dressed in his usual coat, tie, and fedora, splitting cottonwood saplings, obliterating debris floating in the river, and generally blowing things up with bursts from the tommy gun. The crowd cheered every blast.

An Oklahoma editor expressed his contempt for the presence of Texas Rangers at the bridge. "They spend the bulk of their time shooting ammunition which, apparently, Texas furnishes in abundance," he wrote.[25]

As the sun set, many families remained to stroll on the unused bridge, visit with old friends, and tell each other, "It can't be long now."

Sunday's hopeful families wouldn't know until reading Monday's newspaper that Governor Sterling's settlement conference ended soon after it began. The attorney general declared Sterling's contract invalid and said his office remained opposed to paying a penny to the bridge company. The gathered parties dispersed with no glimpse of a settlement in sight.[26]

Exasperation, frustration, and anger burst from a smolder to a blaze in towns and farmhouses on both sides of the river. Community leaders, concerned that the populace might be on the verge of mob action, conferred with city officials, county sheriffs, Hickman, and State Senator Jake Loy about a course of action. Though Hickman and the other law enforcement officers advised against it, the leaders announced a mass meeting in Sherman for Monday night and Denison Tuesday night to send a message to Austin.

Word spread, and more than two hundred people gathered on the Grayson County courthouse lawn in Sherman, determined to send a message to Governor Sterling. The outcome was a "Declaration of Resolution" to the governor and other lawmakers.

If the Sherman meeting was soporific, the following night's meeting soon grew hotter than a honeymoon hotel. Three thousand men and women gathered elbow to elbow in Denison's city park. This time, the crowd controlled the meeting agenda. Hickman and deputies kept a wary eye from the rear of the crowd on a restive "take action tonight" group, but if mob action erupted there weren't enough lawmen to stop it. One of the organizers read a telegram from Governor Murray. The Oklahoma governor congratulated and thanked the people of Grayson County for their "loyal cooperation" in his efforts to secure free bridges for the Red River.[27]

Murray's name brought cheers and shouts of support for the Oklahoma governor. A following speaker called for the county to secede from Texas and join Oklahoma. Alfalfa Bill will take care of us, he said, where Sterling won't lift a finger. More wild cheering erupted, which lightened the mood of a crowd that might have turned ugly.

The Denison meeting adopted a resolution much like Sherman's but with a stronger coda. The highway and bridge, they said, must be made available for immediate use, and all obstruction and objection be discontinued at once. All that was missing was the "or else."

Senator Jake Loy asked for an immediate Wednesday meeting with Governor Sterling to describe his sense of the mass meetings there. Support of Murray and impatience with Sterling were reaching the boiling point.

Just that morning newspapers across the country and in Texas's largest cities had reported Murray's latest "solution" to the stalemate. An excellent idea, Murray said with a straight face, would be to hold a quilting bee, where women from Oklahoma and Texas would meet on the new free bridge, "removing anything that prevents their getting together." The Texas Rangers "probably wouldn't shoot the women if they came along and took a few barricades out of the way," Murray had told smiling reporters. "After the barriers were down, traffic could cross, and the toll bridge would be whipped right there."[28]

Asked if it was true that the Texas Rangers would allow a group of quilters to open the bridge he was guarding, Hickman responded with that unsettling dead-man grin, "Don't count on it."

Governor Sterling was losing the "war" to Murray in the press, and he knew it. His financial supporters were wiring him, telling him that it was time to reach a settlement. Dallas and Fort Worth business leaders wrote to tell Sterling that the bridge closure was killing their summer tourism business. Even friendly newspapers were running editorials calling out his inaction.

The governor saw no way out of the dilemma. Then, Jake Loy walked into the governor's office for his meeting carrying a solution in his briefcase.

Jake Loy was a clothing salesman who had run for the state legislature to advocate for better roads. His ability to listen to people's needs endeared him to constituents; his sales personality made him an effective (and likable) advocate in the legislature. A retired attorney in Denison had whispered to him that the Red River Bridge Company investors simply wanted their day in court, to have Texas honor the contract Sterling had signed and pay the money the contract promised. But the bridge company was prevented by law from suing the state directly. If the state legislature could pass a law allowing the company to sue the state in this one emergency case, the bridge company would ask to set aside the federal injunction and accept the judgment of a state court.

Loy and Sterling—neither of them attorneys—weren't confident of the details, so the governor called in the state's attorney general. "Might work," the attorney general said. The governor reminded Loy that the legislative session was required to adjourn on Friday evening, and it was now Wednesday evening, not nearly enough time to get a bill through both houses of the legislature. "Let me try," Loy said.

Hickman and his Rangers were approaching their second week at the bridge and had fallen into an easygoing routine. Two Rangers would stay overnight in town while the other two camped by the bridge. Each night one Ranger would patrol the bridge while the other slept. The Rangers would swap locations every other day.

Evenings at the bridge had also become routine. Having long ago given up on their campfire suppers, the Ranger enjoyed meals prepared by a Denison diner and delivered to the river encampment by flirty waitresses. Families and romantic couples continued to walk onto the new bridge at the close of day. The sundown stroll came to be called "The Promenade," couples holding hands, families corralling active children, all under the moon and the silvery girders of the truss bridgeworks.

Later in the evening reporters stopped by the Ranger encampment, some to gather any last-minute news, others to enjoy a snort or two around the Ranger campfire. (Hickman was a strict teetotaler, prohibiting his men from any drinking, on duty or off. He was tolerant but was known to have a short fuse when it came to people who over-imbibed in his presence.)

Hickman was good at scaring up entertainment for reporters and others who visited the Ranger camp. He would fetch a wind-up phonograph and an assortment of records from the Ranger equipment trailer. Soon, the Texas Rangers and their visitors were singing along to popular tunes and cowboy ballads, their voices echoing along the dark riverbed.

Reporters from out of state were finding the Texas Rangers to be far different from what they expected. These Rangers weren't scruffy Indian hunters, and they weren't the white-hat, straight-shootin' Rangers from the movies. Hickman and his men were a different type of Ranger: modern, snappy, urban law enforcers who were equally adept at rounding up cattle rustlers or car thieves. They were comfortable in the outdoors but always with a good shave and a shoeshine. The reporters, magazine writers, photographers, and newsreel cameramen who spent time at the contested Red River bridge described to the rest of the country a Texas Ranger of an entirely different caliber: they were Texas Mounties with a drawl (absent the campaign hats, Sam Browne belts, and red tunics, of course).

On Wednesday night, neither the reporters nor the Rangers knew how long this standoff might last. They were unaware of Jake Loy's plan to end it. And they were certainly unaware of what the Oklahoma governor had in mind.

On Thursday afternoon, July 23, a young reporter from the *Denison Herald* was the first to arrive at the Texas Rangers' encampment with the news that had made the wire service teletype in his office ring like the bells of the Second Coming. The Associated Press in Oklahoma was reporting that Alfalfa Bill Murray had declared martial law along a narrow strip of land on the north side of the river. He was sending a light artillery company of Oklahoma National Guard to the Red River under the command of Adjutant General Charles F. Barrett. Murray ordered Barnett to exert "military control against all interference whatsoever."[29]

The *Herald* reporter asked Hickman for a quote, but the Ranger was uncharacteristically silent. He needed to call his boss in Austin for further instructions, he said.

At the state capitol in Austin, Jake Loy was moving faster than small-town gossip from legislator to legislator. Assistant attorneys general had been up all night drafting a bill that *might* end the stalemate. Loy had signed on the two requisite sponsors from the House and was looking for a second sponsor in the Senate. He was on the agenda for a House vote first thing Friday. He'd walk the bill to the Senate if he could talk his way onto the agenda there. This just might work, he thought.

Bill Sterling heard of Murray's order from a questioning reporter. Sterling, also, had no comment except to say that he would be conferring with Governor Sterling about the matter.

Jake Loy and Bill Sterling were probably unaware that Governor Ross Sterling was incommunicado, on his way to Houston for a private family night at his home and a bar association speech the following evening. No governor might be available to sign the all-important bill, even *if* Loy got it passed, or to order reinforcements to the bridge *if* Oklahoma's military should threaten.

Thursday night Hickman and his three men remained at the bridge. They installed acetylene floodlamps on the bridge and used their automobiles to create a barrier at both ends of the span. A reporter noted that, for the first time in the weeks since they had taken their post, all of the Rangers wore holstered sidearms.

On previous nights the Rangers had found patrolling the bridge was quiet, pleasant, solitary duty. Looking over the bridge railing in the dark, they could see little of the river, but the whisper of the water as it flowed over the sandy riverbed was a constant relaxing sound. The occasional splash nearby was from a turtle that fell off a rock into the water, and several times they heard from a mile or so upriver the grinding gears and straining engine of an old high-body Ford. Bootleggers, they guessed, trying to drive across the river to deliver their load on the other side.

There was no relaxing on the bridge that Thursday night. Several hundred armed Oklahoma National Guardsmen were on their way to the bridge with orders Hickman did not know. And four men—Texas Rangers—had been ordered to keep the bridge closed, no matter what Oklahoma dared to throw at them. It was a long night.

Hickman didn't know that sometime during the night Texas Adjutant General Bill Sterling had spoken to his Oklahoma counterpart, General Barrett. "I sent him word that the Texas end of the bridge was being held by four Rangers," the Texan said. "If [Barrett] was sending a brigade to open it, I would keep all four there. If only a regiment was to be used, I'd send a couple of the boys home."

Though Governor Murray had called for a company of National Guard to proceed to the river, Barrett knew that sending a company was like sending a cannon when a fly brush would do. More than two hundred uniformed men gathered at the Durant armory by midnight to draw weapons. Barrett sent home all but thirty of them. He ordered them to march the twenty miles to the Red River and set up near the toll bridge.

With no sign of the National Guard overnight, Hickman walked across the free bridge early Friday to reconnoiter on the Oklahoma side. A farmer told him that several dozen Guardsmen had arrived overnight and were camping in an administrative building a mile away on the north end of the toll bridge. That news, and a later call to General Sterling in Austin, reassured Hickman that he wasn't likely to have his own little Alamo at the new bridge.

Jake Loy started his day early, too. The Texas House passed his bridge bill first thing with a cursory vote, even as the legislators were still reading morning newspapers at their desks. News of armed Oklahoma troops approaching the Red River bridge alarmed Senate members sufficiently to have leaders promise passage of Loy's bill shortly after noon and a pro forma reconciliation immediately afterward.

Loy drove to Houston that night to get the governor's signature on the bill. The next morning he'd meet with the attorneys in the federal judge's chamber to argue that the restraining order be dropped and the new bridge be allowed to open.

Alfalfa Bill Murray had ears everywhere, and by Friday morning he knew two things: First, the Red River Bridge Company was planning to ask a new judge to require that the National Guard, the Oklahoma Highway Department, and any other obstructors withdraw from the toll bridge so it could be reopened for business. Murray intended to keep the pressure on Governor Sterling by continuing to block the toll bridge. Second, he heard about the progress of Jake Loy's legislative solution. Murray had been winning the Red River bridge war narrative, and he wasn't about to let some raw biscuit steal the credit from him.

"I'm sick of this dilly-dallying around," Governor Murray told a group of reporters that afternoon. "The people on this side and in Texas might just as well get together now and have free bridges."[30]

With that, Murray stood up from his desk and told the newsmen he was leaving to be with his soldiers at the river until the matter was settled once and for all. In an hour he had packed his valise with a change of drawers and an old pistol, kissed his wife good-bye, and was napping in the backseat of the state-owned auto that was driving him to the site of the bridge war.

For newspapers across the country, the Red River bridge war had been front-page news. When editors heard that the Oklahoma governor was on his way to command his troops, it was time to put out the extra editions. That evening at the river, Murray posed for photos, "inspected" his troops, and ordered them to march across the entrance of the toll bridge with rifles on their shoulders for the benefit of the newsreel cameramen. Newspapers filed their stories with the dateline, "From the Battle Zone."

Hickman was just as glad that all eyes were now on Murray instead of the Rangers. He caught a ride back to the hotel in town and enjoyed a good night's sleep.

The first visitors to the free bridge arrived early; by ten o'clock hundreds of local men, women, and children milled about near the Rangers' barricade, drawn by curiosity about what the day might bring. Eventually several sheriff's deputies turned up to direct traffic and help control the crowd.[31]

Hickman was at the bridge shortly after dawn. The Rangers again used their autos to block both ends of the span. Scrap lumber reinforced the wooden barricades. Then, like everyone else, they waited.

On Saturday morning Loy brought the signed bill to the federal courthouse, where he met with a passel of attorneys from all sides of the issue. The attorneys argued among themselves in the waiting room before entering chambers and arguing their positions to the waiting judge. The judge said he'd take the matter under advisement and have a ruling before lunch.

Governor Murray was showboating for the reporters and cameramen. He had started the day in the mess line with his soldiers for breakfast. By noon he was seated in a folding chair, greeting visitors, answering reporters' questions, and telling anyone nearby that Oklahoma was on the verge of winning the battle of the bridges. The governor stopped talking mid-sentence, and all faces turned to look when a loud cheer came from the crowd gathered upriver at the new bridge.

In Denison, a Western Union employee handed an envelope to the Denison mayor, who had been waiting in the telegraph office. The mayor rushed off to Tom Hickman at the bridge. Hickman opened the envelope and saw that it was signed by the governor, telling him that the Rangers could open the bridge. Wary that it might be a hoax, Hickman tried to reach Governor Sterling in Houston. Finally, Hickman reached Bill Sterling, his commander, who told him he had spoken with Governor Sterling personally. General Sterling ordered Hickman to open the bridge.

"This ain't the first boundary dispute I've been in," Hickman told the general. "I want to know that it's coming straight." Texas Ranger Captain Tom Hickman gave his men the order to dismantle the barricades and let the traffic flow.

Hundreds of spectators pressed forward, cheering, waving hats and handkerchiefs. Some in the crowd ran to their automobiles, lining up alongside the road in hopes of being among the first to cross the bridge. They sat behind steering wheels, honking horns until the din was so great that it was hard to hear.

The car nearest the fast-disappearing barricade was a new Buick sedan driven by R. G. Gresham of the Denison Chamber of Commerce and crammed full of friends. As Hickman prepared to wave them forward through a gap in the blockade, something shot past him at high speed going north. The Texas Ranger whirled around in time to see a boy pedaling his bicycle hell-bent-for-leather toward the Oklahoma end of the bridge. The first vehicle to cross the newly opened toll-free bridge over the Red River was a bicycle ridden by fifteen-year-old Roy Epps of Sherman. People at both ends of the bridge clapped and cheered him on.

Hickman signaled the Buick to proceed across the bridge, then jumped onto the running board to accompany Gresham and inspect the roadbed for any debris or obstruction. When Gresham expressed his disappointment at not being the first to cross the bridge, Hickman said, "I coulda shot the boy off his two-wheeler if you'd wanted." Gresham was horrified until he glanced up to see Hickman's broad grin.

At the Oklahoma end of the bridge, Hickman stepped off the running board and posed for pictures before hitching a ride back to the Texas side. There, he and the Texas Rangers of Company B packed up their gear and drove away from the Red River bridge to their next assignment.[32]

In 1931 every kid in America who had been to a movie theater knew what a Texas Ranger should look like: young, handsome, and dressed in a bib shirt with buttons running down each side of his chest. A *real* Ranger would be wearing a white cowboy hat and a shiny scarf tied high up on his neck. But that wasn't the Texas Ranger they saw in the newsreels from the Red River bridge. Instead, they saw an older guy with a Thompson submachine gun and a scary, scary smile.

As Hickman and the men of his company guarded the new free bridge across the Red River, writers, still photographers, and newsreel cameramen introduced a new breed of Texas Ranger to their readers. The Rangers carried a hundred-year tradition with them but were no longer the roughshod "Rangers" of the past or popular culture's singing cowboy with a star. Texas had a new kind of lawman. The *real* Rangers of the twentieth century were organized, professional men, cool and competent, and dedicated to enforcing the laws of Texas.

CHAPTER 3

MILDRED "BABE" DIDRIKSON
THE TEXAS BABE STRIKES GOLD

BABE FELT TRAPPED IN HER NARROW SEAT AS THE TRAIN PICKED UP speed leaving Dallas. She wanted nothing more than to sprint up and down the aisle of the passenger car, but she was sure her chaperone would remind her that it wasn't ladylike. She squirmed in the seat, feet tapping. Time after time she pulled off her floppy pink bucket hat and folded it into a different shape before pulling it down over her rag-mop hairdo again. She was full of energy—nervous energy—with no way to work it off. She felt like a fly stuck on flypaper.

Mildred "Babe" Didrikson, an $80-a-month clerk in a Dallas insurance company office, had a growing regional reputation among sports enthusiasts as a skilled all-around amateur athlete. In July 1932, the eighteen-year-old and her chaperone were on the train to Chicago, where Babe would compete as a one-woman team in the Women's National Amateur Athletic Union (AAU) track and field competition. "I am gonna show everyone I have ants in my pants," she wrote a friend.[1]

By the end of that summer, the lanky Texas girl with the rag-mop hairdo would be known around the world as the "Texas Babe," "Texas Flash," "Amazon of the Cactus," "Girl Viking of Texas," or, simply, "Wondergirl."

Venerated sportswriter Grantland Rice would refer to the nervous Texas girl with ants in her pants as "the athletic phenomenon of all time, man or woman."[2]

"Before I was even into my teens, I knew exactly what I wanted to be when I grew up," Babe said in her autobiography. "My goal was to be the greatest athlete that ever lived. I suppose I was born with the urge to get into sports, and the ability to do pretty well at it. I don't guess I have to tell you that I was a pretty competitive type."[3]

Mildred Ella Didrikson was the sixth of seven children of Norwegian immigrants living in Beaumont, a port town on the Neches River in southeast Texas. Her father, a carpenter by trade, and her mother, an accomplished skater in Norway, raised their family in a two-bedroom frame house on the industrial south side of town among other working families. Her family called her "Baby" at first, then "Mildred" or "Millie" as she got older.

"I had a wonderful childhood," Babe said. "That must prove that it doesn't take money to be happy, because the Didriksons sure weren't rich. We generally didn't have any dimes or quarters to hand out to us for picture shows and all that."

The Didrikson parents encouraged physical fitness and athleticism, and the children were vigorous performers on gymnastic equipment built of scavenged scrap in their backyard. Early on, Poppa and Mama Didrikson recognized that Babe was the standout among their seven children. She was exceptionally athletic and self-confident to a fault, with a talent for getting into trouble around the neighborhood.

At ten years old Babe could do more pull-ups in the homemade gymnasium than any of her brothers. She ran everywhere she went, even if it was only next door to return a neighbor's borrowed platter. And when Babe and her sister raced one another to the local market, Babe would hurtle the boxwood hedge fences one after another while her sister would be forced to run around them.

Babe could adopt and excel at almost any skill she could observe. She taught herself how to play marbles just to beat her brothers at the game, and a trip to the circus inspired her to hang a swing in a nearby chinaberry tree to learn the trapeze. She earned the money to buy an inexpensive harmonica and taught herself to play.

After watching for a while, Babe pestered the neighborhood boys to let her play baseball with them. She had a sharp eye and a powerful swing and soon was knocking the ball out of the sandlot into nearby yards. "When I began hitting home runs in ball games," she said, "the kids said, 'She's a regular Babe Ruth. We'll call her Babe.'" The nickname stuck.

Sometimes Babe's interest in sports could get her in trouble. One afternoon her mother sent her to the butcher to pick up two pounds of meat for a special family celebration dinner. On her way home with the expensive package, Babe spotted a baseball game and joined her friends to play. Arriving home later that afternoon, she realized that she'd forgotten the meat. Racing back to the ball field, Babe saw the package next to third base where she had left it. She was too late, though. A stray dog had already found the Didrikson's dinner and was wolfing it down. The incident earned her one of many spankings.

Babe saw a nearby house under construction—just the framing, studs, and rafters—as a climbing challenge. With neighborhood kids following her in a game of follow-the-leader, she swung herself up into the rafters and onto the ridgepole. A large sandpile was below and, after daring the other kids to follow her, she leaped for it from the very top of the house. The sand was hiding a sharp sliver of wood, and it stabbed several inches into her leg.

"After I had that taken care of, I was back out there leading them the next day," she said. "I started up to the top of the house again, and missed my step, and came down on my side with a terrible thump. My whole leg was skinned and bruised. I'd have got a whipping for sure after messing myself up a second time like that, if they hadn't found when I got home that I had three cracked ribs."

Some people in the twenty-first century object to the word "tomboy," feeling it implies that a girl is *aspiring* to behaviors that are boyish rather than accepting her skills as her own. But if you asked anyone in the Didrikson family's Beaumont neighborhood to describe Babe, the first word they would have used is "tomboy."[4]

Even as a child, Babe was a gifted athlete and intensely competitive. If the boys played tougher baseball than the girls, she wanted to play against—and beat—the boys. If her brothers' hand-me-down denim pants and an old T-shirt were better for climbing a flagpole or a long slide into third base, that's what she'd wear. At an age when girls become rounder and softer, Babe remained thin as a slat and muscular.

Junior high school and (especially) high school are happier places for students who are attractive or handsome and succeed in fitting in. Babe had neither the looks nor the personality to make her school years happy ones. But she had extraordinary athletic skills and a white-hot desire to be recognized. It was team sports—not curled hair, patent leather dress shoes, or dimples—that earned her some of the recognition she craved during her school years.[5]

Babe's first exposure to organized sports came in grade school. The junior high and high school teams practiced in the larger, newer gymnasium of Babe's elementary school.

"When those high school girls came over to our courts to practice, I was just dying to get in and play with them," she said. "I'd hang around and pester them. Finally, they did let me in, and I made a few scores. They said they wished I was old enough, so I could play on their team."

Babe made the school team when she was in junior high, but at Beaumont High School the coach turned her down—she was too small and her talent too raw to play on a team that was a contender for the state title. Though she was barely five feet tall at the time, Babe couldn't accept that she wasn't good enough for the basketball team.

"I didn't think the girls who played on it were anything wonderful," she said. "I was determined to show everybody." To improve herself, she went to the coach of the boys' team.

Babe would skip study hall, hunt up the men's coach in the gym, and ask him to watch her for a while. She was probably a pitiful sight: undersized and barefooted (because the family couldn't afford tennis shoes).

"I'd worry him to death with questions about how to pivot and shoot free throws and do this and that," she said. "He'd show me how to do different things and encourage me. He took the time to help me because he could see I was interested."

As erratic and spare as the coaching was, Babe saw the essentials of basketball play, imitated them, and learned them. By her junior year the determined girl won a place on Beaumont High School's varsity basketball team and quickly became a star player. By her senior year Babe was

40

playing on *every* girls' sports team—volleyball, tennis, golf, baseball, and swimming. Team photos from her high school yearbooks show Babe as an unsmiling, slim young woman with broad shoulders and a messy Dutch boy haircut. Her expression betrays a wary anticipation, a performer waiting for the first clap of what she's sure will be a thunderous round of applause.[6]

The applause she was looking for came each time she ran onto the basketball court in Beaumont's Miss Royal Purples uniform. Even her teammates acknowledged that Babe made an excellent team into an unbeatable team. "Babe never let up when she played," said teammate Lois "Pee Wee" Blanchette. "The Miss Royal Purples didn't know what losing was; we never believed we'd ever lose. And we never did."[7]

The high school girls' team traveled through much of south and east Texas, often playing schools larger than their own. Babe was the passing forward, and she could chunk a ball into the basket from any corner of the court. She was invariably the top scorer, and the Miss Royal Purples never lost a game in which Babe played. It didn't take long for the newspaper sportswriters to take note of Babe. She recalled a little write-up headlined "Beaumont Girl Stars in Basketball Game" as her first news clip.[8]

Another man took note of Babe's headlines: a dignified, middle-aged man sitting by himself on an upper bleacher one blustery night in February 1930. He was a Dallas insurance company executive visiting Houston to watch the women's state basketball championship. A powerful Houston Heights High School was facing off against the underdog Miss Royal Purples of Beaumont, and he was scouting a girl on the Houston team.

M. J. McCombs was the manager of the safety department of the Employers Casualty Company of Dallas. Employers Casualty indemnified thousands of families against loss or injury with life, health, fire, and auto insurance policies. It was one of the largest general insurance companies in the Midwest and South.[9]

Despite his job title, McCombs had little to do with safety. He was paid to recruit, manage, and promote winning sports teams that represented the active, healthy lifestyle that the insurance company wished its policyholders to emulate. National publicity that a winning team earned could be worth hundreds of thousands of dollars. For a popular team, turnstile revenue might even make the sponsoring company's costs self-liquidating.

Employers Casualty wasn't the only large company to field a semi-professional sports team. These "amateur" industrial league teams competed under the aegis of the AAU, which required that all team members had to be employees of the company sponsoring their team. It was an open secret, however, that companies routinely hired team members based more on athletic abilities than on corporate skills. McCombs's Department of Safety employed a dozen women typists, clerks, filers, and other administrative assistants to fill the roster of his women's basketball team, the Golden Cyclones.

In 1930, McCombs felt that the Golden Cyclones could snag the AAU national women's title with just a smidgen of improvement. (The Cyclones had been eliminated from the national tournament in the quarterfinals the previous year.) He was scouting for that "smidgen" at the Houston state high school championship finals when he saw Babe.

McCombs knew what to look for in a winning athlete. He had earned letters in four sports while a student at Texas A&M and had coached winning high school sports teams in the decade after graduation. "The only way he could know if a girl was qualified to be a Cyclone was to watch her play," according to one writer. "He placed a premium on a girl's ability to play a smothering defense, including her willingness to deliver fouls with hard slaps and pointed elbows. Far more important than shooting or passing skills was a player's willingness to take and land a punch."[10]

In the championship matchup between the taller, bigger girls of Houston Heights High School and the underdog Miss Royal Purples, it was Beaumont that earned the trophy. The game's outstanding player was the girl with the messy Dutch boy haircut, the not-so-tall, aggressive passing forward wearing the number seven on her purple Beaumont High jersey who scored a game-high twenty-six points.

After the game, his Houston prospect forgotten, McCombs rushed to the locker room to meet the player who would take his Cyclones to the national AAU title: high school senior Babe Didrikson.

Meeting with Babe and her parents after the game, McCombs wasted no time offering Babe a job with Employers Casualty in Dallas. She would be paid seventy-five dollars a month as a typist, be allowed unlimited time to practice basketball with first-class equipment, cracker-jack coaching, and (by the way) wear the gold satin uniform as a starter for the Golden Cyclones.

"You never saw anybody more excited than I was that night back in February 1930," Babe said. "Here I was, just a little old high school girl, wanting to be a big athlete. And now I was getting a chance to go with an insurance company in Dallas and play on their basketball team in the women's national championships."

Poppa and Mama Didrikson weren't quite as excited at having their teenaged daughter move to a city three hundred miles away. Yet Babe's future in Beaumont was likely limited to grimy factory work in one of the local refineries. And seventy-five dollars was an exceptional wage during that first year of the Depression. Poppa's decision eventually carried the day, according to Babe's older sister. "He decided that's what they all came from Norway *for*—to give the kids everything they could in America." Two days later, Babe and her father boarded the overnight train to Dallas.[11]

Babe stepped onto the court as a Golden Cyclone the night of her arrival in Dallas. She wore an ill-fitting uniform retrieved from a closet of extras. "I'd always had the number seven in high school," Babe said. "I went through the extra uniforms, and there was number seven waiting for me." Babe rolled the pants at the waist, all the better to show off her legs.

She was everything McCombs expected: quick, steady, fast, and lithe as a coach whip. "Certain points of her game could stand plenty of polish, but she had that instinctive grace, that natural and easy coordination, that *flash* that hallmarks every champion," he said.[12]

The opposing team wasn't going to make it easy for her. "They'd heard about me, and they weren't going to let this little kid from Beaumont do any shooting at all," Babe said. "They started hitting me that night, and they kept it up the whole season. If one guard fouled out against me, they'd send in another one." Having grown up on the southside streets of Beaumont, Babe had a ready willingness to take and land hard slaps, sharp elbows, and punches. The Cyclones won that first game 48–18, with Babe scoring a team-leading fourteen points.

That first victory marked the beginning of a thirty-month golden period for the Cyclones. With Babe as a starter and most often the high scorer, the Cyclones cruised into the finals of the AAU's national women's basketball tourney in 1930. The Golden Cyclones and the Sun Oilers were tied in the last moments of the championship game, but a missed free throw cost the Cyclones the game by one point. Babe was named an All-American at the end of the season. (She would be recognized as an AAU All-American basketball player in three consecutive seasons.)[13]

The Cyclones won the next year's AAU national championship—with Babe scoring a season average of thirty-one points a game—and made the finals the year after that. Sportswriters noticed Babe's accomplishments on the court, and she was thrilled to see her name in print. "In the newspaper they ran this layout with pictures of the girls on our team," she wrote to a friend in Beaumont. "My picture was in the center, blown up way big. There were just little head shots of the others. Man, I just loved that!"

McCombs was more than pleased with the performance of the girl from Beaumont. Babe received a $5-a-month raise from Employers Casualty.

Babe's salary was modest, but comfortable. (A skilled laborer at the time made less than three dollars a day *if* work was available.) She sent half her monthly salary home to her parents and paid five dollars a month for a private room in an Oak Cliff rooming house occupied by many of her teammates. "We paid fifteen cents for breakfast and thirty-five cents for dinner," Babe said. "I wasn't spending anything on clothes. Sometimes a girl would give me one of her old dresses, and I'd cut it up and make a skirt out of it for myself."

McCombs drove team members to and from work at Employers Casualty each day to save them the cost of carfare. The Golden Cyclones reported to their jobs every morning but could take off most afternoons for team practice or a game.

With the Cyclones, Babe was living, practicing, and playing among a group of skilled athletic women, a community where popularity wasn't dependent on good looks, an attractive hairdo, or store-bought dresses. But it was apparent early on that, despite her skills on the court, Babe wasn't necessarily a popular team player.

Interviewed years later, a teammate recalled that Babe would rush to the press box after games, crowing about her court accomplishments without acknowledging the efforts of the other Cyclones. "She was out for Babe, honey—just Babe. She was out for fame."[14]

At the end of her first season with the Cyclones, McCombs asked Babe if she would like to drive out to a local park to watch a track meet. Though she and her Poppa had listened to the 1928 Olympic Games on the radio, Babe had never seen a meet.

McCombs and his employee walked the grounds, watching the events. "He showed me the high jump and the hurdles and stuff like that," Babe said. "Those hurdles reminded me of all the hedge-jumping I'd done back home. I liked the looks of that event better than almost anything else."

Babe wasn't aware of it at the time, but McCombs had the idea of adding track and field events to Employers Casualty's roster of sponsored sports. A women's track team would give the Cyclones an athletic challenge during the off-season. Told of Babe's enthusiasm for the sport, the company president gave McCombs his immediate approval.

McCombs acquired equipment and coaches and introduced the Golden Cyclones to his plan for a nationally competitive track team. One girl claimed the javelin as the event she intended to specialize in; another wanted the discus. On hearing that the team would have nine or ten events, Babe announced she was going to do them all.

"Everybody nearly died laughing," Babe remembered. "But I was serious. I said it because I thought I could do it." With all her skills and strength, Babe could hardly limit herself to one sport. She was intensely competitive, too. She recognized that an individual who set a record in any one event would have *her* name attached to the record, not the team's name.

McCombs and the coaches showed Babe the basics: how to time her approach to the long jump, the mechanics of the high jump, how to grasp the javelin, and how to spin for greater leverage with an eight-pound shot on her shoulder.

"We had just a few days to get ready for our first meet," Babe said. "Our regular hour or two of practice in the afternoon wasn't enough to satisfy me. I'd go out to Lakeside Park at night and practice by myself until it got dark, which wasn't until nine or nine-thirty at that time of year. If there was good clear moonlight, I might keep going even longer."

At Babe's first meet, the WAAU Texas championships, she won first place in four of the six events she entered: high jump, shot put, javelin, and baseball throw.

Babe was a hard worker and a natural athlete. By the end of their first season in 1930, Babe held southern AAU records in the shot put, high jump, and running broad jump. At the national AAU meet that year, Babe set American women's records in the javelin and baseball throw, leading the Cyclones to second place in overall meet standings. (Babe won fifteen of her team's nineteen total points.) In 1931 Babe's records stood, and she established a new American record of twelve seconds flat in the eighty-yard hurdles for women.[15]

In track and field, as in basketball, Babe seemed to be a one-woman team, especially when newspapers began to refer to "Babe Didrikson and her Golden Cyclones." She was a reporter's dream, always willing to talk about her accomplishments and to forecast her next victories. At the same time, Babe was earning a reputation in the track and field community as a braggart and prima donna. Just as she'd done playing sandlot baseball against neighborhood boys, Babe used taunts and trash talk to distract and intimidate her opponents. She irritated her teammates, too, by bragging about her records and gold medals. Even more infuriating, she invariably lived up to her brags.[16]

McCombs was aware of Babe's jagged personality traits and the dissension brewing in his Golden Cyclones in 1932. But he also knew that Babe was a world-class athlete, the only one of the Cyclones likely to earn a spot on the 1932 Olympics team. The 1932 AAU national women's track and field meet would serve as Olympic team qualifier for the worldwide event to be held in Los Angeles that year.

In early July McCombs rang Babe and asked her to come to his office. "I've been studying the records of the girls on the other teams that will be in the [nationals]," he said. "If you enter enough different events, and give your regular performance, you can do something that's never been done before. I believe you can win the national championship for us all by yourself."[17]

McCombs was placing all his eggs in Babe's basket: she would represent Employers Casualty as a one-person team in the AAU national competition.

He assigned Mrs. Henry Wood, a company bookkeeper, to serve as Babe's chaperone, and Mrs. Wood's first requirement was that Babe wear a proper hat on their train trip to Chicago. Babe eventually chose a shapeless bright pink bucket hat but refused to wear it before stepping onto the train platform. If her office mates saw the hat, she said, "they'd think for sure I'd become a sissy."[18]

Wearing the new pink hat (her first) and carrying a formal white handbag (also her first), Babe Didrikson and her chaperone departed from Dallas's Union Station on Monday, July 11, on the afternoon train to Chicago.

Babe arrived in Chicago with a bad case of nerves.

To others, she was smugly self-confident to the point of arrogance. But Babe was fully aware that the AAU meet and Olympic trials could mean everything to her future. Winning the meet would assure a ticket to the Olympics, and winning at the Olympics meant she could become the world-famous athlete she'd always wanted to be. As a one-woman team, Babe was entered in eight of the ten qualifying events and wouldn't have to depend on anyone else to prevail. On the other hand, she *couldn't* depend on anyone else. It was all up to her.

Babe and Mrs. Wood settled in at the famous Drake Hotel in downtown Chicago, where Babe could do light workouts at a nearby gymnasium and eat well while the chaperone enforced an early curfew.

The day before the meet Babe felt a sharp pain in her stomach. Shooting pains increased through the evening, and her stomach was sensitive to touch. Babe couldn't sleep. She tossed and moaned. Fearing appendicitis or typhoid fever, Mrs. Wood phoned the hotel doctor. The doctor gave Babe a cursory examination, then asked what activities she was planning the next few days. Babe told him about the track meet the next day, and the doctor issued his diagnosis: "There's nothing wrong with her," he told the women. "She's just all excited."[19]

"And that's what it was," Babe said. "I've found out since that whenever I get all keyed up like that before an event, it means I'm really ready."

The Texas women didn't get to sleep until dawn and, exhausted, overslept the morning of the meet. They ran downstairs without breakfast, only to find that most city cabbies wouldn't carry them to Evanston, the site of the meet. A frantic Mrs. Wood finally strong-armed a driver who agreed to take them to Dyche Stadium (now Ryan Field) on the Northwestern University campus. Heavy traffic slowed their progress, and the women worried that Babe wouldn't reach the stadium in time to suit up. Mrs. Wood hung a blanket as a privacy tent in the backseat of the cab, and Babe changed into her track suit as the taxi roared up North Sheridan Avenue.

The frazzled pair arrived just as the announcer was introducing the teams.

More than two hundred women on thirty-two teams were competing for eighteen places on the women's American Olympic team (and, incidentally, the 1932 AAU women's track and field championship) that Saturday morning in Evanston. Twelve former Olympians—with five American records among them—would compete, as would the twenty-two members of the Illinois Women's Athletic Club, which had won the championship the previous three years running.

Coming into Chicago, Babe wasn't exactly an unknown. Due to her self-promotion and outrageous predictions (combined with some slick press agentry by Employers Casualty), Babe's name had become familiar to some prominent national sportswriters. Grantland Rice mentioned her several times in his syndicated weekly column and featured her in one of his weekly sports newsreels. Moviegoers everywhere could see her in action. James Roach of the *New York Times* mentioned Babe in fourteen of his weekly "Women in Sports" columns during the year leading up to Evanston.[20]

Babe had also developed a reputation among women competitors from earlier meets. When she met Babe in 1930, Olympic hurdler Evelyne Hall remembered her as "a modest, likeable girl. She wrote me a couple of letters, telling me about her family." But there was a different Babe in 1932. "When I first met Babe, I liked to hear her talk in that slow Southern drawl. By 1932 I think that drawl was gone. They had started to promote her."[21]

As the women gathered on the sidelines waiting for the announcer to introduce the teams, Babe sought out some of her better-known competitors. "I'm gonna lick you single-handed," she told them.[22]

The announcer's voice boomed out over the field, calling the names of teams competing that day. With each team announcement five, ten, fifteen, or twenty women in matching uniforms ran out on the field to moderate applause from the crowd.

"It came time to announce my 'team,'" Babe said. "I spurted out there all alone, waving my arms, and you never heard such a roar. It brought out goose bumps all over me."

Babe was entered in eight of the ten events. (McCombs advised her to skip the two long-distance running events. Those weren't Olympic trial events and would likely just tire her unnecessarily.) Eight events meant Babe would have to perform twenty-four times that afternoon—a qualifier, a semifinal, and the finals for each event. She paid no attention to the increasing applause and cheers from the stands as she completed each trial.

"For two-and-a-half hours I was flying all over the place," she said. "I'd run a heat in the eighty-meter hurdles, and then I'd take one of my high jumps. Then I'd go over to the broad jump and take a turn at that. Then they'd be calling for me to throw the javelin or put the eight-pound shot."

Three hours after the announcer had introduced her one-person "team" to the crowd, Babe had accomplished what no athlete had done before or since: she won the National AAU track and field championship singlehandedly and earned her spot on the Olympic squad.

"When I came off the field at the end of the afternoon, all puffing and sweating," Babe said, "Mrs. Wood was so happy and excited she was crying. She said, 'You did it! You won the meet all by yourself!'"

Of the eight events she entered, she won five outright, tied for first in another, and took fourth place in another. Along the way she set one world record and tied another. Her thirty points were enough to win the meet outright. (The Illinois Women's Athletic Club was second with twenty-two points.)

The next morning, newspaper readers across the country would read about the scarce-hipped Texas gal with the ten-gallon mouth. They would read how Mildred Didrikson—"who prefers to be called 'Babe'"—can run faster, jump higher, and throw farther than any other woman in America. While other newspaper headlines told readers of job losses, breadlines, Bonus marchers, bank failures, and other distressing news, Babe's story gave readers a chance to marvel and a reason to cheer during dark times. They'd be pulling for the Texas wonder gal to trim the tail feathers of those foreigners at the Olympic Games in Los Angeles just two weeks later.

Babe had no time to return to Dallas. Three days later the eighteen women of the American women's Olympic track and field team boarded a train for Los Angeles. Mrs. Wood was replaced by a chaperone assigned by the Olympic Committee.[23]

"On the train going out, most of the girls sat around watching the scenery and playing cards and gabbing," Babe said. "I was busy taking exercises and doing my hurdle bends and stuff. I'd practice in the aisle. Several times a day I'd jog the whole length of the train and back."[24]

After a stop-off in Denver for some training time, the team arrived at Union Station in Los Angeles, where a greeting committee welcomed them. "The people were just wonderful," team member Evelyne Hall said. "Olympic flags were flying everywhere with red, white, and blue bunting and Olympic banners all across the streets and on the lamp posts. It was a very exciting time."[25]

The 1928 Olympics was the first in which women were allowed to compete, and in 1932 only six women's track and field events were on the program. Many felt that women had no place competing in the games at all. A woman's body, they said, was more suited to swimming, diving, golf, or lawn tennis. Some physicians argued that the more strenuous sports— running, jumping, throwing—could prevent a woman from having children. A few even pointed at the slender, well-muscled, tomboyish Babe as a not-so-feminine product of her dedication to those strenuous sports.[26]

In some ways, Babe made herself a target. She most often wore her droopy wool track suit, avoided make-up, and ignored her hair. She was brash and often roughhoused with other athletes. According to one magazine writer, Babe felt left out when the spotlight fell on more beautiful (but less talented) athletes. "So, she overplayed her antifeminism. When newspaper men interviewed her, she clowned, cursed, and acted the Texas toughie."[27]

"I know I'm not pretty," she told another reporter. "But I do try to be graceful."[28]

Sportswriter Grantland Rice, who had become a major fan of the Texas Babe, believed she outshone any Olympic athlete, female or male. "Certainly, for sheer grace there were few men at Los Angeles who had any edge on Babe," he wrote. "It was a treat to watch her stroll into the high jump. She had less wasted effort than any athlete I have ever seen in action."

Babe had hoped to compete in all six women's events, but in a last-minute ruling, the Olympic Committee—probably reacting to Babe's domination in Chicago—ruled that no athlete could compete in more than three. Though she had qualified and trained for every event, Babe was limited to the javelin, the hurdles, and the high jump.

Babe's first event at the Games was the javelin throw, late afternoon on the first day of competition. Evening shadow darkened half the coliseum field, and the temperature was becoming quite cool. Event judges had placed yardage markers on the field, and, near the 130-foot marker, they planted a small German flag to mark the current world's record—132½ feet set by Ellen Braumiller of Germany.

From the announcer's booth the name Mildred Didrikson reverberated through the bowl. The long-limbed, powerful, graceful girl stepped into the center of things.

"When my first turn came, I was aiming to throw the javelin right over that flag," Babe said. "I drew back, then came forward and let fly. With the coolness and my lack of any real warm-up, I wasn't loosened up. As I let the spear go, my hand slipped off the cord on the handle."

The crowd gasped; it was obviously a bobbled throw. The heave had practically no elevation, sailing in a straight line like a catcher might peg a throw to second base.

At first it looked as if the long wooden spear might reach the German flag. But it kept flying in that straight line, looking like the sharp steel point might go *through* the flag. But it kept flying. And flying.

The fans broke into a roar, wrote Grantland Rice in his syndicated column. "The moment the javelin struck and quivered in the green turf. The crowd knew a world record had been shattered without waiting for any announcer."

Babe beat the world record by eleven feet and won the gold medal in the event, the first medal of all the women on the American team.[29]

Forty-eight hours later Babe broke her own world's record for the eighty-meter hurdles. "The Olympic record here was 12.2 seconds," Babe said. "The world's record, which I had set only a couple of weeks before in Evanston, was 11.9 seconds. I beat both those marks in winning my heat in 11.8 seconds."

Babe was running against a teammate in the eighty-meter hurdle finals. Evelyne Hall was a 1928 Olympian, but Babe had beaten her in the 1931 and 1932 National AAU championship competitions.

Six women lined up for the race. "I was so anxious to set another new record that I jumped the gun, and they called us all back," said Babe. A second false start would disqualify her, so she held back on the next start until she saw the other runners take off. Babe was the last runner to jump the first hurdle, but by the third she was sharing the lead with Evelyne Hall.

"Babe and I went over the last hurdle together," Evelyne Hall said. The women matched stride for stride for the last ten yards and seemed to cross the finish line simultaneously. She added, "When I went back and walked by the athletes from all the foreign countries, they were all cheering and clapping and saying, 'You won, you won, you won.'"[30]

But the race officials were taking their time to determine the placings of the runners. Too much time.

"After a while they came back and announced that Didrikson was first and I was second and that the time for both of us was 11.7 seconds, which was a new world's record," said Evelyne. "I was surprised, and I was disappointed, very disappointed."

In newsreel footage, Evelyne looks absolutely giddy with her second-place medal. Babe, with her gold medal, looks as if there had been a death in the family. "I'm just sorry I couldn't have had a better time," she drawls into the microphone.

Babe's world-record time would stand for seventeen years. (And though the finishing times indicate a tied race, it was Babe's name on the record for having finished in first place.) In two events she had set two world records and earned two gold medals.

"The Babe came here to run amok," a writer marveled. "And she's running two amoks."

Back at their quarters, Babe's boasting and proclamations were getting on her teammate's nerves. Babe bragged to anyone who'd listen that she would be the first woman in Olympic history to win three gold medals once she won the high jump. She didn't consider it boasting; to her, she was simply stating facts, based on her skills and exuberant self-confidence.

Babe was an annoying braggart, but she made good on her brags. One night she and her teammates visited a local amusement park. They stopped at a shooting gallery and, one by one, other women plinked away at the moving ducks, hitting only a few. After watching awhile, Babe grabbed the rifle and flattened twenty-four out of twenty-four of the moving metal targets.[31]

The other American Olympians were learning that when she crowed, you could be sure the sun was up. All that was left was the high jump, an event where Babe was particularly skilled.

"There was a big competition going on because Babe had won the javelin on Sunday and the hurdles on Wednesday," said Jean Shiley, another 1928 Olympian and Babe's main competition in the high jump. "If anybody was going to defeat her it was up to me. It was a friendly competition. We were both on the same team and whoever won it was fine, just so it was for the country."[32]

By the time the bar reached 5 feet, 4 inches, the contest was down to a two-person jump-off between Babe and teammate Jean Shiley. (The previous world record holder at 5 feet, 3 inches was unable to surpass her record and was now out of contention.)

Quarter inch by quarter inch, the judges raised the bar until it stood at 5 feet, 5¾ inches. It was too high. Babe and Jean Shiley both missed their attempts to clear the bar. The judges lowered the bar a quarter inch, and Jean Shiley made a jump that jiggled the standard to the point that it almost fell. Babe cleared the bar with room to spare, but the judges went into a huddle to confer.

Someone had raised the point that Babe's unorthodox jumping style was forbidden by Olympic rules. She would be disqualified from the competition.

The decision is as inexplicable today as it was then. The "western roll" technique—a technique similar to what's known today as the "Fosbury Flop"—was in wide use by the male jumpers, and Babe had been using the technique all day. Babe and the judges shared some strong words (and not a little Texas cussing), but the decision stood.

"Up in the press box Grantland Rice could tell what was happening," Babe said. "He talked to me right afterwards, and said he thought I'd been given a bad deal. So did some of the other writers. That made me feel a little better."

In the end, the Los Angeles Olympic Committee awarded Shiley the gold and Didrikson the silver medal. As first-place winner, Shiley would get credit for the world's record jump that both accomplished. The Los Angeles Olympic Committee's final report reflects its bewilderment at Babe's disqualification: "Miss Didrikson used a western roll that would do credit to any man while Miss Shiley used the conventional style.[33]

Babe came to national attention largely due to the attention paid to her by a new breed of sports writer. Many large newspapers assigned their sportswriters to a single sport, where they could specialize in local personalities and results within their circulation area. The 1920s saw the rise of nationally syndicated sports columnists such as Grantland Rice,

Paul Gallico, Red Smith, and Ring Lardner, who wrote about all sports all over the country. These national columnists could create heroes out of athletes who impressed them. Grantland Rice remained a friend of and adviser to Babe Didrikson for the rest of her life.

Babe never participated in a major track and field event again. Her collection of medals was spoiled forever, she said. "That silver medal for the high jump spoiled it. All the rest were gold—firsts." The public wasn't spoiled on the Texas Babe, however. She was clever, funny, and her slow Texas drawl was endearing. Babe came out of the Olympics with massive name recognition and friendships with some powerful news and sports writers.[34]

She knew her strength: athletics. But professional women athletes had few earning opportunities. For a few years Babe made a living off her name and public curiosity, playing with a barnstorming exhibition baseball team, a girls' basketball league, and even performing in vaudeville.

She found her niche in professional golf. For the next two decades, until her death from cancer in 1956, the Texas Wondergirl was the best-known, most successful woman golfer in the world. She was the driver behind and cofounder of the Ladies Professional Golf Association (LPGA). Year after year she topped lists naming her the greatest female athlete of all time.

Babe's spit-in-your-eye competitive attitude, dry sense of humor, and Texas drawl still resonate. Well into this century, when writers talk about Olympic history, or sports radio hosts talk about women's sports, the Texas Babe is part of the conversation.

CHAPTER 4

BOB THORNTON AND AMON CARTER

DALLAS FOR EDUCATION, FORT WORTH FOR FUN

MARCH 2, 1936, WOULD MARK TEXAS'S HUNDREDTH BIRTHDAY.

This wasn't the anniversary of Texas statehood. (Texas didn't become a star on the U.S. flag until 1845.) But it was a date—to Texans, anyway—akin to the Fourth of July combined with Bastille Day and quadrupled.

On March 2, 1836, fifty-nine mostly Anglo men signed their names to a document declaring Texas independent of Mexico, thereby summoning the Mexican Army, resulting in scuffles at the Alamo and San Jacinto, and ending with the one-legged Mexican General Santa Anna in chains and his army hightailing back to Mexico. These events are celebrated as Texas Independence Day.

Just as other states might plan a statewide historical event, Texans formed committees and issued proclamations calling for community parades, historical reenactments, oratory, pageants, flags, concerts, the dedication of statues and markers, and more oratory. Most Texans anticipated commemorating the centenary of the state's independence with modest local celebrations of its history and culture. The anniversary was shaping up as a date to be celebrated by Texans and little noted beyond the borders of the state.

But two men—bitter civic rivals—each envisioned very different Texas-sized birthday parties. And each expected the rest of the nation would join in to help blow out the candles.

Both succeeded, each in his own way.

After passing a general endorsement of an undefined centenary event (or events) back in 1925, the Texas legislature did little more than form committees and jibber-jabber about a Texas-sized centennial celebration for most of the next nine years. At the beginning of 1934 there was no plan, no financing, and no consensus, and the state was twenty-six months away from marking its one hundredth birthday.[1]

Opinion was divided about whether the state should hold a large central celebration or smaller ones in the towns that were touched by the struggle for independence from Mexico. San Antonio, home of the iconic Alamo, felt that it should hold the central spotlight; Houston said it deserved state financing for a major exposition due to its size and proximity to the San Jacinto battlefield, where Texans defeated Santa Anna's army and won independence. West Texans wanted to bear no additional taxation for monies used to commemorate events in which they had no part in 1836. Politicians faced a choice between patriotism and purse as the need for Depression relief grew and tax revenues stagnated.[2]

It appeared that the state was headed for a centennial birthday celebrated with popguns, not skyrockets.

Texas State Senator Margie Neal, a Carthage newspaper owner and member of the exposition board, refused to let the matter die. When Governor Miriam Ferguson called the next session of the legislature in January 1934, Senator Neal sponsored S.B. 22 and donned battle dress to convince her colleagues to pass it.[3]

Senate Bill 22 required, once and for all, a statewide centennial observance in 1936. A mandated committee would choose the site of the "principal celebration" based on which city offered the greatest financial package and support. Although the committee might endorse holding other events in cities identified with Texas's early history, only the central exposition would be designated the Texas Centennial Exposition.

One city—and one city *only*—would host the signature event. And which city should that host city be? The betting money was on Houston. The city was big enough and rich enough to stage a world's fair-worthy event, and its name and geography had a clear connection to the events of 1836. There was a chance, others opined, that San Antonio could snag the prize based on the presence of the Alamo alone. By general agreement, those cities were the only realistic choices.

Neal's bill passed into law on June 6, 1934, with a streamlined committee already in place. (Although the bill made no commitment to state funding for that "principal event," everyone expected the state to pony up plenty of money once the host city made its plans clear.) Within a month the committee was sending specifications and requirements to the mayors of the state's four largest cities—Houston, San Antonio, Fort Worth, and Dallas—requesting bids to host "a Centennial celebration as big and great and beautiful and inspiring as humanly possible and with the resources available." The committee required that sealed bids be returned by September 1.[4]

The minute Dallas Mayor Charles E. Turner received his bid package, he phoned Bob Thornton.

Robert Lee "Bob" Thornton was born in 1880 in a dugout cabin in Hamilton County, west of Waco. His father was a tenant farmer, and the Thorntons moved to Ellis County, thirty miles south of Dallas, in time for Bob to start the first of his five years of formal schooling.

He proved to be particularly adept at mathematics, a talent that got him out of the fields and into a job at a grocery store in a small town nearby. Within two years he was using his schoolhouse arithmetic to keep the store's books. He received a loan from the grocer to attend business school in Dallas.

For a farm boy who had seen only farms and rural villages, seeing Dallas at the turn of the century must have been like Dorothy dropping into Oz. With a population of 43,000, Dallas was tied with Houston as the second-largest city in the state, behind only San Antonio. The streets of the commercial district—paved with bois d'arc bricks—were crowded with all manner of vehicles: horse drawn and mule drawn, two-wheel gigs and four-wheel carriages, streetcars, delivery wagons, bicycles, and loco-motives. The city seemed to be in constant motion—goods picked up here, delivered there; pedestrians crossed the streets and filled the sidewalks, walking with a purpose, heads down, seeming to talk of important things.

Twenty-year-old Bob Thornton fell in love with Dallas at first sight, he said later. And he spent the rest of his life helping the adopted city he loved remain vibrant, vital, and important.

His first job after leaving business school (and repaying the grocer who loaned him the money to attend) was as a candy salesman rep-resenting lines of confections to dry goods stores in the small towns throughout Central Texas and Indian Territory. He learned salesmanship, organization, customer service, and problem solving as he negotiated sales to experienced merchants. During his travels he met the daughter of a respected Waxahachie businessman, married her, and brought her back to Dallas to start a family of their own.

Thornton learned to operate his own retail business when he and partners purchased an existing stationery store. The store was modestly successful but didn't provide the challenges Thornton had in mind for himself.

In 1916 Thornton found the profession that would challenge and reward him for the rest of his life: banking. With borrowed money, Thornton, his brother-in-law, and another partner founded a private banking house in Dallas, a town that already had too many.

Thornton's customer service and salesmanship skills paid off at the partners' first storefront location. The bank extended its hours to make banking more convenient for its customers, lent money on automobiles, and gambled on entrepreneurs and small business start-ups.

"Any fool can lend money," Thornton is quoted as saying. "It's getting it back with interest that's the trick."[5]

As president of a small bank, Thornton could give an immediate answer to any loan application or business request. He brought a country boy's horse sense to his customer's needs, and only rarely did he have to consult with his partners about any transaction.

Dallas County State Bank prospered and moved to a larger "uptown" location. In 1925 the bank received a federal banking charter, changing its name to Mercantile National Bank and becoming one of the city's larger banks. Business and civic leaders recognized Thornton's business and professional skills, tapping him for involvement in their organizations. He was appointed to city boards, elected president of the Texas Bankers' Association, served as president of Industrial Dallas, Inc., and in 1929 was named director of the annual State Fair of Texas.

"It is certainly possible to be a good citizen and not be a banker," Thornton said. "But it is impossible to be a good banker and not be a good citizen."[6]

Older civic leaders welcomed Thornton's involvement. He was not a "follow me, boys!" leader, claiming credit for achievements. Instead of directing others, he enlisted them to complete necessary tasks and gave them full credit when they did so. His objective was always to make Dallas a bigger, better city for those who lived there.

Thornton got things done quickly and efficiently, he said later, because he filled his address book with the names and phone numbers of the city's "yes and no" people, businesspeople who could, on the spot, commit their companies to support financially any civic project or issue. "We didn't have time for no proxy people," Thornton said. As the Depression made itself felt in Dallas, he used his yes and no people to raise whopping amounts of money for emergency relief.

In 1933, as the Depression tightened its grip on Texas and the rest of the country, Thornton was elected to the first of his three terms as president of the Dallas Chamber of Commerce. Business across the state had slowed to a crawl, and in Dallas, progress was stalled.

But when Bob Thornton reviewed the Texas Centennial Commission's bid package in July 1934, he saw a clear path out of the doldrums.

Of the four cities asked to submit bids to host the "central celebration" of Texas's birthday, San Antonio and Houston were odds-on favorites. Fort Worth was "Cowtown," the central market for west Texas's cattle industry, but it probably didn't have the resources to host a significant event. Dallas had the resources but had no historical claim on the state's birthday party. The executive committee of the Texas Centennial Commission would receive sealed bids from the cities on September 1, schedule on-site tours of the cities, and announce the results shortly.

With a salesman's enthusiastic optimism, Thornton saw Dallas as the *only* reasonable choice to host the centennial celebration. He would nod to the historical aspects of the event, but the real value, Thornton believed, was to showcase the progress Texas had made in the previous century and what it could accomplish in the next. And progress just happened to be Dallas's long suit.[7]

There was also the matter of money. The legislature had not yet appropriated money to help pay for the celebration, but the choice of the site would be based on which city offered the greatest financial package and support.

Thornton opened his address book and began phoning his "yes and no" people.

The centennial commission came to Dallas for the first of its three visits to prospective cities on September 6. (Fort Worth, assuming that Houston or San Antonio had a lock on the competition, declined to submit a bid.)

Thornton held the commission spellbound, promising a "Texanic" Texas event that would highlight the state's progress of the past one hundred years and the progress of the next one hundred. Accompanied by colorful architectural renderings, charts, and maps, he described Dallas's location as a gateway city with more than nine million persons living within three hundred miles (more than San Antonio and Houston combined). Maps demonstrated that Dallas was the center point of all state transportation systems—train, roads, and airlines—and that visitors to Houston or San Antonio would have to travel through Dallas anyway.[8]

He took the commission on a tour of the Dallas fairgrounds and reminded them that the city had forty-six years' experience with staging a profitable exposition: the annual State Fair of Texas. At one point a commissioner asked Thornton if Dallas planned a grand esplanade on the grounds. "Of course," the banker answered. "We'll have a Texas-sized esplanade." Later, he turned to the architect and whispered, "What the hell's an esplanade?"[9]

There was one final item. The commission chairman posed a question that he said he would put to all competing cities: "Assuming you are chosen as the Centennial city, would you carry on anyway without any state or federal aid?"

"Dallas has already said 'Yes,'" Thornton replied without hesitation. "The Dallas bid stands firm for the Centennial."

At the end of the tour, members of the Texas Centennial Commission boarded a train to Houston for that city's presentation.

Houston's showing was half-hearted, at best. A county judge escorted the commissioners down the Houston Ship Channel to the San Jacinto battlefield, a hot, swampy lowland infested with mosquitoes, for lunch, where they heard an overlong patriotic speech. Back at the hotel meeting room, the commissioners, sweaty and mosquito-bitten, heard a list of existing buildings—a hospital, city hall, the municipal library—that might be used to house exposition exhibits.

Houston officials had failed to engage the support of the business community, and wholehearted financial support was lacking. Asked if the city would carry on with the event without state or federal aid, Houston Mayor Oscar Holcombe said Houston would not be interested. "In that case, it would be a Houston fair and not a Texas Centennial, in reality," he added.

The commission moved on to San Antonio.

The San Antonio presentation merely set forth its claim as the logical Texas Centennial site. Special emphasis was placed on the public's historic interest in San Antonio—particularly the Alamo—as a drawing feature. The San Antonians offered up a laundry list of scattered parklands for use as centennial sites, estimating their total value at close to $5 million.

San Antonio's proposal was contingent on at least a million dollars of state or federal funding.

On September 9, the commission members met in Austin in private session to discuss the bids and visits. Deliberating until late afternoon, commissioners finally revealed their choice to the reporters waiting to phone their home newspapers.

In the end, Dallas money smothered the centennial hopes of Houston and San Antonio. The commission chose Dallas as the exclusive host of the Texas Centennial Exposition.

The Fort Worth newspaper correspondent phoned his boss, *Fort Worth Star-Telegram* publisher Amon G. Carter. Told of Dallas's Centennial coup, a writer said, "Amon set a record for consecutive gawddamns."[10]

In many ways, Amon G. Carter and R. L. Thornton were cut from the same bolt of fabric. They were born within six months of one another, both the sons of farmers. They both spoke in a manner that betrayed their rural origins and made no attempt to hide them. Both were passionate civic boosters, fostering and promoting the interests of their adopted cities. The two men were salesmen at heart, proud of the attributes of their chosen communities and eager that others view them the same way.

And that's what made them bitter (if usually courteous) rivals. Thornton was from Dallas, and Carter was from Fort Worth, competitive north Texas cities just thirty miles apart.

"What does Fort Worth have that Dallas doesn't?" Thornton would ask when pitching a company to locate in Dallas. His answer: "A major city just thirty miles east of it." "You'll want to come to Fort Worth, where the West begins," Carter might say in a similar circumstance, "not to Dallas, where the East peters out."

The rivalry was famous. Stories abound that when Carter was forced to attend a meeting in Dallas, he would bring his lunch in a brown paper bag, refusing to spend a dime in a Dallas restaurant. Thornton was said to have a sign on his desk saying, "Fort Worth Passports Validated Here."

Amon Carter, like most Texans, had figured San Antonio or, maybe, Houston would be chosen to host the Texas Centennial Exposition. But Dallas pulled a fast one. Dallas, which wasn't even a city in 1836, pledged to stage an event every bit as educational, historical, entertaining, and *commercial* as the 1933 Chicago Century of Progress World's Fair. City fathers in Dallas sealed the deal by making personal pledges of $8 million to supplement state funds.[11]

Carter was furious that Dallas would get the prestige, tourists, and money that came with hosting the Texas Centennial celebration while Fort Worth, just thirty miles away, would get nothing. He called together a group of Fort Worth businessmen to plot retribution. He'd show the neighboring city "just how the cow ate the cabbage."[12]

Starting from scratch less than a year before the Dallas event was set to open, Carter set out to upstage the bigger city to the east.

Amon Giles Carter was born in a log cabin in Wise County, Texas, in 1879. His formal education ended after the eighth grade when he left home to earn his living with an assortment of scams, cons, dodges, and penny-ante businesses. He found his calling as a salesman at age eighteen when he went to work for the American Copying Company of Chicago selling color portraits and frames. He was a dogged, creative salesperson and was soon brought to the home office as the company's national sales manager.[13]

Recognizing that his prospects were limited (and wanting to see more of the country), Carter found employment with a San Francisco advertising agency. Advertising agencies were new to the media landscape. National manufacturers, having little patience with researching and placing small ads in hundreds of newspapers across the country, would hire an advertising agent to do the work. The ad agency would place the ads, collecting a small commission from the newspaper for each ad placed. Carter gained an extensive knowledge of national newspapers, their rates, and their ad sales strategies but eventually grew bored with the work.

He returned to Fort Worth in 1905 to find that the raw frontier outpost he'd known as a youngster was now a booming city. The livestock industry and railroads had helped transform Fort Worth into a city with electric lights, a good water system, a workable form of city government, and a respectable bond rating. Carter was soon asked to invest in a start-up newspaper, but his only capital was a skill at selling ads and a knowledge of the national ad market, skills none of the other investors possessed. When the first issue of the Fort Worth *Star* appeared in February 1906, it was with Carter in the role of advertising sales manager. The *Star* was a bedraggled rag competing with the powerful Fort Worth *Telegram*'s circulation of more than eleven thousand, but Carter was a powerful salesperson.[14]

As successful as he was at filling the *Star*'s columns with ads, Carter could never match the *Telegram*'s circulation or resources. The *Star*'s main investor was soon impatient and ready to close the paper. As a last-ditch effort, he placed Carter in full charge of the newspaper.

Carter didn't spend a lot of time flogging his corpse of a newspaper. Instead, he hatched a plan to purchase his larger competitor and merge the two newspapers into a monopoly afternoon daily. Through an intermediary, Carter offered $100,000 for the larger newspaper, using three diamond rings and a diamond-and-pearl stickpin as collateral for a down payment of $2,500. His connections with several Fort Worth businessmen—the Monnigs and Striplings were savvy retailers who saw the advertising cost savings in having to advertise in only one afternoon newspaper—and a little financial black magic provided the remaining $97,500. The combined *Star* and *Telegram* debuted in January 1909.[15]

Given his sales background, expansive personality, and talent for promotion, Carter built the *Star-Telegram* into a major metropolitan newspaper. In just four years the paper had a circulation of 40,000, making it the fourth largest newspaper in the state. He acquired the Hearst-owned Fort Worth *Record* in 1924 and merged it with the *Star-Telegram*, giving him a virtual newspaper monopoly in the city. Carter plowed every cent of profit back into the newspaper; he wasn't wealthy, but he was traveling in that direction.[16]

In his anecdotal biography of Carter, *Amon: The Texan Who Played Cowboy for America*, longtime *Star-Telegram* columnist Jerry Flemmons describes Carter's inspiration for further growth. Carter first looked eastward, Flemmons says, and saw only Dallas.[17]

He then turned to the west, toward the rural, barren, and primitive expanses of West Texas. Population was sparse, and established newspapers were already in the area. But no single town was larger than Fort Worth all the way to the Pacific Ocean, and most newspapers published in West Texas were generally small-town affairs.

It didn't hurt, in Carter's eyes, that oil discoveries in West Texas were bringing unprecedented wealth to the area.

The *Star-Telegram* had two audiences: its Fort Worth readership and the two million farmers, ranchers, and small-town folks who populated the eighty-four counties of West Texas. Local Fort Worth readers received their share of news about city government and local schools; West Texans could rely on the *Star-Telegram* for news about their own town, news of local festivals and graduations, and the all-important high school football scores. Weather was another topic of great interest to the largely agricultural region, and the *Star-Telegram* took a chamber of commerce approach. The word "drought" was never used, but the paper reported on "prolonged dry spells." Every rain in the area, even one resulting in flash flooding, was described as "beneficial showers."

Amon Carter built the *Star-Telegram* into the largest newspaper in the state by "owning" West Texas, and Fort Worth was the gateway and host city to that unique area. As the state's centennial year approached, Amon Carter had fashioned Fort Worth into the city "Where the West Begins."[18]

In the immediate aftermath of the announcement that Dallas would host the centennial celebration, Thornton's mind was on money, not Fort Worth. Dallas bit down on a hard biscuit when it committed to fund the exposition with no expectation of state or federal support. Thornton knew that government money could be had; he just had to shake it loose. His "yes" people went to work in Washington and Austin.

Dallas announced a citywide vote on a $3 million bond package to help finance its centennial celebration. Far from the hoped-for $15 million, the Texas legislature eventually passed a $3 million appropriation, with less than half going to Dallas for the express purpose of building and furnishing a permanent Hall of State on the exposition grounds. A reluctant U.S. Congress passed an additional $3 million after Vice President John Nance Garner, a Texan, shamed members into (at least) matching the state's contribution.

But Dallas couldn't wait for the money to arrive. On September 10, 1934, the day after the selection of Dallas, committees and groups began to execute battle plans that had been drawn up earlier and were sitting at the ready. A publicity group prepared ads to run in newspapers and magazines across the country. Another group contacted business organizations, encouraging them to hold their national conventions in Dallas during the exposition. Still others met with executives of some of the largest companies in the country to enlist exhibitors. By the time the gates opened, the Texas Centennial Exposition would amass $25 million from government funding, sponsorships, licensing fees, and other sources.

Few people in Dallas were giving any thought to Fort Worth, but Amon Carter wasn't about to stand around and allow Dallas to collect every egg in the henhouse.

As the *Star-Telegram* grew more successful under Amon Carter's management, so did his enthusiasm for and control over Fort Worth. He was not a city "boss" in the way New Yorkers or Chicagoans would understand the term. ("He managed the city civilly and politically, but rarely out front," according to a former employee.) Instead, he was at once the benevolent uncle who wanted only what was best for his city and the impatient dictator using his newspaper as a cudgel. He knew how to find money when his beloved city needed it.[19]

Carter was determined to stage a centennial celebration to rival the Dallas event, and for that he'd have to tap every one of his business and political connections. "You'd think Dallas invented Texas just because they bid higher for the Centennial than any other city," he grumbled.

He had applied for a $250,000 grant from the Texas Centennial Commission, an amount he was certain to receive once the Texas legislature passed a centennial appropriation. But that was just a drop in the bucket compared to the $1.1 million budget Carter had in mind, so he set out to claim a share of the federal largesse that was pouring out of New Deal Washington. The Public Works Administration turned down his request for $700,000, but after Carter's personal appeal to President Franklin D. Roosevelt, the agency reconsidered and put a check in the mail. Vice President John Nance Garner found an additional $250,000 in federal funding for Carter.[20]

Back in Fort Worth, the city council authorized $150,000 for purchase of a 138-acre tract west of downtown, the former site of WWI-era Camp Bowie. The city also appointed some of the city's most prominent citizens to a board of control to oversee the day-to-day operations of the planned exposition. And a $1.25 million bond issue was in the works.

By the end of January 1936, Carter and control board chairman Walter Monnig had the location and funding set for a Fort Worth Frontier Exposition intended to steal the thunder and the customers from Dallas. They wouldn't be breaking ground, however, until they decided just what a Frontier Exposition ought to be.

Meanwhile, the Dallas Texas Centennial Exposition was due to open its gates in three months.

Seven thousand men were working twenty-four hours a day to put finishing touches on the Dallas Centennial grounds. All the buildings were complete, waiting only to be filled by exhibitors. Pavers finished the walkways while landscapers filled greenhouses with ornamental plants and grasses that would be planted shortly before opening day.

There had been problems, of course: soil composition, strikers, late deliveries, and a few petty political squabbles, to name a few. But the supervisors under Bob Thornton's management sorted out the issues and maintained the work schedule. "Construction has been handled with a circumspection that comes from careful banker management," *Business Week* reported.[21]

The Centennial management group wasn't content to merely prepare the grounds and open the gates; committees were working full-time on publicity, advertising, and education. The publicity campaign kicked off on January 1, 1936, when Texas Governor James Allred bantered with Hollywood star Ginger Rogers on a coast-to-coast radio hookup during halftime at the Rose Bowl, where the Southern Methodist University football team faced off against Stanford. Later that day, the radio audience for the Sugar Bowl heard Lieutenant Governor Woodul during halftime of the Texas Christian University-Louisiana State University showdown. Millions of sports fans heard one or both broadcasts. The message: "Come to Texas for the biggest show you've ever seen." Governor Allred also hopped aboard the Texas Centennial Press Train, joining a blue-ribbon collection of newspaper publishers, political leaders, and celebrities to visit every major population center in the country during the spring. They gave interviews, shook hands, and gave out ten-gallon "Centennial hats," all while inviting everyone within earshot to come to Texas for a Texas-sized birthday celebration."[22]

Ads for the Centennial appeared in all mass-circulation magazines. Every daily and weekly newspaper within nine hundred miles of Dallas received a schedule of paid ads. The major dailies in the rest of the country also carried ads inviting readers to come to Texas. The Texas

Centennial Exposition rented more than six hundred billboards on routes leading to Dallas.

Newspapers across Texas urged their readers to prepare for and make welcome the expected out-of-state visitors that summer. They editorialized on the civic benefits of travelers coming through their towns on the way to Dallas.

Bob Thornton and other Centennial executives regularly spoke to Lions Clubs, Rotary clubs, chambers of commerce, and church groups in scores of small towns surrounding Dallas. Thornton eschewed any mention of Texas history or tradition, saying that the principal benefit of the Centennial to Texas is the influx of visitors who want to buy things. "Everybody is seeking a new hope, a new place, a new opportunity. Texas offers that opportunity."

The City of Dallas did its part, too. The city commission made sure all arterial roads leading to the exposition grounds were resurfaced and rut free. The commission ordered rigorous inspections of residences and businesses along those routes to be sure that they would "represent our city in the best possible way." Even the entertainment establishments along Elm Street pledged that "Dallas' hospitality to Centennial visitors will not be confined to the fair grounds."[23]

Amon Carter, standing on the 138-acre vacant land that was supposed to become Fort Worth's biggest show, could only imagine the sounds of saws and hammers hard at work in Dallas. By the first of March, his Frontier Fiesta was still nothing but goats grazing in an open field. Carter and Monnig had heard plenty of ideas. The cattlemen wanted a livestock show, cowboys wanted a rodeo, and the historical society ladies wanted to stage an amateur historical pageant—"Texas History, Watch It Grow!"—that sounded about as rousing as watching potatoes bake. Nothing yet was big enough, nothing rip-roaring enough to outshine Dallas, and certainly nothing deserving enough for his people of Fort Worth and West Texas.[24]

Carter could only mutter a string of "gawddamns" and pray for a miracle.

Amon G. Carter's miracle arrived in Fort Worth in the person of Billy Rose, a 5 foot, 1 inch, semi-successful Broadway producer wearing a pinstripe suit with spats and talking faster than Texas ears could understand him. Using his Hollywood contacts, Carter had drawn the New Yorker to Fort Worth.

A Tin Pan Alley songwriter with an abiding love for vaudeville, Rose had produced one successful revue, one musical flop, and was now enjoying his biggest audience hit yet. *Billy Rose's Jumbo!* was a musicalized circus featuring comedy by Jimmy Durante, songs by John Raitt, music by Paul Whiteman and His Orchestra, actual circus acts, underdressed women, and a white elephant named Rosie, all wrapped around a thin story line.[25]

Billy Rose needed another big event to cement his reputation as a producer of theatrical extravaganzas. Amon Carter needed a big show on an impossible deadline. They needed each other.

On March 7, Rose signed a $100,000 contract for a hundred days to act as Frontier Centennial's full-time producer and general director. He would create, direct, and manage all the shows, acts, concessions, and entertainment "of such magnitude and appeal as to be the outstanding of all Centennial celebrations."[26]

Carter and the producer visited the 138-acre open field that Rose was expected to fill with buildings and attractions in time for a July 4 opening. Rose also toured the almost-complete grounds of the Texas Centennial Exposition, purportedly sharing his opinion of the Dallas event with Carter. "There's only one thing that can compete with twenty million dollars' worth of machinery," Rose said. "And that is girls—pelvic machinery." While Dallas might educate its visitors with a look at a cold, mechanical future, Rose added, Fort Worth will entertain them.[27]

Rose's immediate task was to increase the level of ballyhoo surrounding the Frontier Centennial. He fed the press a steady stream of top-of-the-head ideas and sold them as set in concrete: a musicalized rodeo featuring a thousand beautiful girls dressed in pioneer garb, signing Shirley Temple for the first week of the show, a dramatic pageant called "The Fall of the Alamo," and stagecoaches to carry visitors around the grounds. All this was from the oiled tongue of a master promoter, and few of the promises came to fruition. The stories served their purpose, however, by sparking enthusiasm over an event that once threatened to die on the vine while buying Billy Rose time to work out what the *real* Frontier Centennial would look like.[28]

The people of Dallas were experienced at ignoring Fort Worth, though some of Billy Rose's more outlandish ideas found their way into the local papers. The city was too busy polishing the turnstiles and sweeping the streets in preparation for its own Opening Day on June 6 to pay any mind to the Broadway blowhard thirty miles to the west.

He may have been a little free with the facts, but Rose knew one thing to be absolutely true: "The exposition in Dallas will show the progress of art, education, and culture during the last hundred years, but my exposition will show just the opposite."[29]

On the morning of June 6, 1936, a three-mile-long parade proceeded up Main Street of Dallas. Texas Governor James Allred was in the lead car, grinning and waving at the crowds stacked five deep on the sidewalks like a politician facing reelection. Ornate floats representing the six national flags that have flown over Texas and scenes from the history of the state followed. Marching bands, military men, mounted riders, and circus folk filled the intervals.[30]

Governor Allred arrived at the entrance to the Texas Centennial Exposition at 10 a.m. After a brief ribbon-cutting ceremony, the gates swung open, and the parade drove onto the fairgrounds. Immediately inside the grounds were the fountains of a lighted reflecting basin with the broad quarter-mile walkways of Bob Thornton's "Texas-sized esplanade" on either side. The basin focused the eye on the still-incomplete Texas state building, the Hall of State, where the Lone Star and national flags flew.[31]

Two immense buildings flanked the esplanade: the Transportation Building and the Varied Industries/Communications Buildings were decorated with monumental Southwest-themed statuary, colorful murals, and allegorical bas-reliefs. On the two-hundred-acre grounds were other buildings—Natural History, Food & Fiber, Fine Arts, Aquarium, Hall of Religion, Hall of Negro Life, and the Museum of Domestic Arts housing exhibits of the latest in arts, culture, and science—just as dramatic in appearance and content. The buildings of the livestock section exhibited every animal and reptile—natural and domesticated—commonly found in Texas. The agriculture building included plots of growing crops, foodstuffs made from Texas agricultural products, and the latest in farm equipment. To counter the Texas summer heat, 75 percent of the indoor space was air-conditioned, a luxury for fairgoers in 1936.

The *New York Times* described the public buildings as "architecturally striking. The exposition buildings symbolize the spirit of Texas and the Southwest. Modernistic designs and bright coloring blend with Spanish Colonial architecture, in turn combined with a background of the native cultures of the Mayans and Aztecs."[32]

Ford, General Motors, Chrysler, the great oil companies, electric corporations, and rail systems all had exhibit buildings with regular demonstrations and performances. ("There is a very big reason these industrial concerns are making a big splurge in Dallas," *Collier's* reported. "Texas provides them with a tremendous market for their products.")[33]

There was a midway, of course, with the usual collection of the latest thrill rides (the Rocket Speedway), games of chance (two shooting galleries with fifty guns each), and carnival attractions (Midget City and the Anthropoid Ape Show). With a little searching, the grown-ups could find plenty of adult attractions in an area called Streets of Paris. (City officials strictly enforced laws banning outright nudity and the purchase of alcohol on the fairgrounds. Enforcement was more casual in the city's hotels and nightclubs.)

Texas Centennial organizers in Dallas were intent on showcasing their city as a progressive, successful, can-do, modern city, and they succeeded. But even a focused banker such as Bob Thornton acknowledged there had to be *some* nod to a century of Texas history at its hundredth birthday party. The Cavalcade of Texas was more than a nod: it was a throw-your-hat-over-the-windmill, paint-the-town-red resurrection of the Texas mythos.

Once inside the Centennial grounds, visitors could pay an extra fifty cents for a seat at the "Cavalcade," an oversized pageant played out on a three-hundred-foot movable stage near the racetrack. Hundreds of performers (human and animal) acted out the heroic four-hundred-year history of Texas, beginning with the expeditions of Coronado and La

Salle, the rise and fall of the missions, opening of trade routes, the pira-
cies of Jean Lafitte, the appearance of frontiersmen to aid in Texas's fight
for freedom, the Alamo defeat, and the rise of such leaders as Austin and
Houston. It was a spectacular and emotional telling of Texas history as
Texans like to tell it.

As exposition visitors—116,000 of them the first day alone—departed
the fairgrounds that evening to the booms of a massive fireworks show,
they could marvel at Texas's industrial might and its unique history. But
did they have *fun*? A billboard with lighted letters, the biggest ever seen
in Dallas, across the street from the exit gates offered a solution:

WILD & WHOOPEE
45 MINUTES WEST
FORT WORTH FRONTIER
In Person:
PAUL WHITEMAN, SALLY RAND
CASA MAÑANA REVUE

Billy Rose ordered the billboard; Amon Carter paid for it. Together,
the promoter and the publisher had settled on a theme for their Frontier
Centennial: "Dallas for Education—Fort Worth for FUN!"

Billy Rose was performing just as Amon Carter had hoped, enlisting
some of the country's top-named talent, working with designers and
architects to create the major buildings, choreographing acts, and issuing
a constant stream of P. T. Barnum-like press releases intended to keep the
Frontier Centennial front-page news around the country. Three days after
his March 7 signing, Rose organized a (largely ceremonial) groundbreaking at the site to signal that Fort Worth's event was making progress.

Rose's plan was to feature four major entertainment attractions. First,
he'd import his popular Broadway musical circus, *Jumbo*, to a home on
the grounds. Second, he envisioned a four-thousand-seat theater suited
for dining, dancing, and presentation of Ziegfeld-like revues. The third
attraction was the Pioneer Palace, essentially a giant-sized honky-tonk
with a forty-foot-long bar, a huge dance floor, western bands, and a
saloon-girl chorus line. Finally, Rose had no intention of allowing Dallas

to upstage him in the pageant department. His Last Frontier Pavilion would present the history of Texas without all the flag planting and crumbly old missions, told around a steamy love story, marauding Indians, singing cowboys, a rodeo, and an appearance by the famed Black Horse Troop of the United States Cavalry.

"What the hell are they doing over there?" asked one Texan about Fort Worth's plans. "Is Texas celebrating its independence or the birth of musical comedy?" If the purpose of the Frontier Centennial was to show the *opposite* of Texas's progress in art, education, and culture during the past hundred years, this seemed to Carter the way to do it.[34]

Rose's plan was ambitious, and they had just ninety days to meet the July 4 opening deadline. By mid-April, three contracting firms and more than two thousand workers toiled at the site, trying to decipher drawings and plans still wet from the blueprint machine.

Rose himself worked seventeen hours a day auditioning acts and chorus girls, approving designs, and inspecting every detail. Nothing escaped his attention. Every day he would dictate a list of minute defects—"The ninth wheel on Pinwheel Boulevard isn't spinning" or "One letter on the front gate sign is out." The diminutive New Yorker took to wearing cowboy boots, holstered six-shooters, and a large cowboy hat with an extra-wide brim. With tongue in cheek, Rose told a reporter that the guns were necessary for "protection against Dallas's angry city fathers."[35]

The national press wrote that Fort Worth was likely to make up in liveliness for what it lacked in the cultural aspects. *Business Week* magazine acknowledged that Fort Worth was underfunded and late to the game. "However, Fort Worth is under the unchallenged leadership of Amon Carter, whose exploits are swift and spectacular." "So, Dallas was going for education, and statuary, and modern marvels, was it?" the *New York Times* asked. "Good! Then Fort Worth would set up a brawling, noisy jamboree where the footsore, the weary, and the thirsty could rejoice and revel unrestrained!"[36]

As the opening date grew closer and the nature of the event became clearer, concerns were increasing that Rose's big top might be over the top, even for the Lone Star State. Billy Rose would only promise, "You stick with me, and I'll make a big state out of Texas!"

The Fort Worth Frontier Centennial opened on July 18 with Amon Carter and other dignitaries riding through the entrance atop a stagecoach. Visitors surged through the main gates, following the stagecoach, under a sign proclaiming, "Welcome Stranger." According to one writer, it was the Texas way of saying, "Step in, yank the bridle off, and go as fur as you like in the way of havin' a good time."[37]

The gates led onto Sunset Trail, a detailed reproduction of a frontier western Main Street. It included a working barbershop with rows of shaving mugs, a sheriff's office, a little newspaper office with a printing press, the Astor Hotel, a blacksmith shop with the blacksmith at work, a train station, a country chapel, and beside it, a graveyard with wooden crosses. "Before the summer ended, a real wedding actually was held in the chapel," a publicist said. "But we never got around to really burying someone in the graveyard."[38]

While the women visitors strolled down the wooden sidewalks and visited the quaint shops, male visitors might slip into Sally Rand's Nude Ranch, featuring the (nude) fan-dancing sensation of the 1933 Chicago Century of Progress Exposition. Rand's classy show included performances by a chorus line of well-proportioned women who managed (in publicity photos, anyway) to keep their private parts hidden with ten-gallon hats and board fence rails.

Next was a performance of *Jumbo*, Billy Rose's Broadway musical circus sensation, transported lock, stock, and elephants to Fort Worth and housed in a red-and-gold building designed to look like a circus tent. It was, said *Time*, "a circular theater with a circular curtain to show a circular audience the great show."

If visitors were thirsty, they could relax in the Pioneer Palace, where drinking and gaming were encouraged. The enormous replica of a Texas honky-tonk featured a dance floor, a rodeo arena, a forty-foot-long bar, and a wall of nickel slot machines. Periodically, doors behind the bar would open, a stage would rise, and a troop of vaudeville performers—dish spinners, acrobats, singers, comedians, and other second-tier acts—would perform a show called "The Honky-Tonk Parade." The featured dance act that (almost literally) brought the house down each performance was the Tiny Rosebuds, six women whose average weight exceeded two hundred pounds.

Dallas had its "Cavalcade of Texas," the live, outdoor pageant of Texas history and heroes; Fort Worth presented "The Last Frontier," an outdoor pageant that ignored history and heroes in favor of live buffalo, timid settlers, a surprise Indian attack, and a rousing rescue by the mounted cavalry. "It is a show," columnist Damon Runyon wrote, "where is unveiled the life of the Old West, wild and wooly and full of fleas, and never curried below the knees."[39]

But Billy Rose's Casa Mañana was his piece de résistance. It was a 4,200-seat dining and entertainment venue with the world's largest revolving stage: one hundred thirty feet in diameter. The stage appeared to float on a lagoon larger than a basketball court and could be made to move toward or away from the seated audience. Fountains hidden in the lagoon could throw up a curtain of water, allowing actors to enter or exit and stagehands to set the stage unseen by the audience. A control room hidden in the center of the revolving stage controlled the state-of-the-art lighting and sound systems and the waterworks.

Nineteen gently rising tiers of tableside seating fanned out from the stage. Two hundred black waiters in crisp white tunics served dinner and delivered fresh cocktails from the fifty-foot-long bar at the rear of the theater. Famous jazz bandleader Paul Whiteman and His Orchestra provided dining music.

The nightly show featured famous Broadway and Hollywood acts— Eddie Cantor, Bing Crosby, Martha Raye, Jimmy Durante, Frances Langford, Faye Emerson, and Eddie Foy Jr. There were songs by popular singers and elaborate production numbers featuring chorus girls in lavish costumes.

"If you took a big-league baseball stadium and converted it into a café," Damon Runyon wrote, "And then you added the best scenic effects of an old time Ziegfeld production, you might get something approximating Casa Mañana."[40]

Amon Carter brought Billy Rose to Fort Worth, and Billy Rose brought Broadway with him.

The Texas Centennial Exposition in Dallas and Fort Worth's Frontier Centennial combined drew almost eight million attendees during the summer and fall of 1936. Attendance for both events was lower than expectations due, in part, to a blisteringly hot August, a rainy September, and an unseasonably cold October. Dallas would repeat the 1936 event the following year as the Texas Pan-American Exposition. Vowing not to be "out-entertained" by their neighbor to the west, Dallas organizers hired their own version of Billy Rose to build a swanky nightclub and assemble a program of entertainment to match that of Casa Mañana. George Preston Marshall, a sometime theatrical producer and owner-promoter of a Boston football team, signed on as entertainment director. The resulting Exposition nightspot, the Casino, didn't outshine the Fort Worth venue, but it sparkled with stardust and added to Dallas's second-year revenues. Fort Worth opened its centennial grounds as the Frontier Fiesta in 1936 and 1937. Casa Mañana continued drawing audiences through its final 1939 season. The building was razed in 1942.[41]

If you're inviting nine million people to a party, you better let those potential guests know when the party starts and at whose house it's being held. The Texas Centennial organization in Dallas did just that. They staged one of the largest integrated multimedia ad campaigns of the decade. Newspapers, magazines, billboards, direct mail, posters, ad specialties, and radio reached every family in the five states surrounding Texas an average of seventeen times before opening day. In addition to paid media, civic clubs, churches, schools, and books were used to include the people of Texas. It was a campaign that equaled or exceeded any national branded product of the time. The majority of Fort Worth's advertising and publicity budgets went to bring attendees the thirty miles from Dallas to Forth Worth.

Judging strictly by their balance sheets, both centennial celebrations ended up in the red. But it didn't matter.

Tourists left plenty of money in Dallas and Fort Worth. Hotels and restaurants reported annual sales increases of up to 50 percent. Retailers showed similar gains. The railroads saw a 35 percent increase in the number of fares to Dallas during the months of the Texas Centennial. At a time when the Depression still held many cities in its clutches, Dallas and Fort Worth provided more than three thousand jobs to construction, maintenance, and operations workers.[42]

More important, perhaps, were the forty-five thousand out-of-state visitors who entered Texas each month, their primary destinations being the centennial celebrations in Dallas and Fort Worth. According to the Texas Highway Department, more than one in five admissions were sold to non-Texans.

Many of the non-Texans who entered Texas for the first time came expecting to see the Texas of the movies: tumbleweeds and cactus, marauding Indians, and dusty cowboys armed with six-guns. Instead, they saw modern, thriving cities of commerce, broad new highways, thriving farms and ranches, and friendly hosts.

Dallas demonstrated the modernity, innovation, and entertainment that marked it as a city of the future. Fort Worth provided the Old West experience, albeit one more akin to Broadway than Hollywood.

For many non-Texans (and Texans alike), this was the year that America discovered Texas.

CHAPTER 5

SAM BAUGH

MR. BAUGH GOES TO WASHINGTON

IF THERE WAS ANY FOOTBALL GAME THAT SPECTATORS WOULD REMEMber for the rest of their lives, that sportswriters would dissect and discuss for the next ninety years and would justify without question the creation of the Pro Football Hall of Fame, it would be the game played in Chicago on December 12, 1937. The powerhouse Chicago Bears faced off against the new-to-Washington Redskins for the NFL Championship in what was then considered the world's pro football championship title.

Three days before the game a heavy snow fell on Chicago. Groundskeepers at Wrigley Field had covered the field with tarpaulins and straw, but a hard freeze, the bitter cold, and a strong northwest wind left the playing field a solid sheet of ice on game day. The twenty-degree weather, frozen roads, and a snarling wind discouraged even rabid Chicago fans; attendance was less than sixteen thousand.

Football historians still refer to the game as "The First Ice Bowl."

"The ground was like a skating rink and certainly in no shape for a football game," said the Redskins' rookie quarterback, Sam Baugh. "This was definitely the roughest game of football I ever played in."[1]

Football *was* rough in Sammy Baugh's day. It was a brutal game of kicking, punching, gouging, scratching, cutting, and full-body hits. Players had little protection from the barfight mayhem on the field. Some of the canvas pants had pouches that might hold cotton pads to lessen kidney injury or deep bruising, but players had none of the customized structural shoulder pads, elbow pads, or reinforced footwear worn today. Cleats in 1937 were long, hard, rubber cones, sharp as a chef's knife and screwed into the soles of leather shoes. Forget about modern molded and padded helmets with the "bird cage" face masks. Instead, by 1937 most pro football teams had given up the "glove" helmet in favor of a reinforced leather hat that offered more protection against scalping than brain injury. For most of Sammy Baugh's career as a quarterback, no rules protected the passer after the ball had left his hands. Run or pass, Baugh could expect to end up buried under a mountain of linemen every play of every game during his sixteen-year career in pro football.[2]

Newsmen made a lot of Sammy's Texas toughness, his fearlessness, his self-confidence, and of course, his ability to pass a football. He is known today as the man who weaponized the forward pass, a tactic that, up to his time, was most often a desperation play. "What Babe Ruth's home runs did for Major League Baseball in the 1920s," one writer observed, "Sam Baugh's passing did for the National Football League." Sam could fill football arenas with crowds eager to see how the Texan performed his aerial magic of moving teammates down the field. "Slingin' Sam" changed forever the way football was played, and he demonstrated it during the Redskins' 1937 title game on the Chicago ice.

Funny thing is, Baugh almost chose to play baseball instead.

Samuel Adrian ("Slingin' Sam") Baugh was born in Temple, Texas, on St. Patrick's Day, 1914, but nothing in his boyhood hinted at leprechauns, rainbows, or pots of gold. Sammy's was a farm family, living on a little patch outside the town proper. In his early teens Sam's family moved into town when his father hired on with the railroad.[3]

Life in town wasn't particularly difficult for the Baughs. Sam took on part-time jobs for spending money while attending school. Like other youngsters, he played whatever sports were in season—baseball, football, basketball, track—but didn't have a particular interest in or aptitude for any of them. When he entered high school, Sammy went out for the football team and was slotted into the end position. The Temple football team was a laughingstock, losing consistently but mercifully hidden in the shadow of the school's winning basketball team.

Family lore has it that Sam had a competitive streak in him that spurred him to excel in at least one aspect of the gridiron sport. He salvaged an old tire and hung it from a tree limb. He'd get the tire swinging from side to side and practice throwing the football through it. Day after day in the off-season he practiced with the old tire—faster swings, greater distance—learning timing and how to lead a pass receiver.

During a preseason practice session, his coach saw Sammy throw the football and switched the young man from end to the backfield. His first two passes were interceptions. "I didn't make a damn bit of difference that I could tell," Sammy said. "We just kept on losing."[4]

While Sam was focused on football, the Depression struck central Texas. Farm prices crashed, banks closed, and workingmen were out of jobs. Sammy's father lost his job with the railroad, but the company had a similar job available in West Texas for lesser pay. At the end of Sammy's sophomore year of high school in 1931, the Baughs packed up and moved to Sweetwater.

Sam entered high school and won a spot on the football team. The team played for the state championship, but Sam's contribution was negligible. He played baseball in school, where his throwing arm was appreciated but not worshipped. Perhaps he was distracted by his home life. Sam's father left the family to take up with another woman, leaving Sam's mother with three children, no support, and no way to earn a living. She took in washing, and the children all found part-time jobs. Sammy graduated with hopes of a baseball scholarship, but none materialized. He had no job and no prospects.

Treading water, Sam caught on with a barnstorming semipro baseball team known as the Oilers. Baugh was the youngest on the team. They called him "High Schooler," and he traveled with these men in their twenties and thirties from small town to small town throughout West Texas, challenging local teams to exhibition matches on parched diamonds. The Oiler players were paid a share of the gate (after deductions for food, travel, and equipment); at some stops they didn't earn anything but bruised bodies. But it was baseball, and Sam loved it.

A college baseball coach was also barnstorming that summer. Leo Robert "Dutch" Meyer made it a practice to spend the weeks before school started with his baseball team barnstorming West Texas, his boys taking on everything from high-school teams to hardened professional teams. That summer of 1933 Dutch Meyer and his Texas Christian University Horned Frogs baseball team took on the Oilers in a two-game series in Abilene.[5]

Meyer was captivated by the tall, loose-jointed kid at third base. The boy had a good eye and a great arm, Meyer thought. The coach saw the kid make a side-armed clothesline throw from third base to first and turn away before the ball hit the first baseman's glove, confident the ball would arrive exactly where he wanted it to.

Meyer desperately wanted the boy for the Horned Frogs baseball team. Trouble was, he was out of baseball scholarships.

Toward the end of August, the University of Texas baseball coach called Sam with a last-minute offer. Play baseball for us, the coach offered, and we'll put you through school here on a baseball scholarship. As quickly as he could pack his bags and kiss his mother good-bye, Sam was on the bus to Austin.

The University of Texas team would be a high-profile entrée into major league baseball. The coach was becoming a legend, the team had a winning record, and several recent graduates had signed pro contracts. But Sam had a condition: he wanted to play football in the off-season. That was impossible, the coach told him. Sam would play baseball only.

After four days of practice with the University of Texas team, Sam got back on a bus, northward this time, to Fort Worth and TCU. Coach Meyer had managed to scrounge an athletic scholarship, and Baugh enrolled there as a student athlete in September 1933.

At first, Dutch Meyer didn't expect a lot out of Sam. The kid had a good eye, a better arm, and a quiet self-confidence. Sammy was an exacting punter, too, so maybe he could do a little kicking during football season. But the more he watched Sammy on the diamond—his consistency, his willingness to learn, and the practice, practice, practice time he put in—the more Coach Meyer thought the Sweetwater boy might fit into some plans he was hatching.

Football's forward pass wasn't accepted as a legal play in college ball until 1905, thought to be a safer alternative to the flying wedge of the time. Most schools ignored it, thinking it was "sissified" somehow to gain yardage in the air instead of grinding it out with brute strength on the field.

One college coach—a coach whose players were not so large but exceedingly fast—adopted the forward pass right away. Coach Glenn Scobey "Pop" Warner saw an opportunity for the undersized (yet speedy) Native boys of the Carlisle Indian Industrial School. Using forward passes as trick plays when needed, Pop Warner's teams defeated such nameplate schools as Penn and Harvard. In a 1913 victory over Army, Notre Dame got credit for "pioneering" the forward pass, based largely on the name of speedy receiver Knute Rockne.[6]

By 1933, Texas colleges, mostly smaller schools compared to their eastern and midwestern rivals, included passing plays as a minor alternative to their ground games. Dutch Meyer of TCU was considering an offense built around passing but only if he could find the key player to execute his strategy.

Sam first qualified to play on the varsity football team in 1934. His sophomore year was the year the Southwest Football Conference (SWC) came into its own. The conference—which included mostly Texas schools, with Arkansas and Oklahoma schools in some years—had been around since 1914 but was generally ignored by national sportswriters and team rankings. When they played teams in other conferences, the SWC teams were often considered "practice" matchups for their larger rivals. On October 6, 1934, things changed. That afternoon the Rice Owls beat the unbeatable Purdue Boilermakers with a score of 14–0. Several hours later the Texas Longhorns edged past Notre Dame 7–6. Big-city sportswriters and wire service reporters were thunderstruck, especially when both SWC teams went on to near-perfect records that year. Sponsor Humble Oil and Refining Company assembled a radio network to broadcast SWC games live, and the excitement of Texas college football literally filled the air in Texas and beyond.

The year was not so golden for Sam Baugh. Meyer alternated Sam with another player at quarterback. His kicking was good, but his passing was inconsistent. The season ended with a wait-till-next-year record of 8–4.

During his first year, Sam's inexperience showed. In the off-season Meyer took advantage of Sam's willingness to learn and coupled it with his practice, practice, practice work ethic to make a more consistent player. As a punter, Sam learned to drop the ball just out of bounds behind the opponent's ten-yard line. He became better at reading the other team's play and adjusting accordingly. Meyer gave him the freedom to run whatever play looked like it might work, regardless of the yard line Sam stood on. His passing needed little help, but Sam insisted it be a part of the training regimen.

The 1935 season would be Sam's season.

"I remember our first [team] meeting," he said. "We were in the room waiting for coach to come in, and up on the blackboard were three S's, just three S's, one up under the other. All us idiots, we got to wondering what those S's stood for. And he came in and said, 'This is our passing attack. That first S is for short. The next one: safe. Third one: sure.' I'd never heard of such a thing." Coach Meyer unveiled a plan called the "Meyer Spread," similar to the modern shotgun formation. "They said I had my ends sitting in the stands," he told a writer, "spread out so wide they would sell soda water between plays." Meyer introduced a pass-oriented short yardage system with Sam's arm the key element. Short passes could eat up yardage bite by bite while preventing the opponent from controlling the ball.[7]

Meyer's plan and Baugh's arm worked like clockwork. September, October, November—TCU won every game. They were undefeated going into a November 30 home game with SMU, their thirty-miles-away rival. The Dallas school was coming to Fort Worth with a matching undefeated season. They were playing for a national championship and a trip to the Rose Bowl. On game day, with the score tied and four minutes left in the game, SMU faked a kick and connected a long pass for the winning touchdown.

The TCU Horned Frogs lost that afternoon, but Sam Baugh won a lasting supporter in Amon G. Carter, the influential newspaper publisher who saw his town's spirits soar and cash registers ring at every TCU home game that year. And the year wasn't over. Southern Methodist University played a lackluster game in the Rose Bowl, losing to Stanford

7–0, while the "Cowtown Christians" won an invitation to a rain-soaked Sugar Bowl, beating LSU 3–2.

Williamson Rating Service, the dominant college football ranking voice at the time, voted TCU the nation's top college team. The ranking drew even more national attention to TCU and, especially, to the passing arm of Sam Baugh.

"Texas may run dry of oil, the cows may die of old age or the butcher's knife, and the Alamo might crumble like fresh Graham crackers," a New Orleans sports columnist wrote, "but as long as Texas has Sam Baugh, the Lone Star Staters are home on the range, footloose, and fancy free."[8]

By autumn of 1936, crowds at Fort Worth's Frontier Fiesta and the Dallas Centennial celebrations were dwindling as enthusiastic summer tourists returned to their homes and jobs. Dallas promoters, however, were completing an expansion and renovation of the stadium on the Dallas fairgrounds with plans to call the new facility the Cotton Bowl, and college senior Sam Baugh was beginning his final season with the TCU Horned Frogs.

Dutch Meyer had recruited a worthy backup and eventual replacement for Baugh in the person of sophomore Davey O'Brien, a 5-foot 7-inch, 140-pound dead-eye passer from Dallas. Even so, the season didn't exactly lift off like a rocket for the Horned Frogs. After some lackluster opening games by TCU, the fired-up Arkansas Razorbacks arrived in Fort Worth with heads shaved and prickly like a razorback hog, determined to knock TCU off its pedestal. The Horned Frogs' line couldn't seem to protect Baugh and, although Arkansas was the better team that day, TCU scraped by with an 18–14 win. Sam Baugh left the game injured and would miss the next two matchups.

By the time TCU took the field against SMU, the Horned Frogs were still in contention for the conference title. Arkansas's only loss was against TCU, and TCU had lost only one conference game. A win over the Mustangs would put the Horned Frogs at the top of the Southwest Conference. The SMU game was played in a downpour, with water running over the players' shoe tops and the fat leather football soaked and heavy. The game ended in an unsatisfying 0–0 tie, leaving Arkansas with the conference title.

The final regular game of Baugh's college career pitted the Texas Christians against the California Christians of the undefeated Jesuit Santa Clara University. Amon Carter planned a treat for his home team: he chartered a train to take the team, coaches, marching band, and boosters to California for the game and a weeklong pre-Christmas celebration in San Francisco. To the surprised Santa Clara fans—but not the national press—TCU polished off the California team 9–0. For TCU's graduating seniors, the week in the San Francisco Bay Area was an unrestrained spree of touring (by day) and nightspots (by night). Wherever they went—Fisherman's Wharf, Chinatown, restaurants, clubs, or bars—Amon Carter would find an opportunity to stand, hush the crowd, talk about the wonders of Texas and Fort Worth, and finally, introduce "my boy" Sam Baugh, the finest football player in the nation. The accompanying press ate it up.

The weary Horned Frogs found they had one more game. Promoters of the now-complete Cotton Bowl hadn't yet struck a deal to host the SWC title winners each year, so they arranged a New Year's exhibition game between the best passing teams in the country: TCU and Wisconsin's Marquette University, who'd come within a single game of a national championship that year.

The brand-new bowl drew a sellout crowd, many of whom had never seen Baugh play. "Slingin' Sam" gave them a show. By halftime TCU was leading a dispirited Marquette team 16–6, and Meyer started pulling his seniors off the field. Still leading well into the fourth quarter, Dutch Meyer pointed at one of his bench players, and Samuel Adrian Baugh strolled onto the field to deafening cheers and a standing ovation.

When he left the field that day, he had thrown for four thousand yards in three years and won twenty-nine games with thirty-nine touchdowns. The "Sweetwater Stringbean" had put his name in college record books and helped bring a previously overlooked Texas college football program to national prominence.

Sam Baugh was ready to graduate and find a real job. He was hoping to get back to his first love: baseball.

Amon Carter hated to lose "his boy" to baseball. He reached out to George P. Marshall, the "1937 Billy Rose" that Dallas had hired as its entertainment director for the Dallas Pan-American Exposition. Marshall's theatrical background and promotional skills had more in common with the big-as-Texas Carter personality than with the dry bankers of Dallas, and the two men remained in touch. Marshall confided that he would be moving his Boston Redskins pro football team to Washington, DC, that summer and planned to redouble his promotional efforts on behalf of the team. Carter offered to introduce "his boy," Sammy Baugh, to Marshall. Whether Carter sold him on Baugh or Marshall sold himself on his need for a headline-making player, the team owner began to covet the still-in-school TCU passer.

It's unlikely that Sam knew any of this. He had convinced himself that baseball was his best sport, a sport where he'd likely have a longer career as a player. As a senior, he was wrapping up a nine-letter year at TCU—three years a varsity player in three sports: football, basketball, and baseball. Unfortunately, the numbers showed that baseball was his weakest sport.

That June, after graduation, he went back to the baseball Oilers to showcase his talents on the diamond. The ragtag traveling team that had known him as "High Schooler" had found a civic sponsor and was playing in a scheduled semipro league. From time to time a reporter would ask Sam about his plans. He'd say TCU had invited him to be the freshman football coach that fall, or that he'd be coaching baseball at a private high school in Phoenix. But nothing seemed to pan out.

Marshall continued to contact Baugh throughout the spring and summer with increasing salary offers, urging him to consider playing pro football with the Redskins. The courtship played out in the press, but Sam made no commitment.

The annual *Denver Post* charity baseball tournament drew noted pro players and coaches to mix with successful semipro teams from the West. It was a scouting series of sorts. On August 8, the chief scout of the St. Louis Cardinals showed the press a baseball contract signed by one Samuel A. Baugh. The scout said the contract barred Sam from playing pro football. The nationally known TCU football passer had already checked out of the hotel and was on his way to St. Louis for a baseball tryout.[9]

Marshall was frantic; it appeared that his star prospect had slipped away. The facts get cloudy at this point, with different parties reporting differing conversations, contracts, and conditions. What's likely true is that George Marshall, with his first game just days away, made a last-ditch offer of $5,000 for the first year. (The Redskin's highest-paid player at the time made a little less than $2,000.)[10]

Sam went to Coach Meyer for advice. It's a good offer, Meyer told him. Most college coaches don't make that much. Sam asked how he might get the offer up just a little bit. Hell, boy, Meyer is reported to have said, tell him the figure you want and see if he'll meet you halfway.

Sam called Marshall, asking for $8,000. Marshall didn't negotiate. All right, he said, it'll be $8,000. "To me, that looked like a million bucks," Sam said later.[11]

Sam arrived in Washington on September 9, 1937, and by that afternoon he was in the middle of heavy scrimmages with his team. Sam had missed nearly a month of practice, but it didn't matter. Seven days later the Redskins—playing their first game in Washington—took the field against the New York Giants, winning 13–3.

By mid-December the Redskins were Eastern Division champs, needing only to face down the Chicago Bears for the NFL's 1937 version of a Super Bowl showdown.

There's not a lot of winter in Sweetwater, or Fort Worth for that matter. The twenty-three-year-old Sam Baugh had never experienced temperature that cold, and only three weeks before he had seen snow for the first time in his life.[12]

When the rookie looked out over the ice sheet that was Wrigley Field on December 12, 1937, he may have wished he'd remained a baseball player after all—the soft green turf of a baseball diamond didn't threaten frozen fingers or broken legs. He'd shown his skills as a defensive back and quick-kicker—team members were expected to play both offensive and defensive positions—but his reputation was built on passing a football. And this was not passing weather.[13]

The Redskins had earned their 8–3 Eastern Division in 1937 based on Baugh's passing game. The Bears won their Western Division title with a 9-1-1 record due to their ability to roll over their opponents and smash them flat. Chicago's rollers and smashers were known as the "Monsters of the Midway."

At 1:15 p.m., a coin toss at midfield determined that the Redskins would kick off to the Bears. Catching the ball at his one-yard line, beefy Bronko Nagurski slipped on the ice. The big man got to his feet and lumbered downfield until Baugh bumped him out of bounds at the Chicago 33-yard line. The Monsters smashed into the Redskins' line gaining a first down, but they stalled out and punted, giving it to Washington on their own 7-yard line. Baugh threw long from his own end zone to future Hall of Famer Cliff Battles, who was brought down a yard into Bears' territory. The weather was taking its toll on Baugh, however; he missed two throws and skidded over the ice. His sideline punt went out of bounds at the Bears' 6-yard line.[14]

Ice and cold hobbled both teams; Baugh struggled to complete a string of passes, and Chicago couldn't break through. All the players were angry at the weather and frustrated at their lack of progress. A writer in the press box noted, "the tackling was vicious and bad blood was apparent."

Halfway through the first quarter the Redskins received the ball on their 47-yard line. Baugh refused to let the weather dictate his game, but his first two passes were incomplete. He finally hit Riley Smith for a first down on the Bears' 39. Short pass by short pass (with a few fakes thrown in), Baugh took the ball to within seven yards of the Bears' goal. On the next play, Battles dove in for touchdown.

Washington led 7–0, but the touchdown was enough to kick over a hornet's nest on the Chicago bench. Starting from their own 28-yard line the Bears made a four-minute march downfield to score a touchdown of their own.

The score was tied 7–7 going into the second quarter, and the Bears intended to run up the score, whatever it took. After a few more back-and-forth possessions, Baugh faked a pass and ran through the center of the Bears' line for a 17-yard gain.

His run wasn't worth the yardage; he ended up in the middle of Chicago's beefy and belligerent linemen. George Musso, a 250-pound Bear guard, 250-pound tackle Danny Fortmann, 230-pound Joe Stydahar, and at least one other Bear behemoth were sprawled across the skinny Texas quarterback, squashing him to the frozen ground. A referee rolled the Chicago players aside, looking for Baugh's body like a fireman searching debris for plane crash victims.

"Somewhere, somehow in the pile, somebody gave Baugh's leg an awful wrench," a newsman wrote. When the referee finally untangled the man mountain, he found Sam on the bottom, splashed with blood and clutching his knee. When the Texas quarterback finally got to his feet and tried to limp to the huddle, he felt a stabbing pain in his hip. The Redskins coach called a time-out and pulled Sam from the game in the middle of the second quarter.[15]

Sam watched from the bench as the teams battled back and forth for small yardage. A trainer had wrapped his pelvis in a tight bandage and placed ice around his knee. Sam didn't tell the trainer or the coach about the bloody gash across the palm of his throwing hand; he put on a new glove and wrapped the hand in a towel to cover up the bloody mess.

At halftime, the Bears led 14–7, and the Redskins' key player was benched with a twisted knee, a half-paralyzed leg, and a lacerated passing hand. The Monsters of the Midway might finally win their national title.

Baugh's injuries were bad news for Washington Redskins' owner George Preston Marshall. He was a rich man, but his football ventures had put him deep in a financial hole, and he was counting on the Texas All-American with the howitzer passing arm to pull him out. Things had been going well until Baugh limped to the bench.

Marshall had always envisioned a theatrical career for himself. After college he was cast in a few small parts only to realize that, one, he was not much of an actor; and two, the real money and recognition came from producing shows. He managed a group of theaters in Washington, DC, and found he had a knack for getting butts into seats. He put his plans on hold when he was drafted during WWI.[16]

He returned from Europe to find that his father had died, and his mother was trying to manage the family's barely profitable chain of laundries in Washington. The twenty-two-year-old entrepreneur believed his show business skills applied to the laundries and set out to (as we would call it today) "rebrand" the chain. He painted the laundry storefronts and delivery vehicles blue and gold. He adopted the phrase "Long Live Linen" and spent heavily on ads touting the company's cleanliness and professionalism. The laundries—eventually fifty-seven of them—became a cash cow for him and his mother.

Marshall had always been interested in sports. Pro football was beginning to catch on in the bigger cities of the northeast, and the new National Football League was at work setting schedules and common game rules. The Boston Braves had failed after a single season in 1931, and the NFL was eager to establish a new team there. Marshall had attended several pro games. He appreciated the intensity of the game but felt it lacked the theatrical sizzle that he could bring to it. The actor/laundryman brought in three more investors, acquired the Boston Braves, and signed a one-year lease for Braves Field, several miles west of the city.

Boston hated football. Despite fielding a respectable team and ending their first season at 4-4-2, the Braves drew small crowds their first year and lost $46,000 in 1932. The partners pulled out, but Marshall chose to hang on.

Marshall made some drastic moves: moving to Fenway and rechristening his team as "Redskins." (He made his players wear warpaint during games until they rebelled.) Little improved, even though pro football overall had its best year yet. He grew exasperated by the Boston fans' apathy (and the money he was losing), even after winning the division title in 1936. Marshall reached the breaking point when *Boston Globe* sportswriters gave bigger headlines and more ink to a girls' field hockey team than to his professional players. The frustrated owner announced that he was moving his team home to Washington. Marshall had a final snub for the city that gave him the cold shoulder. Instead of playing the prestigious NFL championship game in Boston, the league allowed him to play the Packers in New York. Bye, Boston.

Sam Baugh flew into Washington, DC, on September 9, 1937, greeted by a front-page headline and a photo of the "wiry Texan." The congressional delegation included plenty of Texans, and based on what they'd heard back home during the summer recess, they were ready to hoist the Sweetwater phenom on their shoulders for a parade down Constitution Avenue.

Prewar Washington was still a sleepy southern town with not much competitive entertainment. Marshall planned to provide a show along with top-level football. He assembled a marching band to perform at pep rallies and halftime and hired a lyricist to write a team song. The players wore flowing feather headdresses as they entered the field. Fans began bringing purple feathers they wore in headbands at games. Many of those same fans boarded reduced-fare special trains and buses to travel to out-of-town games. (Three thousand of the twelve thousand fans attending the icy 1937 league championship in December arrived on a special train that Marshall chartered.)

Baugh's first appearance for the team was in an exhibition home game against the Giants. Twenty-five thousand Washingtonians showed up to see "their" new team in person. It was a close-fought game, and Sam didn't get that much time on the field. He threw sixteen passes and completed eleven of them, just enough to show the coaches and his team that he was more than a flashy college boy. Marshall was thrilled.

The crowds—home and away—increased as the year progressed, and Sam took center stage. The quality of Sam's throwing continued to improve. He could rocket the ball to a receiver's hands while running to his left, running to his right, or standing still, even as eight hundred pounds of linemen barreled toward him. His open-stance sidearm throws were deadly accurate. By the time they were preparing for their 1937 NFL championship game, Marshall, his coaches, the sportswriters, and the other players agreed that the Redskins' league title and the possibility of winning the national championship rested on Sam's arm.

At halftime of the icy Chicago championship game, Baugh joined his teammates in the locker room. He had one unstable knee, a semi-paralyzed leg, miscellaneous bruises, and a slashed passing hand. There's no record of what the coach said in the locker room that day, but

Sam carried his own motivation with him. He used the time to wrap his palm with training tape to stop the blood from making the football slippery. He wasn't much for running on his injured knee, but he could plant his numb leg and swivel the other leg and hip around it, much like a draftsman's compass.

When the referee whistled a game-time warning, Sam was leading his team onto the field for a score settling with the Bears.

The Redskins received the kickoff, then moved down the field courtesy of Baugh's passing arm. A final cross-field pass to Millner, and Millner's twenty-five-yard run across the goal line tied the game at fourteen points each. A brutal drive by Chicago's Monsters ended with a touchdown. The Bears reclaimed the lead, 21–14.

The combination of Baugh to Al Millner (with Millner's ability to outrun the beefy Chicago defenders) once again evened the score, 21–21.

The chopped-up turf was refreezing, turning the churned-up field to broken glass. Men on both teams bore cuts over their bodies from falling on the ice shards. An enraged Nagurski made little progress on the ground, and after four downs, the line judge turned the football over to the Redskins.

With a flurry of passes—short and long, left and right, jumpers and shoestrings—Slingin' Sam took the team downfield for eighty-six yards and a touchdown. At the end of the third quarter the Redskins took the lead, 28–21.

Neither team made progress for most of the fourth quarter. Frozen hands, bruises, cuts, and sheer exhaustion slowed the players, some staggering like prizefighters in the fifteenth round. Chicago players were angry that they couldn't knock Baugh out of the game; Washington players were angry because the Bears had tried. Tempers were short.

With four minutes left in the game, the Bears caught a break. The Redskins were threatening to score when a fumble gave the Bears the ball on their 14-yard line. Chicago's first play was a long pass to receiver Dick Plasman. Baugh, on defense, ran Plasman out of bounds at the 50-yard line, and the men tumbled to the ground in front of the Redskins' bench. Plasman aimed a fist at Baugh's eye, and Baugh returned the punch. The Redskins' bench emptied to teach Plasman a lesson, and the Bears raced across the field to mete out justice of their own. The melee—some called it a brawl—at midfield allowed members to settle scores; fans jumped out of the stands to join the fray, swinging walking canes, insulated jugs, and any other cudgel that came to hand.[17]

The fist slinging finally ended when the referees (who were likely the only ones watching the game clock) blew their whistles to end the game. The Washington Redskins, a team still getting used to its Washington digs and fielding a rookie quarterback, won the game and the National Football League title in 1937. The fans, the owner, the sportswriters, and the other players credited Texan Sam Baugh with the victory.

"What the heck," he drawled. "Anyone can do the pitching, but it takes real ball players to do the catching."[18]

Commercial radio became a reality in 1922. As the number of stations and listeners increased during the 1920s, some stations began broadcasting local football games. From the start, it was apparent that football was well suited to entertain a listening audience. The pace of the sport was neither too fast nor too slow for fans at home. Football's scoring system allowed for dramatic swings in the lead, which added to the drama of the sport. Because players played both offense and defense, it was easy to identify heroes in the game. By the time Sam entered TCU in 1933, more than a thousand licensed stations were broadcasting to millions of living rooms across the nation. Radio networks formed and broadcast games from coast to coast, and Sam's winning ways made him one of the early heroes.

During every one of his sixteen years with the Redskins, the man known as "Slingin' Sam," the "Redskin Rifle," or the "Sweetwater String-bean" remained a fan and sportscaster favorite. The Texan was the subject of magazine articles, movie serials, children's books, newsreels, and product endorsements.

In 1941 he starred as a Texas Ranger in a twelve-part Western serial for Republic Pictures. Baugh and the producer agreed that he looked natural on a horse; they also agreed Sam had no talent for acting. Even still, an independent producer invited him and eleven other well-known pro football players to make cameo appearances in a cheapo football drama in 1948.

"In his rookie year," an NFL history says, "Sammy Baugh had beaten pro football's best with a style of play fifteen years before its time." The game of football was much different in 1937 from the game of today. But when George P. Marshall ran up the championship flag in Washington, pro football had discovered its base.[19]

CHAPTER 6

STANLEY MARCUS

DESIGNS ON TEXAS WOMEN

THE AFTER-HOURS INSTALLATION WAS GOING POORLY, AND THE WORK-ers were frantic. One woman lost her head. Another lost an arm.

Stanley Marcus received an after-midnight call and, after dressing in a pair of khaki slacks and matching pullover sweater, drove to downtown Dallas. The first International Neiman Marcus Fashion Exposition would begin the following day, and no problem, no detail, was too small for Marcus's attention. The installation in the Main Street display window was the first thing his guests would see as they entered the store.

The glass, wool, and resin mannequin who lost her head proved to be no problem. The installer was trying to fit the head to the wrong torso. Marcus switched one head for another. Problem solved. The disartic-ulated arm on the other mannequin was more of a puzzlement. After several middle-of-the-night phone calls to the sculptor and the manu-facturer, Marcus and his merchandising manager realized that an internal armature connector had dislodged and fallen inside the figure. Unable to extract it, Marcus gave his car keys to an assistant, telling her to drive to his home and retrieve a can of wood putty from his garage. Putty finally in hand, Marcus affixed the runaway arm in a stylish pose, then stepped aside to let the dressers do their work.[1]

As the sun was rising, Marcus drove home to dress himself for the day, a day that would earn a high-fashion reputation for a Lone Star State not known for stylishness.

Stanley Marcus did not found Neiman Marcus—his father, his aunt, and her husband did.

The family of Herbert Marcus came to Texas in 1893 when he was fifteen years old. The family settled in Hillsboro, a small cotton gin town fifty miles south of Dallas. Herbert worked in a general store there, delivering merchandise, stocking shelves, sweeping up, and clerking whenever the owner allowed it. After four years he moved to Dallas, again finding work at a small retail store and learning to keep a mental record of every item in the store. Herbert Marcus's sister, Carrie Marcus Neiman, went to work for the A. Harris and Company store, and Herbert eventually went to Sanger Brothers, where he worked in the women's shoe department at fifteen dollars a week. A. Harris and Sanger Bros. were the two largest department stores in Dallas at the time. His salesmanship earned Herbert promotions to assistant manager of the boy's furnishings department and then to buyer. Herbert abruptly resigned from Sanger Bros. in 1905 over a salary dispute. (He believed a $1.87 raise was too little to account for his added responsibilities.)[2]

Herbert Marcus and brother-in-law Abraham "Al" Neiman departed Dallas to launch an advertising and sales promotion agency in Atlanta. The business was apparently successful; within a year, other companies were offering to buy out Marcus and Neiman.

Decades later Stanley Marcus would tell interviewers about that Atlanta business venture. His father and uncle faced two attractive alternatives in early 1907. First, they could swap their ad agency for shares in a new Atlanta soft drink bottling company, Coca-Cola, plus the lifetime exclusive Missouri franchise for the beverage. Or they could take $25,000 in cash for their business and return to Dallas.

They took the cash instead of the shares and a franchise that would have made the families bazillionaires in a few short decades.

"And that's why I tell people who ask," Stanley Marcus would say with a twinkle in his eye, "that Neiman Marcus was founded on bad business judgment.[3]

At the beginning of 1907, Herbert Marcus; sister Carrie; and her husband, Al Neiman, held $35,000 in capital for a business of their own. But what kind of business? And where? They settled soon enough on retail clothing, a specialty store offering fine garments, millinery, notions, and toiletries, but they vacillated between New Orleans and Chicago. In the end they settled on Dallas, where they could remain near family members in the area and where Herman and Carrie had developed a customer following.

On September 10, 1907, the trio opened Neiman Marcus. (The Neiman name came first because two of the three founders bore that surname.) Elegant fixtures and mahogany cabinetry filled the rented twenty-six-year-old wood frame building, and every surface was polished to a shine. Their business plan was to bring fashionable ready-to-wear to a less-than-cosmopolitan city of 86,000.

"Fashionable" and "ready-to-wear" were contradictory terms throughout most of the South at the time. Rural general stores had always carried ready-to-wear clothing, but much of it consisted of formless shifts (for women) or baggy shirts and overalls (for men). Demand was too low and the range of sizes too large for most stores to stock broad assortments of styles or sizes. Mail-order retailers such as Sears, Roebuck and Co., and Montgomery Ward took up some of the slack when the U.S. Congress funded Rural Free Delivery postal service in 1905. The catalogers, however, offered sizes, fabrics, and colors more suited to a national market. (And Texas cotton farmers rarely wore red flannel shirts.)

Women of means could hire a dressmaker to design, sew, and fit their garments. Local dressmakers were generally not, in the main, inspired dress stylists; they often depended on a more or less distinguished couturiere, a local arbiter of style who studied whatever fashion magazines might come her way and traveled to the European fashion centers every decade or so. As a result, what might be fashionable in Richmond one year might appear laughable to a Dallas woman and vice versa. Likely, both women would be easily identified as rubes on the sidewalks of New York, Boston, or Chicago. Women of more modest means—those who were unlikely to attend a soiree in another state or stroll between the skyscrapers—could settle for sewing their own clothes from the same paper patterns that might be used by a neighbor.

In their first ad, Marcus and the Neimans promised that Dallas women could find ready-to-wear fashion at affordable prices at Neiman

Marcus. "We will improve ready-to-wear merchandising," the threesome pledged.

At the end of the first year the store showed a profit, quite an accomplishment for an undercapitalized family business. The three owners participated equally in day-to-day operations, each settling into their own specialty. Carrie Neiman had an unerring sense of style and chose many of the lines the store carried. Herbert Marcus was the arbiter of quality. He inspected each garment for irregular stitchery, a fabric color shift, or an uneven hemline. Al Neiman's role was advertising, sales promotion, and merchandising to bring enthusiastic buyers to the store. One of the three owners would always be on hand in the store. Always. They refused to take lunch together or enjoy family vacations so as not to leave the store unattended at any time.

The store remained profitable during its early years, though it occasionally fell victim to the usual assortment of bugaboos: cash flow, inventory duds, late shipping by suppliers. They worked hard, weathered the storms, kept their banker happy, and earned a modest living.

Another thing Herbert Marcus and wife, Minnie, worked hard at was raising a family. Their first child, Harold Stanley Marcus, was born in 1905, two years before the family store opened. Stanley (as he preferred to be called) was soon followed by three brothers—Edward, Herbert Jr., and Lawrence—at regular intervals.

As the store grew up, so did the boys. The Marcus's had no maid, so when the boys' mother went downtown to visit the store, she deposited the youngsters in the alterations department in the basement, where Stanley recalled making toy trains from empty thread boxes and spools. Stanley could later say truthfully that he started at the store at the age of two and "from the ground up."[4]

The Marcus boys grew up surrounded by a large family of aunts, uncles, cousins, and grandparents, but the store was always the focus of their parents. The Neimans often came to the Marcus home in the evenings, and Stanley remembered that "over the dinner table they discussed the events of the day, how one or the other had made a great sale, the weaknesses of the stock, or of salespeople."

Those modest but comfortable days ended on a May Sunday morning in 1913. "Building Occupied by Neiman Marcus is Practically Destroyed," the newspaper reported the following morning. A fire of unknown origin burned the Neimans and Marcus out of business; what little stock that could be salvaged was water soaked and smelled of smoke. Fixtures and cabinetry were a total loss.[5]

As family members considered their future and awaited an uncertain insurance settlement, they held a fire sale to raise needed cash. Fire-damaged goods in wearable condition were freshened up as much as possible and displayed on temporary tables in a vacant building rented for the purpose. Two weeks after the fire Al Neiman placed ads announcing a one-day fire sale the following morning at eight o'clock. No alterations. No exchanges. No dogs. No men. Cash only.[6]

"At six o'clock in the morning the first ladies appeared and got a stand at the door," said an observer. "By seven o'clock the sidewalks for some distance around were blocked and many stood in the streets." Police came to keep automobiles moving after dropping off shoppers near the door. People were arriving from twenty and thirty miles away.

By the time the sale ended, everything but Herbert Marcus's pocket watch and Carrie Neiman's shirtwaist had been sold for cash. That cash, a modest insurance settlement, and short-term loans from family members gave the founding trio hope that there would be a new Neiman Marcus store.

Al Neiman located an open property at Main and Ervay Streets in Dallas and showed it to Herbert and Carrie. The property was so far uptown as to be almost out of town. It was "surrounded by wagon yards and grocery stores and the inevitable saloons and a few residences." By husbanding their resources, the partners could build a hundred-foot by hundred-foot building with a basement and four stories. Once again, they took the plunge, and the new store opened ten months after the original went up in flames.[7]

The move was a good one. In the year before the fire, the store did $380,000 for a profit of $20,000. The first year at the new Main and Ervay store, sales volume was $700,000 for a profit of $40,000.

It's likely the four Marcus brothers—they were known locally as the Marcii—were unaware of and uninterested in store sales and profits. They were the typical active, rowdy boys, always into mischief and always deeply regretful when caught at it.

Herbert Marcus had no desire to see his sons grow up as pampered rich boys. They attended public schools and were expected to have part-time jobs. During the summers the boys worked at the store as messengers, delivery boys, elevator operators, cashiers, and junior floorwalkers.[8]

Oldest brother Stanley always seemed to be the leader, the instigator. They sometimes fought among themselves, often to the point that their mother had to pull them apart and take the flat side of her hairbrush to their backsides. But they always seemed to end the day arm in arm, loyal to one another and assured of the others' support. One by one the boys left home to attend college or for other pursuits, but each eventually would return to Dallas, working together in the store their father helped found.

By 1921, when Stanley entered Amherst College, Neiman Marcus had attained more than a million dollars in annual sales. Herbert Marcus insisted that his son should attend the prestigious school dressed as the son of a successful businessman. Father and son traveled to New York, where Herbert helped outfit Stanley with new made-to-measure suits, custom dress shirts, and designer neckties. "It took me no more than two days to recognize the mistakes in my wardrobe," Stanley said. His first call home was to request extra funds for the purchase of a lilac tweed suit with plus-fours. His aunt and uncle treated him to a full-length raccoon coat, another fashion necessity for the eastern college student.[9]

Stanley's freshman year at Amherst was a painful one. There, he encountered institutional anti-Semitism for the first time in his life. Though the other students were cordial in class and in passing, Jews were restricted from joining campus fraternities and left out of the social activities of the school.

Stanley was accepted to Harvard for his sophomore year. He found the campus and Cambridge enthralling. He was an active participant in campus activities and spent his spare time haunting the dusty used bookstores of Boston. He graduated in 1925 and, on advice of his father, attended Harvard Business School before returning to Dallas to work in the family business.[10]

Stanley Marcus found a very different Neiman Marcus when he returned. The familiar storefront at Main and Ervay Streets was surrounded by scaffolding and shrouded with tarpaulins. Herbert, Aunt Carrie, and Uncle Al had decided to acquire the rest of the city block and expand the store to cover it all. The outside of the store would be sheathed in stone to provide a uniform appearance all around; intervening interior walls would be removed and the enlarged space redecorated as if it had been part of the original building.

Herbert took on his son as a junior executive, an up-and-comer with no specific portfolio. Stanley was encouraged to involve himself in any part of the business, if he didn't overspend, didn't disrupt the regular operation of the store—and run every decision by his father first.

"I was eager to apply some of my new knowledge of statistics and advertising to Neiman Marcus," Stanley said, "but at the moment they weren't ready for my college expertise." He sat in on meetings, went on buying trips with the store's buyers, helped build displays, tried his hand at ad copywriting, and asked questions ad nauseum.[11]

Stanley's exposure to every part of the store would prove valuable. With its expansion, Neiman Marcus became an aggregate of specialty stores, and one of the guiding principles was to equip women with ensembles rather than a single item of dress. "The store would much rather sell a woman a dress, jacket, and scarf than two dresses," a writer explained. This allowed a salesperson to escort a customer to different parts of the store—past other tempting merchandise—to complete the outfit. Herbert Marcus and Carrie Neiman made a special point to be sure that buyers coordinated their purchases, that their accessories matched the dresses, and the dresses matched the coats.[12]

This emphasis on ensembles and coordination had two beneficial results. First, it gave the shopper full confidence that the items in her shopping bag, worn together, would result in a stylish, attractive appearance. Second, it characterized what came to be known as the "Neiman Marcus Woman." Though many copywriters and journalists (and Stanley

Marcus himself) have tried to define precisely what a Neiman Marcus Woman is, the specifics remain elusive. Perhaps the best definition came from Banks, a longtime elevator operator who ferried thousands on thousands of Neiman Marcus women from one floor of the store to another. "We-l-l-l," Banks drawled, "she's a lady who just kind of goes together."[13]

The expansion provided room for more specialty departments, and Stanley wanted more responsibility. He was named merchandising manager of the new sportswear department, a new category for the younger, more active woman. He made the mistakes common to a green buyer—buying a little of everything instead of concentrating in depth on a few items—but he was learning lessons he could pass on to subsequent buyers.

Al Neiman had begun to quarrel with Herbert and Carrie about inventory levels, personnel policies, buying decisions, and the like. But Al Neiman's vote was only one of three because his wife usually sided with her brother. Unhappy with the course of his business, his partners, his nephew, and his marriage, Neiman decided he couldn't continue as things were, so he made a buy-or-sell offer to Herbert and Carrie in 1928. After lengthy negotiations, Herbert Marcus took out a personal loan for $250,000 and bought out Neiman's share of the business. During the negotiations, Carrie Neiman discovered that Al was involved in a long-term relationship with a woman in New York. She filed for divorce immediately.

By the end of 1928, Al Neiman was no longer involved with the store he had helped found twenty-one years before. Herbert Marcus and Carrie Marcus Neiman were in complete control of all aspects of the business. Their second in charge (not a family member) resigned when Neiman left, and Herbert gave the position to a twenty-four-year-old Harvard man with only two years of full-time business experience.

"My father certainly could have found someone with more mature business credentials," Stanley wrote later. "Instead, he decided to take a chance on me. He threw me into the water, not positive whether I would sink or swim. Fortunately, I was able to swim."[14]

As Stanley learned to swim in his new executive position, a bit of good luck helped keep him afloat initially. The stock market crash of

1929 threw much of the national economy into free fall, but Dallas was a regional cotton market, and cotton prices remained high through 1930 and 1931. Neiman Marcus's clientele of middle- to upper-middle-class women still had money to spend.

Then came the East Texas oil boom.

The Spindletop oil discovery in 1901 on Texas's Gulf Coast led the nation into the oil age. The 1919 West Texas oil boom in Eastland County sparked the biggest boom in American history. The East Texas oil discovery in 1930—centered just a hundred miles east of Dallas—was bigger yet. Oil flowed at more than a million barrels a day, producing new livelihoods and new ways of living for thousands of families.[15]

"Dirt farmers, florists, anyone who owned a piece of land in the area, were transformed overnight from poverty to riches," Stanley observed. "Fortuitously, Dallas was located midway between the new oil fields to the east and the oil fields to the west, and Neiman Marcus was in Dallas."[16]

(There are tales of the barefoot newly rich oil queen walking into the store saying, "Dress me up. Give me the works." Stanley said that story wasn't true, but he did appreciate the cartoon that showed a farm woman standing in front of a shack with an oil well gushing in the background. "How late does Neiman Marcus stay open?" she's asking.)[17]

Neiman Marcus weathered the Great Depression handily, showing profits in all but two years of the 1930s. Even during hard times, Neiman Marcus remained the guiding star of fashion for Dallas's well-dressed women of means; but a brighter star hovered over New York fashion retailers, and Stanley worried that the Dallas carriage trade might follow that one.

In 1934 Stanley was considering the policies of the national fashion magazines, which limited their editorial credits to stores that advertised with them. A Dallas woman who picked up a copy of *Vogue* or *Harper's Bazaar* might come to believe that the fashion lines advertised there might only be available from Bonwit-Teller, B. Altman, or Saks Fifth Avenue. With his father's approval, Stanley launched an advertising campaign in the national consumer fashion magazines.

"We reasoned that we would make our local customers proud that 'their' store was being nationally advertised," Stanley said. The magazines added the name of Neiman Marcus to the credits that accompanied each editorial spread. "As the first store in Texas to advertise in the fashion publications, we became the object of instant scrutiny by potential customers, designers, and the news media."[18]

Texas women were duly impressed, and so were fashion-conscious women from Atlanta to San Francisco. Many of those out-of-state women had the opportunity to visit the fashion institution at Main and Ervay in Dallas when they were among the six million visitors to attend the Texas Centennial Exposition in 1936.

The store marked the opening of the exposition with a gala fashion show depicting fashions from 1836 to 1936. Stanley oversaw "a collection of clothes and accessories inspired by the colors and motifs of the Southwest." Fifteen hundred selected customers from all over the state (and Edna Woolman Chase, senior editor of *Vogue*) attended the event.[19]

The fashion magazines weren't the only national publications intrigued by Neiman Marcus. In November 1937, Henry Luce's new *Fortune* magazine profiled Neiman Marcus with a cover story titled "Dallas in Wonderland." The business magazine marveled at the selection of designer merchandise available to a Texas clientele: Hattie Carnegie gowns, Lilly Dache hats, Palter DeLiso shoes, Marghab linen, Steuben glass, Georg Jensen silver, and Godiva chocolates. In a region ill-suited by climate to the wearing of furs in spring or fall, Neiman Marcus had fur sales of more than a half million dollars in one year alone.[20]

Neiman Marcus built its business, the mostly laudatory article said, on selling Godiva chocolate in a Hershey bar town.

Some years after Stanley Marcus rose to international prominence for his management of Neiman Marcus, Texas writer Green Peyton characterized Stanley precisely, saying that "he has the soul of an impresario like Florenz Ziegfeld."[21]

If Stanley Marcus was the impresario, the exquisite little jewel box that is the Neiman Marcus store was his stage. Wide aisles, subtle color on the walls, custom display cases, lighting designed to make heroes of the merchandise, and large display windows fronting three of the busiest streets in downtown Dallas would provide the perfect mise-en-scène for an idea that had been brewing for several years.

"One day I came across the phrase 'presenting a veritable exposition of fashion,'" Stanley said. "This triggered an idea: why not create an event of such importance that we could make it an exposition in fact as well as just words." As he discussed it within the organization, the idea blossomed like a hydrangea. He would invite noted designers to make personal appearances, just like movie stars at a movie premiere, artisans would demonstrate their work in the store, and the whole event would be topped off by a fashion show featuring the designers' newest lines.[22]

Neiman Marcus's first annual International Fashion Exposition and Awards was born.

Fashion designers prior to 1940 were a tight coterie of couturiers, an insular bunch who rarely found it necessary to travel from Europe to the United States or from New York to anywhere west of the Hudson River. They accepted little advice from manufacturers and almost none from even the largest apparel retailers. Their designs might use fabrics too heavy to wear comfortably in the sweltering Southwest or be constructed in shapes more suited to a stalky mademoiselle than a San Antonio society matron. Stanley believed that, by bringing the designers to Texas, they might see and appreciate the market for garments that should exist in the real world. Such an event would also provide Neiman Marcus customers a chance to mingle with the celebrity designers whose work they already knew.

But how to get those big-name designers to leave their familiar environs and travel to an alien country like Texas? The answer, Stanley thought, also lay in the world of show business: professional awards. He would conjure up a prestigious award for design excellence, then present it at a special ceremony during the exposition.

The exposition could take place in September, Stanley reasoned. September was the apparel industry's traditional "fall opening" month. If he could schedule the event early enough in September, he could get the jump on high-end New York specialty stores.

Planning for the September 1938 event began in January and, right away, Stanley ran into an obstacle. The designers had no interest in coming to Texas, a land of tumbleweeds and ten-gallon hats. Just send us the plaque or statue or whatever, and we'll put it up on a wall, they said. Attending the exposition in Dallas was a requirement for receiving the award, Stanley explained in a series of purposeful phone calls to each designer. If you choose to decline the award for fashion excellence, he said, we're sure a competitive fashion house would be pleased to accept. By April, seven big-name designers of dresses, separates, footwear, millinery, and specialty fabrics committed to attend and ship early samples of their fall lines to Dallas.[23]

Stanley's father threw another hitch in the works. Herbert Marcus was of the opinion that "Neiman Marcus would be showing a lack of hospitality if any out-of-town guest was left to his own devices." So, Stanley hired a team of party planners to arrange transportation, meals, lodging, and entertainment for his temperamental guests.[24]

Using an outside venue for the fashion show was out of the question. The event must occur in the store itself. Stanley engaged an architect to plan for a runway and seating for fifteen hundred guests on the main floor. Using the architect's schematics, he contracted with a builder to fabricate the runway in pieces and install it after the store closed on the night of the show.

How would he represent the "Neiman Marcus Woman" to out-of-towners unfamiliar with his clientele? The normal posturings and gestures affected by professional runway models wouldn't do, so Stanley put out a call for local girls and women who could learn to perform naturally on a runway and not outshine the apparel.[25]

If professional runway models weren't representative, neither were the display mannequins and body forms. Stanley ordered his art director to oversee sculptures of the archetypical Neiman Marcus Woman and have them cast in the new, more lifelike glass, wool, and resin.[26]

Samples from the designer honorees began arriving almost daily in August, organized for Stanley's perusal by a small group of Neiman Marcus merchandising managers and the fashion coordinator. They scrutinized the garments, ranking and reranking them for use in the big show. Jewels, scarves, hats, shoes, and other accessories came and went daily until Stanley decided on the perfect ensembles to represent every honored designer. Even then, he reserved the right to change his mind, and the whole process might start over again.[27]

There were a thousand details—small and large—to be attended to: gifts for the visitors, flowers, ashtrays, window design, wording on the awards, the paper on which the show programs would be printed, and all the other particulars a shopkeeper sees but only the most discerning customer notices.

Stanley Marcus involved himself in everything. By the night before the first out-of-town guests arrived, the thirty-three-year-old impresario was as weary and worn as Warner Baxter in *42nd Street*. He drove home at nine o'clock, determined to get a full night's sleep and be refreshed in the morning.

Shortly after midnight the telephone rang, and Stanley was summoned back to the store. It was the window display manager. A mannequin had lost her head.

Sunday morning, September 11, 1938, as Stanley was dressing following his sleepless night with the mannequins and show windows, his honorees were flying into Dallas from New York. At his father's suggestion, Stanley had arranged white-glove service for his guests.

Brother Edward Marcus and his wife accompanied the honorees on their flight from New York to Dallas aboard American Airlines newest DC-3 flagship. With a refueling stop in Nashville, the party arrived in Dallas at noon. Waiting on the tarmac was a fleet of black 1938 Cadillac sedans to whisk the guests to a welcoming lunch at the Lakewood home of Mr. and Mrs. Ray E. Hubbard. (Baggage was loaded into a jitney, driven to the respective hotels, and placed in rooms.) During his lunchtime toast, Stanley apologized to the guests that they would not be able to tour the store that day. The store was closed to customers on Sunday, Stanley said, and his employees were working to make Neiman Marcus ready for the following day's awards. Besides, he teased, I've arranged a special preview for you this afternoon.[28]

The group loaded into the Cadillacs for the drive to their hotels, a drive that took them by some of the grander homes in Lakewood and Highland Park and through the grounds of the Dallas Country Club.

Later that afternoon the Cadillacs returned to the hotels to pick up the guests for a short ride up Main Street to the entrance of the Neiman Marcus store. An ebullient Stanley Marcus waited on the curb and directed them to the first display window, the Nettie Rosenstein store window.

Rosenstein was a highly regarded American designer and an awardee. "Her" store window, like each of the others, was "outlined in a massive frame of natural wood to create the illusion of a picture." Within the frame was one of the new "Neiman Marcus Woman" mannequins, posed standing, looking into the full-length mirror in front of her. She wore a breathtaking floor-length black crepe dress with a high necktie that flowed into voluminous sheer billowed sleeves. The mannequin seemed ready for a night on the town in one of Rosenstein's signature "long black dresses." A tall, bunched hat sat on a chair behind her, a brocaded wrap hung on the back of her chair, and she sported more than $10,000 of fine jewelry around her neck, wrist, and on her fingers.[29]

Stanley pointed out various items in the Nettie Rosenstein window, a narration that was essentially the rehearsal of his fashion show script. "Nettie is famous for her classic simplicity. She makes distinctly lady-like clothes, avoiding the eccentricities so prevalent in many Parisian designs."[30]

Then he directed the sidewalk crowd to the adjacent window, the Dan Palter window. A half dozen shoes—toeless pumps, open-heel shoes, some with straps and some without—sat on alabaster-looking pillars of differing heights, each with its own colored spotlight. In the center, however, intended to be the focus of the display, was a pair of cranberry-red strappy sandals of dyed kid leather with heels, a stunning style and color for 1938. "Dan Palter, half of the firm of Palter DeLiso," Stanley said, "is largely responsible for many innovations in feminine shoemaking, such as the open toe, the sandal, and the glove-like shoe."

In this way, Stanley led the group from store window to store window around the perimeter of the building: Richard Koret, handbag manufacturer; Dorothy Liebes, American textile designer and weaver; Mr. John (Fredericks), New York milliner; Louise B. Gallagher, coat and suit designer; George Miller, American shoe manufacturer; Germaine Montiel, French-born designer (and later, cosmetics entrepreneur). Every honoree viewed the window dedicated to their designs while basking in the applause of their peers.

The afternoon was warm. Stanley ushered his party back into the Cadillacs for their trip to Herbert Marcus's Oakwood Lane home, where the senior Marcus served a lavish buffet dinner.

That night Alice Hughes typed her weekly column, a column syndicated by Scripps-Howard and appearing in more than six hundred newspapers. "I've met a heavenly creature, a little bit aloof and remote," she wrote. "But she'll be the talk of the town after today. She is the Neiman Marcus Woman, and she stands resplendent in the store windows." Hughes suggested that designers who have difficulty putting their concept of beauty into words should stop trying. "Just look at the Neiman Marcus Woman. She's the answer."[31]

Monday was a workday for Stanley and his awardees. Stanley attended to last-minute preparations for the show that evening and attempted to mollify the comptroller for the monies spent on this first-time event. The out-of-towners received personal escorted tours of the store. Glass display cases had been polished to near invisibility, wooden fixtures gleamed from recent waxing and rubbing, and the sales floor was banked with fresh flowers. After the tour, designers went to the workrooms for a last look at the apparel that would represent them in the fashion show that evening.[32]

At five o'clock the store was closed, and frantic preparations began. While some workers moved display cases and platforms back from the center of the store, others erected the runway that began at the mezzanine steps and stretched nearly to the front door. Twin grand pianos were rolled to a spot behind the stairwell, and padded salon chairs were placed in lines along the runway.

Neiman Marcus had sold a thousand tickets to the event—all proceeds donated to the Dallas Museum of Fine Art—but many more people crowded the sidewalks outside the store. When the doors opened for the show, some of Dallas society's richest and most notable jostled and elbowed one another for the best seats. By seven o'clock, 1,750 attendees filled the store, many of them standing, packed into the outside aisles or leaning against perimeter walls. Light music from the two Steinway pianos was barely audible over the expectant whispers of the large crowd.

Suddenly, the store lights dimmed, leaving only bright spotlights over the runway and another spotlight on Stanley Marcus as he stepped before twin microphones. The room erupted in applause. "We celebrate our thirty-second anniversary by not only bringing you the finest merchandise," Stanley said, "but we bring many designers of fashions you have worn and bought."[33]

Stanley called the designers, one by one, to walk down the runway to the stairs, where he would hand them a gold medallion of honor. (Each would also later receive an engraved plaque.) As they walked the runway, Stanley narrated their accomplishments, much as he did at the store windows the previous day.

After introducing the syndicated fashion columnist and the editor of *Brides* magazine, Stanley called for the visiting editors from *Vogue* and *Harper's Bazaar*. The women emerged on the stairway landing with an oversized pair of scissors between them. Together, they clipped the ribbon of a huge bonbon box to reveal a spotlighted mannequin: the Neiman Marcus Woman posed in mid-wave and wearing a French lace party dress. As the spotlight over the mannequin dimmed, Stanley described "the Neiman Marcus Woman" to the audience. At the end of his short narration another spotlight illuminated another figure, a *real* woman of the same size and coloring, in the same pose as the mannequin and wearing the same French lace party dress. She walked down the stairway onto the runway, and the fashion show was on.[34]

"We had created a totally new sales promotion device!" Stanley marveled later.[35]

Women reading the style section of six hundred local newspapers the following week read the verdict of fashion arbiter Alice Hughes: "These high style notes make Neiman Marcus in Dallas New York's strongest contender in a style tug-of-war." *Collier's* magazine, writing about the exposition, took it one better: "At this moment the eyes and ears of the fashion world are focused not on Paris. Not on New York. Not on Hollywood. But on Dallas." Within two years most large consumer magazines, including *Life, Saturday Evening Post,* and *Atlantic Monthly*, published laudatory features on Texas fashion and Neiman Marcus.[36]

The Neiman Marcus Fashion Exposition and Awards put Neiman Marcus and Texas fashion on the national map, just after New York. The event was staged every year for the next three decades. It grew into a five-day festival honoring such fashion icons as Elsa Schiaparelli, Lilly Dache, Christian Dior, Adrian, Jacques Fath, Elizabeth Arden, and many more.

The Neiman Marcus Fashion Exposition and Awards disproved the fashion myth of the sunburned Texas woman in her Hoover wrap and sunbonnet. Instead, fashion designers, manufacturers, writers, and buyers embraced the Neiman Marcus Woman.

"She is a woman in her thirties, not a great beauty," as one magazine described her. "She is a womanly woman, obviously well-bred. Smart, but without the harsh brightness associated with the word. She wears slacks like a lady, not a hoyden. She has dignity, sweetness and poise, instead of glamor, poise, and heavily overplayed sex appeal."[37]

Stanley Marcus and the Neiman Marcus Fashion Exposition and Awards brought an appreciation of regionalism to designers of fashionable ready-to-wear. At first, the resulting sense of regionalism was more midwestern than southwestern, but Stanley remedied that in subsequent years. By the 1950s designers of fashion garments, footwear, and accessories were adopting southwestern colors, lighter fabrics, and looser fits in their designs to better accommodate the lives and nature of postwar women.

To the rest of the world, the Neiman Marcus Woman became the Texas Woman.

CHAPTER 7

ENID JUSTIN

A 2,000-MILE TEXAS-SIZED HORSE RACE

At 8:45 a.m. on Wednesday, March 1, 1939, she walked out of her office, down the stairs, through the factory work room, and out the front door to stand in the middle of Clay Street in downtown Nocona. From where she stood, she could see people standing shoulder to shoulder on the sidewalks, crowding windows for a better view of the street, and perching on roofs and marquees of the buildings overlooking the town's main street. Some people waved at her; she didn't wave back.

The woman was tall—six feet at least—and somewhere in her mid-forties. She was dressed stylishly, especially for a woman on a workday in a small Texas town. A felt western hat with flat crown and wide brim was cocked forward and to the left, exposing tight pin curls on the right side and rear of her head. Her suit was made of a supple antelope leather dyed deep blue; the jacket, dyed the color of Santa Clara wine, was of the same material. Her boots had silver tops on which were painted bluebonnets, the state flower of Texas, and gold poppies, the state flower of California.

She might have been a more attractive woman if she smiled. Instead, her expression was austere that morning, dour, as it often was when she appeared in crowds or among people she didn't know. There were frown lines around her mouth and between her eyes that even the opaque makeup of the day couldn't cover. A smile softened her face considerably when Zana, a seven-year-old tomboyish favored niece, ran out of the crowd to stand beside her.

Enid Justin was sole owner and manager of the Nocona Boot Company, the largest employer in town, and she was the sponsor of the morning's festivities. In fifteen minutes, fifteen cowboys and one cowgirl would gallop out of town to begin a Pony Express-style race from Nocona across Texas, New Mexico, Arizona, and up the length of California. It was a two-thousand-mile competition that newspapers were already calling "the world's longest horse race."[1]

Enid Justin was a rare breed in 1939: a single female entrepreneur who founded, owned, and ran a successful regional manufacturing business in a small Texas town. She was not given to excessive warmth or jollity (except with children, customers, or in close social gatherings). Enid was determined, focused, and fiercely protective of a business she rebuilt from remnants remaining after it had been stolen from her father.[2]

In 1879, H. J. "Daddy Joe" Justin opened a boot shop on the Chisholm Trail just south of the Red River, taking orders from cowboys going north to Kansas and having the custom footwear ready in time for them to pick up on the way south. The business flourished, and Justin developed a statewide reputation for quality custom-made boots.[3]

The boot company was a family endeavor; all the Justin children—three boys, four girls—were expected to pitch in. Enid was the fourth oldest, born after two brothers and one sister. At twelve years old she spent her after-school hours inserting order forms in boot catalogs. More than any of her sisters, Enid loved being around the boot plant—the smell of the raw leather, the careful cutting of each hide to get the greatest number of boot parts out of it, the constant *b-dap-b-dap-b-dap* of the treadle sewing machines. But, most of all, she loved being around Daddy Joe.

"I had a legible hand," Enid told an interviewer. "It was not a very pretty one, but legible, so I did all his correspondence and ordered his materials." When needed, she also stitched the patterns on boot tops.[4]

Young Enid earned a reputation for willfulness within her father's company and without. Suspended from school for dancing, Enid walked away from her eighth-grade classroom and never went back. Hard as a horseshoe nail and twice as smart, Enid at fourteen years old became a full-time boot company employee in 1908.

That same year Daddy Joe named his older sons, John and Earl, partners in the business and changed the name of the company to H. J. Justin & Sons. The youngest son, called Avis, was only ten years old, but his father expected he would become one of the "& Sons" when he reached his majority. As for the daughters, in 1908 little was expected of them but that they would marry well.

That's the path that Enid followed. In 1915 she married a promising young telegrapher from a neighboring town. Her husband went right to work in the shop.

H. J. Justin died unexpectedly in 1918 at age fifty-nine. He left his three sons more than half of the company's stock; the four daughters and his wife shared the rest. The Justin boys effectively controlled the company.[5]

For a while, the sons continued their father's tradition in Nocona: making quality boots, paying decent wages, and earning a profit. Even so, they saw the need for better rail services, a larger labor pool, and a bank with more resources.[6]

And that's when, in Enid's opinion, the brothers stole the company.

"My daddy would never allow his company to leave Nocona," Enid said. The brothers' decision to move the family factory to Fort Worth caused an estrangement among the Justins that never healed. Enid fought the move with every argument she could muster, but the brothers were majority owners, and the decision was theirs to make.

"It broke my heart when I saw those great big old vans loading up all the machines," she said. The sounds, smells, equipment, and people she had known since she was a toddler were gone in a day.[7]

Whether her stubbornness grew from wanting to honor her father's memory, a festering resentment that she had no say in the business, or a desire not to move from her hometown (all reasons she offered in the years following), Enid dug in her heels. She would open her own boot-making operation. "They took all of my daddy's machines," she said. "We had to start from scratch."[8]

Enid pledged her Justin stock for a $5,000 loan to lease equipment, hired some of the experienced boot makers who hadn't moved to Fort Worth, and took over her father's old building. She made sure that she owned 100 percent of the new Nocona Boot Company and named her husband the company's president. But no one in town was confused about who was in charge.

Enid designed the styles and chose the colors of the boots Nocona Boot Company manufactured, and she had a good eye. Even as the Depression began to choke businesses in other parts of the country, Enid's sales continued to climb, thanks partly to the growth of oil exploration in north central Texas. She designed and sold an over-the-calf lace-up boot perfect for navigating the gooey mud and gunk of the oil patch, and the boot proved immediately popular.

By the time Enid divorced her husband in 1934, he was irrelevant to the business anyway. A local attorney made sure that Enid kept her house, her stock, his stock, her family name, and a $3,000 cash settlement. The husband left town for Oklahoma.[9]

By 1938, as the Depression years lingered with their dust storms, bank failures, and drought, Nocona Boot Company's sales leveled off, and profits dipped only slightly. However, the rest of the town wasn't faring quite so well.

L. A. Parton, a man with a hearty handshake, a toothy smile, and an air of irrepressible optimism, had a solution: a long-distance horse race.

Anyone who dug into L. A. Parton's background would have found that he had arrived out of nowhere at other small Texas towns, earned the trust of the town movers for his civic enthusiasm, sold them on some can't-lose promotional plan, then departed on a fast train with a stack of unpaid bills or (at the least) a stain of embarrassment behind him.

In 1932, Parton was editing a small South Texas newspaper controlled by the county boss. When a reform party overthrew the boss and began looking into county finances, Parton was nowhere to be found. In 1935 a Texas hill-country town loaned him money to run its beloved community swimming hole, based on his promise to build an amusement park there. The first season's receipts and Parton left town on the night train.[10]

After running as a spoiler for county judge in Coryell County, Parton chose Lampasas for his next sure-fire, can't-miss, million-dollar idea. To Lampasas merchants he described a marathon horse race from Lampasas to the gates of the Texas Centennial Exposition 180 miles away. Parton promised a publicity bonanza for Lampasas businesses and more than two hundred entries in the race. The merchants handed Parton the several thousand dollars for prize money and expenses. When the race fizzled, Parton and the prize money were nowhere to be found.[11]

Two months later Parton had convinced the businessmen of Marlin to sponsor "The Ankle Express," a hundred-mile footrace. Despite all the ballyhoo and seed money provided by Marlin merchants, the event never occurred.[12]

For the next two years Parton was involved in a number of civic promotions that never quite lived up to all his puffery. He ran weekend horse races in Goldthwaite in 1936 until the Texas Rangers shut him down for fostering illegal gambling. Guymon, Oklahoma, merchants paid Parton to hire a lively old cowboy as a "Pony Express" rider for a marathon ride to the Fat Stock Show in Fort Worth.[13]

Like Harold Hill arriving in River City, L. A. Parton arrived in Nocona from out of the blue in 1938 with a hearty handshake, a toothy smile, and sure-fire, can't miss ideas. His enthusiasm for Nocona's mercantile prospects and a cascade of ideas for shaking the dust off the town of 2,500 quickly earned him a job as secretary-manager of the local chamber of commerce.

Within several months of Parton's arrival, an announcement of "the longest horse race ever run" appeared as an eight-column, front-page headline on the February 3, 1939, issue of the *Nocona News*. The race was being backed by "a number of Nocona businessmen," according to the newspaper, and "L. A. Parton, manager of the Chamber of Commerce, is in charge of details." Though that first article makes no specific mention of Enid Justin, it's apparent that she had already taken the whip hand. The purpose of the race, the paper said, "is to advertise Nocona throughout the West and the nation as the 'Leather Goods Manufacturing Center of the Southwest.'"[14]

There are no meeting minutes, no records, no newspaper accounts, and no living memories of how or why Nocona civic boosters adopted the idea of a two-thousand-mile Pony Express–style horse race. There is only this: Enid Justin was too smart and too hard to be hornswoggled by some tinhorn promoter. She likely recognized Parton for the slickster he was, but she also knew that her small hometown needed to plant itself on the map to avoid the fate of other small towns that were drying up and blowing away. And then there was her beloved boot company. Nocona Boot Company was a strong competitor in Texas, Oklahoma, New Mexico, and Colorado, but Enid thought a huge promotional stunt involving Arizona and California would expand sales there. If she oversaw the details, the benefits of Parton's horse race might well prove more valuable than the cost to support it.[15]

In later news stories Parton announced that Enid Justin "has underwritten with five thousand dollars a proposed Pony Express race from Nocona to the Golden Gate Exposition in San Francisco," and she was named sponsor of the event. Whether Enid spent that amount is a matter of conjecture. It is certain, however, that she didn't let Parton get his hands on the cash. She put a thousand dollars of prize money—$750 for the winner and $250 for the runner-up—directly into the hands of exposition officials in California to avoid any hanky-panky in paying the winners what they were owed.[16]

Parton published a set of official rules for the event: riders would travel a specified route and must ride down the main street of designated towns on the route. Entrants would be required to make the race using only two horses, changing them out every twenty-five miles. The rider must be accompanied by a two-man crew that would trailer the spare horse to the next exchange location. If one of the starting horses was unable to complete the entire race, the rider must finish the race on the other animal; no mid-race substitutions were allowed. Under no circumstances could a rider step into any motorized or wheeled transport.

A competitive race of two thousand miles through open country— even while switching between two horses—is a remarkable challenge. The distance is the equivalent to running two back-to-back Iditarod sled-dog races, seventy-six marathon footraces, or fifteen hundred Kentucky Derbies. The most active thoroughbred race horses run on carefully groomed tracks; these latter-day Pony Express riders would race on grass, dirt, sand, mud, rock, and asphalt.

The race would be a grueling one, and riders paid their entry fee knowing that they would have to stand for their own expenses on the trip. Food for the rider, crew, and horses was the responsibility of the rider's team; Mother Nature would provide lodging under the stars in the open air. Some riders planned to cover their expenses through the sale of commemorative stamps and trinkets, and they would be sorely disappointed.

To serve the Pony Express theme, Parton required every rider to carry five pounds of U.S. mail. Spectators along the route would give mail to the rider, who would affix a special stamp reading "Nocona Texas, the leather goods manufacturing center of the Southwest, via Pony Express to Golden Gate Exposition, San Francisco, California." The envelope would receive a Golden Gate Exposition postmark on arrival in San Francisco. The stamps cost fifty cents, and the riders were promised twelve-and-a-half cents for each one they sold.

Except they weren't really stamps at all, at least not in the sense of being official U.S. postage stamps. (The *Fort Worth Star-Telegram* and some other newspapers refused to call them "stamps," referring to them instead as "stickers.") Parton talked the Nocona chamber into printing thousands of sheets of these stickers as a moneymaking venture, selling them to the chambers of commerce in towns along the race route. "Philatelic devotees the world over are already making demands for the stamps," a chamber member in Electra told the newspaper editor there.[17]

To Parton's credit, he knew how to get publicity. His announcement garnered plenty of publicity from newspapers in Texas, New Mexico, Nevada, and California. Most of the larger out-of-state papers published the short announcement that the Associated Press distributed. Many of the smaller papers, however, published Parton's claims for the race verbatim. "Three women and forty men have already entered," he wrote the *Reno* (NV) *Evening Express*. "About 100 entrants are expected," Parton told other editors. The promotion man's claims may have been exaggerated, but most of the stories mentioned Nocona Boot Company and Nocona. The townspeople of Nocona were thrilled. It appeared that the North Texas town might be about to shake loose of the hard times gripping the rest of the country.[18]

The big race wasn't the only thing driving civic euphoria; a wildcat oil company found deep oil just a mile west of Nocona, and it appeared that the underground pool extended beneath the town site. And oil wasn't the only good news. Steady (but gentle) rains fell over the area for much of February, breaking a two-year drought and giving hope to farmers that they might make a good crop that year. Even the Nocona high school basketball team had come out of an early-season slump to lead the district.[19]

In the end, only sixteen riders and crews showed up to make the race.

Standing in the middle of Clay Street on Wednesday morning, March 1, 1939, Enid Justin could see, to the north, the riders adjust saddles and calm horses spooked by the crowds. To the south of her as far as she could see, people and cars lined the street to cheer on the riders. She saw several press photographers and two newsreel cameramen ready to film the start of the race. Nocona Boot Company appeared to be getting its money's worth in publicity.[20]

Enid continued across Clay Street to a decorated wooden platform. Amon G. Carter, owner and publisher of the *Fort Worth Star-Telegram*, was already standing on the platform, and he extended his hand to assist Enid up the rough steps.

Carter was born in Montague County and lived with his family as a child in Nocona. He had had a long relationship with the Justin family—Daddy Joe before he died, the brothers in Fort Worth, and Miss Enid. Nocona Boot Company was a longtime sponsor of Fort Worth's Fat Stock Show and Rodeo, an annual event dear to the publisher's heart, and an occasional *Star-Telegram* advertiser. Carter wore a battered Stetson he said had been given to him by Will Rogers and a tooled leather holster that held a silver-handled pistol that the county sheriff had loaned him for the occasion.

At a signal from a radio reporter who was broadcasting the event live, the president of the Nocona Chamber of Commerce stepped up to a microphone at the front of the platform. After a few brief remarks thanking the community for its support of the race, he turned over the microphone to Enid. She wasn't timid in front of a microphone; her voice was strong and confident as it echoed from speakers up and down Clay Street as she introduced Amon Carter.

Carter was no shrinking violet when it came to public speaking, either. He talked about childhood incidents in Nocona and his friendship with "the greatest American citizen of all time, that sweet old Will Rogers." Carter then launched into a history of the original Pony Express. When some impatient spectators began calling out, Carter pulled the silver-handled revolver from his holster and fired it into the air.

At the sound of the pistol shot and the cheers of five thousand spectators, fifteen cowboys and one red-haired girl and their horses jogged down the road toward Wichita Falls, forty-eight miles away.

Enid's sharp eyes noticed something amiss as the horsemen passed by; one of the racers was wearing a competitor's boots. She turned to the chamber of commerce president. "If he's not wearing Nocona Boot Company boots by the end of the day, disqualify him," she ordered.

The "World's Longest Horse Race" was under way.

For the first few miles the riders trotted their horses at a steady pace, riding on flat land adjacent to the roadway, taking time to get a fix on the other riders' horses, and judging their own chances in the race.

The one female in the race was Bennie Greenwood of Bowie. Her gender and her flaming red hair had been the subject of much news coverage. (Promoter Parton had taken a special interest in the girl and unilaterally had given her the title of "Miss Nocona.") Eighteen-year-old Lige Reed Jr. rode a thoroughbred cow pony, wiry and quick. Reed's father was manager of the Tom Burnett Triangle Ranch outside Iowa Park, and he equipped his son with two of the best horses from the ranch. T. J. "Tolly" Sykes, the only Oklahoman in the race, was a farmer, not a rancher, and he was riding plow horses that plodded along with head low to the ground. Twenty-two-year-old Shannon Davidson lived on a small farm in Motley County with his mother and siblings. He cared for and trained horses in the area to help support his family. For the race, he rode big, muscular animals—Rocket and Ranger weighed close to twelve hundred pounds each—figuring that endurance, rather than speed, would win the race.

Wichita Falls, near the Red River, was the first destination. From there, the route turned southward toward High Plains country through the small towns of Archer City, Olney, Albany, and Throckmorton to Abilene. From Abilene the riders would turn west for a grueling four-hundred-fifty-mile desert stretch to El Paso. The riders would spend at least eight days on horseback before ever leaving Texas.

Race organizer L. A. Parton had called on the network of chambers of commerce in towns along the route to stage welcoming events as the riders came through their town. He sold the organizations stacks of his "commemorative stamps"—the printed stickers—to resell locally and promised that the riders would take their stamped envelopes to San Francisco and be posted there. Dozens of towns signed on, forming welcome committees and collecting money for cash prizes to the first arrival.

At first, the lead in the race changed hourly as riders pushed for the honor (and cash bonuses) of arriving first in a town along the route. Shorty Hudson led the race the first day but was overtaken in Olney by Tolly Sykes.[21]

Taylor Tuck was running a close second, but fifty miles south of Wichita Falls his trailer crew saw him slide off the side of his saddle and fall headfirst to the ground. The crew scooped him up and raced toward a hospital in Olney, where he was diagnosed with influenza. Tuck was out of the race.[22]

Thursday brought another disqualification. Several riders and a judge reported seeing Bennie Greenwood riding with her horses in her support trailer. The sixteen-year-old red-haired girl sobbed as organizers told her she was out of the race. (Later, Bennie's mother visited a local newspaper editor to tell him that Bennie hadn't actually been a race contestant. She had signed a personal services contract with L. A. Parton to accompany the riders for publicity purposes, her mother said.)[23]

Tolly Sykes built up a twenty-mile lead by sleeping in his saddle while his muscular plow horses plodded on, but by the time he arrived in Abilene on Friday afternoon, his lead had been whittled down to just three miles.[24]

Chris Uselton and Shannon Davidson rode into town thirty minutes after Sykes. Stopping only long enough to change horses, the two got back into the saddle and began the four-hundred-fifty-mile ride to El Paso, leaving Sykes in third place.

Enid was following the race with daily newspaper reports and calls from her judges. The *Fort Worth Star-Telegram* had a reporter following the West Texas leg of the race route and filing daily reports. The Dallas papers depended on wire service accounts, but they occasionally published details the *Star-Telegram* didn't. The *Nocona News* was a weekly newspaper and not useful for daily updates. But Mr. Perry, the owner-editor, was placing long distance calls to newspaper editors along the race route and bringing news of the riders' standings to Miss Enid's office every day. The race judges were less conscientious about reporting daily progress.

By the time the riders crossed the Pecos River two days later, the lead had changed twice. The cowboys had been sandpapered and half blinded by a vicious sandstorm that had blown into their faces for more than twenty-four hours.

Sykes's strategy of sleeping in the saddle while his horses continued plodding along seemed to be working. He had overtaken the other riders who were forty miles behind him when he rode through the town of Pecos. Shannon Davidson had a small lead on Chris Uselton, but the rest of the riders were strung out for sixty miles or more.[25]

A delegation from Electra waited in Pecos for their hometown favorite, eighteen-year-old Lige Reed. The Electra Chamber of Commerce sponsored the sale of Pony Express stamps, and the town had taken up a collection to print envelopes with Reed's picture on it. The delegation would give the young rider a packet of envelopes addressed to forty-eight states and two foreign countries for Reed to post when he reached Oakland. The delay in Pecos temporarily set the young wrangler back to sixth place.[26]

When the riders entered the Trans-Pecos area of far West Texas, they were riding through the driest, most desolate area of the state. The Trans-Pecos lies across the upper region of the Chihuahua Desert, a landscape that few of the riders and none of their horses had navigated before. Jake Clifton withdrew from the race when one of his horses gave out in the sand dunes. Shannon Davidson chose to ride bareback to spare his mount the heat of a saddle and blanket. Most of the riders rode the remaining two hundred miles to El Paso at night, sleeping during the day under what little shade they could find.

The sun was setting as the first of the Pony Express riders approached El Paso on Wednesday, March 8, after eight days in the saddle. Shannon Davidson overtook Tolly Sykes twenty miles outside El Paso when Sykes's plow horse wandered off the route as Tolly napped in the saddle. Chris Uselton, the Nocona favorite was in third place; Lige Reed was making up for lost time and running fourth.[27]

El Paso marked the one-third point of the race. Davidson got a 5:30 a.m. start the next morning. He and the other riders still had twelve hundred miles to go.

Shannon Davidson maintained his lead across the southern edge of New Mexico and into Arizona, pressed by Tolly Sykes, Chris Uselton, and Lige Reed close behind. Sykes apparently pressed too hard; one of his patient plow horses refused to take another step, and Sykes withdrew from the race near Deming.[28]

As the riders approached California, the larger newspapers began printing daily reports about the race. Readers in Albuquerque, Tucson, Phoenix, Los Angeles, Oakland, San Francisco, and elsewhere read daily updates about race leaders; their progress; about little Nocona, Texas; and about the world's only lady bootmaker, who was sponsoring the contest. Welcoming crowds in cities along the route grew larger and larger.

As Davidson approached Phoenix on Tuesday, March 14, a police escort led him up Central Avenue. Well-wishers crowding the sidewalks waved and shouted encouragement. Several local cowboys appeared and rode along with him to the state capitol. Arizona Governor Bob Jones greeted Davidson on the Capitol steps as the two posed for photos. Davidson declined the governor's offer to spend the night in Phoenix, switched out his horse, and rode off toward Wickenburg fifty-three miles northwest.[29]

In Arizona, Davidson stretched out his lead to seventy-five miles, almost a day's ride ahead of his nearest followers. Slim Mathis, King Kerley, Chris Uselton, and George Cates pressed on, knowing that any mishap could knock Davidson off his pace or out of the race. Eighty miles behind those runners-up were the tail-enders: Shorty Hudson, Lige Reed, Bob Moyer, Art Helm, and V. H. Henderson.[30]

Davidson entered Blythe, California, on Thursday afternoon, March 16, after sixteen consecutive days in the saddle. Blythe marked the two-thirds point of the race; twelve hundred miles behind him, six hundred miles to go. The lanky twenty-two-year-old was maintaining a blistering pace; he started at five-thirty each morning and rode until eight in the evening, averaging eighty miles a day. After spending five minutes in Blythe, a dusty and windburned Davidson departed for Indio.[31]

Back in Nocona, Enid Justin heard some disquieting news. L. A. Parton and the five chamber of commerce members serving as race judges were supposed to drive the race route, back and forth between the lead rider and the last rider. As the distance between first and last place grew longer, however, the judges decided to cut back on the driving and let the riders come to them. (As a later report put it, "Promoter Parton and his pals had a rare outing, a lot of it in wayside saloons.")[32]

Enid was also concerned about the reception for the race winner at the Golden Gate Exposition. The Oakland Chamber of Commerce was planning a lavish, well-organized welcome. Now, at Parton's unexpected invitation, exposition officials were stepping in to run the show.

As quickly as she could secure an airline ticket, Enid flew to San Francisco to sort things out.[33]

As Davidson's horses carried him from town to town—Indio, Palm Springs, and Banning in the Southern California desert—the size of the welcoming crowds grew, and the greetings grew flashier. The Indio Fire Department welcomed him with sirens and lights. In the smaller towns, rural communities with people not much different from those of his own hometown, assorted local cowboys joined up with him and rode alongside. Small-town mayors presented him with proclamations and posed with him for photos.[34]

Crowds were even larger in the agricultural towns—Arcadia, Riverside, San Bernardino—east of Los Angeles. Davidson camped outside of Pomona Saturday night, but not before the town staged a parade and escorted him out of town with the police chief leading the Texan and a mile-long string of cars.[35]

In Los Angeles, Davidson got an update on how his competitors were faring. George Cates dropped out of the race when one of his horses went lame. Lige Reed's horse suffered a fall, rolling over on the young cowboy. Reed was trying to continue the race with an injured leg, but he was expected to drop out soon. Slim Mathis was falling further behind, but Chris Uselton, King Kerley, and George Cates were picking up the pace. They were following Davidson by only a half-day's ride. Davidson seemed unfazed by the news. He posed for an Associated Press photographer as he changed out horses and asked only, "How far's the ocean?"[36]

The twenty-two-year-old cowboy (who had never been more than a half-day's ride from his home in Texas) got his first glimpse of the Pacific Ocean at daybreak on Monday, March 20, as he reached the coast highway near Santa Monica. He turned northward toward Oakland and the finish line four hundred miles away.

Newly arrived in San Francisco, Enid Justin was trying to get a handle on plans for welcoming the race winner. L. A. Parton had been out of touch for a week, supposedly following riders in Arizona or California.

Welcoming crowds grew larger still as Davidson rode through coastal towns—Oxnard, Santa Barbara, Santa Maria, and San Luis Obispo—on the route to Oakland. There were the town's businesspeople, of course. But there were also ranchers, farmers, field hands, store clerks, cars full of families from nearby towns, housewives, and children with toy cap guns in holsters and cowboy hats out to cheer him on. Davidson was too good-natured to turn away anyone, so he signed autograph books, answered questions about Texas, sampled local fruit, and even had his horses blessed at one of the old Spanish missions. With every minute of delay, however, he was aware that the other riders were closing the gap on his lead.[37]

He needn't have worried.

On Wednesday, March 22, fewer than a hundred miles from Oakland, Davidson learned that an automobile had struck Chris Uselton and his horse in Oxnard the day before, breaking two of the horse's legs and bruising Uselton. Davidson's nearest competitor was out of the race.

When Davidson awoke in Salinas on Thursday morning, he knew he could make it to the finish line by late that night. Oakland Chamber of Commerce officials recommended that he delay his arrival until midday Friday to allow time for the welcome party to gather. They had arranged for Davidson to spend the night at the Patterson Ranch near Centerville, twenty-five miles from the finish line. His nearest remaining competitor, King Kerley, was a hundred miles back, chamber officials reported, and couldn't overtake him before he reached Oakland.

Davidson galloped into San Jose at 3:15 p.m. He delayed only long enough to sign autographs and make a short talk to the crowd that turned out to greet him. By 4 he swung into the saddle once more and was off toward Centerville and the Patterson Ranch.

On March 24, his twenty-fourth day in the saddle and final day in the race, Davidson rose early to brush out his dress hat and put on his best denim shirt, purple tie, and leather jacket. His road crew had oiled his boots, saddle, and tack the night before. At 7:30 he saddled Rocket, shook hands with his road crew, and trotted off to Oakland.[38]

Davidson's progress slowed as he passed through the towns of Hayward and San Lorenzo, despite the California Highway Patrol escort and some outriders from nearby ranches. Thousands of people lined the route, crowding in to see the Texan from Matador, shake his hand, or pat his horse. Miss Haywood Area stepped up to plant a kiss on his cheek; Davidson blushed and politely stuck out his hand for a shake, instead. Mayors, police chiefs, and fire chiefs made welcoming speeches and read proclamations as Davidson patiently sat his horse, waiting to continue to the finish line.

Sirens, a marching band, and more than a thousand spectators (including a large Texas contingent) greeted Davidson when he finally clip-clopped across the official finish line at 38th and Market Streets in downtown Oakland at seven minutes before noon. City officials welcomed him, representatives of the Oakland Chamber of Commerce welcomed him, the band played Texas songs, and the crowd whooped, yipped, and cheered at every opportunity. Through it all, the cowboy stood on the outdoor platform and grinned as well as his chapped and cracked lips would allow.

But Davidson's ride wasn't over. He still had to cross the San Francisco-Oakland Bay Bridge to reach Treasure Island, site of the Golden Gate Exhibition.

Treasure Island is a man-made island created from landfill in the middle of San Francisco Bay. The Bay Bridge passes alongside the island, and an access road, named the Rainbow Ramp, is the gateway from bridge to island. Race organizers, local chamber planners, and even fair officials assumed that Davidson would ride his horse over the bridge, down the ramp, and onto the exposition grounds to a finish line there. But bridge officials wouldn't hear of it; they had a strict rule that no live-stock was permitted on their $77-million bridge, and no Texan was going to break the rule. An appeal to California's governor failed to get results.

Davidson helped load Rocket and Ranger into his support trailer and climbed in after them for a six-mile ride to the Rainbow Ramp, where he saddled Ranger for the final two-hundred-yard ride to the exposition gates.

Enid Justin and fifteen carloads of friends, supporters, and family from Davidson's hometown of Matador were waiting. (Enid had paid for their train tickets and lodging.) Enid presented Davidson with a hat filled to overflowing with seven hundred fifty shiny silver dollars, recently produced at the San Francisco mint. Enid kissed Davidson on the cheek, prompting a noticeable blush under the cowboy's deep tan.

"I'm not very tired," Davidson told a reporter. "But I wouldn't want to make another trip like this one."

King Kerley of Quanah, Texas, arrived in Oakland the following evening to claim his $250 second prize. Other riders with their full mail sacks straggled into town over the next few days to find no welcoming committee, no newsreel cameras, no accommodations, and no free entry to the exposition.[39]

They had expected to have their horses cared for in the livestock barn on Treasure Island, to have a place to sell souvenirs, and to ride in the Wild West Show. They had worked as exposition emissaries all along their route through the Southwest, they told a reporter, and disappointment was their only reward. All of them were stony broke, and they were seeking cowboy work to earn funds to get them back to Texas.

L. A. Parton had assured the Nocona chamber president, the Oakland chamber, and Enid Justin that all arrangements had been made with the exposition management, but exposition management was ignorant of any such arrangements. Parton hadn't been seen in ten days and failed to show up in Oakland. (Two weeks later, the Nocona Chamber of Commerce would receive his letter of resignation but no accounting of the funds raised from the sale of his commemorative "stamps." The riders never received their share for the stamps they sold.)[40]

Enid Justin was still in San Francisco when the news of the riders' complaints hit the front pages. She called the *Oakland Tribune* to say that she would pay their way home, buy tickets to the exposition for each one, and present each entrant with a pair of custom boots from the Nocona Boot Company. Her response drew favorable headlines the next day.[41]

Enid Justin's Nocona Boot Company and her little town of Nocona certainly benefited from the publicity given her sponsorship of the "World's Longest Horse Race" across the Southwest and up the length of California. But she wasn't finished.

On April 3, Enid and Shannon Davidson took the train to Los Angeles for a weeklong stay in a suite at the Biltmore Hotel. Local papers noted their arrival—"the only woman cowboy bootmaker in the world" and "a sure 'nuff cowboy." Their names opened the doors to the Hollywood movie studios. As publicity men toured them through MGM, Columbia, Warner's, Paramount, and RKO, they met stars and influential moviemakers. To each one she pitched the benefits of wearing "authentic" Texas cowboy boots, calling attention to the stitchery and the quality of the finish. For some, she offered to make a pair of custom boots if they would send her their measurements.[42]

Some Hollywood moviemakers adopted the high-heel Texas boots right away, finding them comfortable and practical when shooting on location. Others wore them, perhaps ironically, as a fashion statement. But it was Hollywood's "sure 'nuff" cowboys—the wranglers, extras, and bit players—from the movie business that spurred demand for authentic Texas boots and allowed Enid Justin to sign up dozens of new retail accounts in California.[43]

The Nocona-to-the-Golden-Gate horse race was a publicity stunt no less than a tightrope wedding or waiters dressed as lobsters. But Enid's race was a Texas-sized stunt spanning two thousand miles, three weeks, and four states, proving, once again, that everything was bigger in Texas. Yet, it was a personal event. Thousands of people in small towns along the race route had a chance to meet Shannon Davidson and the other riders personally, to shake their hands, and to discover that folks across the country weren't all that much different from one another.

The country also met Enid Justin, a tall, determined Texas woman who ran a successful business producing an iconic product in her own hometown. It was through the "World's Longest Horse Race" that Hollywood discovered Enid Justin and the Nocona Boot Company, and through Hollywood movies that the rest of the country discovered *authentic* Texas cowboy boots and Texas people.

CHAPTER 8

AUDIE MURPHY

THE TEXAN WHO ALWAYS SHOT FIRST

THERE WAS NOTHING HEROIC IN THE FACE OF THE BOY ON THE MAGA-zine cover: none of the clenched jaw, squinty determination of a Gary Cooper; nothing of an Errol Flynn's I-laugh-in-the-face-of-danger smirk.

The photos in *Life* magazine in July 1945 document the small-town homecoming of a boyishly handsome twenty-year-old who's slightly pudgy around the jawline and smiling like a shy high schooler on his first date. He appears joyful and unaffected, just as every mother with a son in uniform remembered her son to be when he left to fight a world war.[1]

A photo inside the magazine shows the same young man in full U.S. Army officer's uniform, standing at a rural roadside chatting with a much older man, apparently a local farmer. A cotton field stretches out behind them. The younger man is tilting his head upward as he listens to the farmer; the top of his round service cap barely reaches the older man's chin. He could be a youngster dressed for a costume party in the photo, not a battle-worn soldier who has pushed an enemy back across two continents while watching men to his left and right die.

Another image in the photo spread shows the young man giving his thirteen-year-old sister a look at a war souvenir brought home from Europe: a German Mauser Karabiner 98k sniper rifle factory-fitted with a Zeiss Zielvier 4x scope. He grins like a Boy Scout with a new merit badge as he points out features of the rifle, but he doesn't tell her that the dark stain on the elmwood rifle stock is the blood of the German he shot between the eyes to claim the rifle.

By the time the boyish-looking Audie Murphy returned to Texas from the European theater of operations in 1945, the smiling twenty-year-old had personally killed more than two hundred German soldiers in combat. He had earned the Congressional Medal of Honor, and *Life* was calling him America's "most decorated soldier."

America was calling this boyish young Texan a hero.

The reporters and columnists who described Audie Leon Murphy as having "grown up in the backwoods of Texas" never visited Hunt County. Rural Hunt County is open country, crisscrossed with creeks and shallow streams, with brushy thickets, berry patches, and trees scattered here and there. By the time Audie Murphy was born at home on June 20, 1925, most of the land was under the plow. Sixty miles east of Dallas, Hunt County lies in the Blackland Prairie region of Central Texas, where the soil is a black clayey loam perfectly suited to growing cotton.[2]

Audie Murphy was born on some of the richest, most productive agricultural soil in the state, but the Murphy family knew only the hard work and little of the profit from the land. The Murphys were hand laborers, cotton sharecroppers, who prepared the soil, planted the seed, harvested the crop, and received only a small share of the proceeds when the landowner ginned and sold the cotton.

"To say that the family was poor would be an understatement," Audie wrote later. "Year after year the babies had come until there were nine of us children living, and two dead."[3]

The large family moved from community to community around Hunt County—Kingston, Hog Eye, Quinlan, Celeste—as the seasons changed, and they contracted with different landowners. They found lodging in whatever dilapidated shelter the landowner might rent them or allow them to use. In Kingston, their home was a four-room clapboard cabin with newspaper insulation and no running water; in Celeste it was an abandoned railroad boxcar.

Every member of the family worked. "As soon as we grew old enough to handle a plow, an ax, or a hoe, we were thrown into the struggle for existence," Audie said. The Murphys weren't the only ones scratching out a living on the bottom rung of the economic ladder. In 1930, 72 percent of Hunt County's agricultural workers were tending crops on land that belonged to someone else.[4]

But things seemed to be looking up.

Through the 1920s, Texas cotton prices had increased from a low of nine cents a pound at the end of the Great War to twenty cents by the end of the decade, almost an all-time high. At picking time, hundreds of the five-hundred-pound bales could be seen stacked near the train depot platform, fifty thousand bales a season, and each bale worth a hundred-dollar bill to the landowner.[5]

Even in those better times, however, Audie's father couldn't seem to find a way to improve his family's lot. "He wasn't lazy," Audie said. "But he had a genius for not considering the future."[6]

Like a giant asteroid, the Great Depression slammed into Texas in 1930, scorching crop prices, demolishing the state's economy, and rattling confidence in markets and institutions. Farmers who planted twenty-cents-a-pound cotton were soon picking fifteen-cent cotton. And prices continued to plummet to nine cents a pound the following year and as low as four cents a pound by 1935. Those five-hundred-pound bales—each representing two hundred man-hours of physical labor—were selling for about twenty dollars. Oil prices were in freefall, too; refiners and shippers were laying off workers as fast as they could shed them. Farmers who had taken mortgages to buy additional acreage or invest in oil leases were facing foreclosure or bankruptcy. And share-croppers like the Murphy family competed for fewer and fewer acres in production.

The banks that loaned money based on higher prices began to fail when customers couldn't repay their loans: banks in Aubrey, Post, Ennis, Merkel, Jefferson, Henderson, Brownwood, and two dozen more in the last five months of 1930 alone. Thousands of families lost their savings, small-town merchants lost their lines of credit, churches lost their building funds, and small towns lost their collected tax money when the local banks closed. The impact was as devastating as it was inexplicable.

Audie was only five years old when the Depression arrived. He would spend the next eleven years, his formative years, living under a form of peonage that judged human beings only by their labor and rewarded them with pennies. Still, he never blamed the social structure, never turned to lawlessness. He developed a close acquaintance with hard work, a sense of responsibility to provide for his family, and a desire to find any work other than farming as soon as he was able.

Children of sharecroppers were lucky to get any formal education at all, and Audie didn't enter elementary school until he was nine years old. He was a good student, his teachers said later, earning mostly As and Bs. One schoolteacher described him as "intelligent, industrious, quick to anger, but very loyal and devoted to the ones he loved."

Audie's temper could be explosive, particularly when teased about his size, his age, or his hand-me-down clothes. "At school, I fought a great deal," he acknowledged in his autobiography, *To Hell and Back*. "Perhaps I was trying to level with my fists what I assumed fate had put above me."[7]

He may have been a promising student, but he left school—barely literate after five years—to help support his family.

Audie caught a glimpse of a pathway out of lifelong poverty in the stories his uncles told as the family worked the cotton fields. Several uncles had served in the Great War, and they told him stories of army life. They told tales (probably exaggerated) of what it was like to be a soldier: the exploits, adventures, outdoor life, and the satisfaction of seeing a German raise his head above a barricade and into the sights of an Allied rifle. But Audie was also drawn to the idea of a fresh new uniform, a bunk of his own, clean bedding, indoor toilets, and the dream of three full meals a day.[8]

Audie was already a deadeye with a .22 rifle. Starting with thrown rocks or a homemade slingshot, the boy graduated to a firearm and an unerring ability to stalk and kill small game animals. He could drop squirrels from their trees, rabbits in mid-jump, and grazing deer with a single shot. The game he killed went to help feed his family. He had to be accurate, he said, because he couldn't afford more ammunition. "If I missed, we didn't eat!"[9]

He dreamed of one day becoming a soldier. "I was only twelve years old," Audie said, "and the dream was my one escape from a grimly realistic world." If he felt that his family existed at the bottom of an economic barrel, in 1940, when Audie was barely fifteen, the family's world became grimmer still.[10]

Audie Murphy's father was the kind of Irishman who gives the Irish a bad name: a lazy, drunken wastrel with too many children. He was prone to unexpected absences, sometimes sleeping off a bender in a neighbor's barn, sometimes spending a night or two in jail following a barroom row, and sometimes gone for weeks with no reason offered.

Then, one day, he never came home at all. "He gave up," Audie said. "He simply walked out of our lives, and we never heard from him again." For the rest of his life, he would despise quitters.

Audie's mother didn't last long after that. When her husband disappeared, she was already showing symptoms of tuberculosis and died of the lung disease in May 1941. The younger Murphy children were left to fend for themselves.

On leaving school, Audie took a series of salaried jobs as a hired hand, a filling station attendant, and a radio repair trainee. His employers found him to be a hard worker, and a large portion of his earnings went to support his remaining family. For a short time after their mother's death, Audie's salary and small contributions from an older married sister (along with meals delivered by the social aid and church ladies) sustained the Murphy children, but it was obvious to everyone that what was left of the family would have to split up.

Audie, at sixteen years old, handsome, with a captivating smile, was declared emancipated, a ward of his older sister, Corinne. The three youngest siblings were taken in by the Boles Orphans Home outside Greenville. No closer to escape from his life in Hunt County, Audie went back to work to repay the money he had borrowed for his mother's burial.

American newspapers in 1939 and 1940 devoted plenty of front-page space to news of the war in Europe. Congress passed the country's first peacetime conscription act in September 1940, but it was more of a "just-in-case" measure for a nation determined to avoid entanglement in another European war. As much as Audie Murphy wanted to be a soldier, the plain fact was that there was no war for him to fight.

That changed on December 7, 1941.

When the Japanese attacked Pearl Harbor, and Germany declared war on the United States, the public became aware of what military planners had known all along: America was woefully short of the men in uniform necessary to wage a global war. On December 20, 1941, amendments to the Selective Training and Service Act made all men between the ages of twenty and forty-four liable for military service. (An amendment four months later made eighteen- and nineteen-year-olds eligible for the draft.)

The United States needed men in uniform—*fast*—but they weren't yet ready to accept Audie.

"I was half-wild with frustration," Audie said. "Here was a war, and I was too young to enlist." He was only sixteen years old; he wouldn't turn eighteen for another year and a half. "I was sure that it would all be over in a few months, and I would be robbed of the great adventure that had haunted my imagination."[11]

Sister Corinne had the solution.

As with many bottom-rung, born-at-home rural youngsters of the time, Audie lacked a birth certificate. His birth should have been reported to the county when he was born, but the Murphys or the attending country doctor had neglected that bureaucratic detail. Corinne and Audie called on the old country doctor who had helped deliver Audie, asking him to complete a form attesting to the boy's birth years before. Perhaps the old doctor had no accurate records of his participation in the birth or was confused by all the births he had assisted in the Murphy household. Maybe he fudged his records a bit in the spirit of patriotism. Whatever the reason, the result was that the Murphys left the physician's office with a document attesting to Audie's birth on June 20, 1924.

After receiving an official delayed birth certificate from the Texas Registrar's office, the now-eighteen-year-old could present himself to a recruiter's office, where he would be disappointed again.

"I hurried to a Marine Corps recruiting station," Audie said. A glance at the young man's diminutive physique—five-and-a-half feet tall and weighing in at just over a hundred pounds—was all it took to know Audie wasn't leatherneck material.[12]

Audie next tried to enlist as a paratrooper because it sounded rough. "There was another point in its favor," Audie said. "Paratroopers wore such handsome boots." The recruiter didn't turn him down cold. He recommended that Audie go on a bananas-and-milk diet to bulk up. "That sergeant was only the first in a long list of uniformed authorities that I requested to go to the devil."

Reluctantly, Audie enlisted in the infantry. "With a pocket full of holes, a head full of dreams, and an ignorance beyond my years, I boarded a bus for the induction center." The underage recruit had never been more than a hundred miles from home.

Audie completed his basic training at Fort Wolters in West Texas and his advanced training at Fort Meade in Maryland. In February 1943, he boarded a troopship in New York and landed at Casablanca in North Africa a week later. Along with a thousand other young men from farms and towns across the country, Audie Murphy was about to become an American fighting man.

The baby-faced boy from Hunt County, Texas, was assigned as a replacement to Company B, 15th Infantry Regiment, Third Infantry Division, Fifth U.S. Army. The Third Infantry Division carried with it a reputation earned in WWI when, with backs to the Marne River, surrounded on both flanks, and facing a withering frontal assault, the division commander assured his French allies, *Nous resterons la*," (We shall remain here). The division stood firm (at a terrible cost) and became known as the Marnemen.[13]

Murphy's Third Infantry Division upheld its tradition of steadfastness and unremitting action in WWII. The division led four amphibious assaults and spent 531 days in combat, more than any other unit in the European theater of operations.

The Third Infantry suffered the most casualties of any U.S. unit in the European theater, and Audie would be one of only two men remaining out of the two hundred men on the original Company B roster to see V-E Day. His cotton field imaginings of being a soldier were about to meet the dirt, cold, thirst, blood, mud, horrendous casualties, and grisly death of warfare.[14]

To recount details of Audie Murphy's wartime experiences—the amphibious landing on Sicily, the race to Messina, the drive north through the mountains of Italy to Cassino, the bloody Anzio beaches, an amorous encounter in Rome, another amphibious landing in southern France, the brutal slog up the Rhone Valley, winter warfare in the Vosges Mountains, and the advance to the Rhine River near Strasbourg—would be a disservice to Audie's own account in his autobiography, *To Hell and Back*. Written with the help of a ghostwriter and published in 1949, *To Hell and Back* appeared at a time when generals were writing about their grand strategies, and politicians were describing events in nations' capitals. "It is a fighter's story of a fighter's war," one reviewer wrote. "Stark, grim, and straight from the shoulder. There is no civilian conscience in *To Hell and Back*."[15]

His story makes it clear that Audie—just seventeen years old when he enlisted—learned the soldier's business, and the business of a soldier is to fight and kill. A soldier wounds, cripples, and kills his enemies at will and impersonally. If he doesn't, the enemy will do the same to him. He writes, "Now get this straight in your head. If a man comes over that hill, he'll be a German. One of you is going to get killed. The man that shoots first will be the one that lives."[16]

As a soldier, the sharecropper's son who used rocks, slingshot, and a .22 rifle to kill so his family could eat was most often the man who shot first. His skill with a weapon, determination, self-confidence, and compulsion to care for and protect his foxhole "family" were a collection of traits his superiors took to be valor, and they rewarded him for it with the only currency they had: promotions and medals.

Audie was promoted to corporal during the Sicilian campaign; at Anzio he was named staff sergeant. His battlefield promotion to lieutenant came as the German army reluctantly gave ground in the snowy forests of the Vosges Mountains and a colonel summoned him back to the command tent. "You are now a *gentleman* by act of Congress," the officer said as he pinned on the gold bars. "Shave, take a bath, and get the hell back into the lines."[17]

In addition to the standard infantry and campaign medals, Audie received the Purple Heart (with a second oak leaf cluster), the Bronze Star (with a "V" and cluster), the Silver Star (and cluster), and one of the nation's highest awards for valor in combat, the Distinguished Service Cross. All this was before the division entered Germany. (He would later receive the French Croix de Guerre/with Silver Star and the Belgian Croix de Guerre.) And for one of the most spectacular single heroic events of the war near Holtzwihr, France, on January 26, 1945, he would earn the Congressional Medal of Honor.[18]

Audie relates the events of that day in *To Hell and Back*, and it's a powerful narrative. But the matter-of-factness of Murphy's account lacks the specifics that made his actions so exceptionally courageous that the regimental commander, Lieutenant Colonel Keith Ware, chose to recommend Murphy for the nation's highest honor for bravery in combat. Sworn statements from three men of Murphy's Company B accompanied Ware's recommendation to battalion headquarters.[19]

The Third Infantry was tasked with removing experienced and well-equipped German forces from their last foothold on French soil, a strategic area known as the Colmar Pocket. It was a bloody, acre-by-acre contest, and a forested area had been wrested from enemy control the night before at a cost of much blood. The area was of cardinal importance, Ware wrote, "as the woods dominated the town of Holtzwihr, reduction of which was essential."[20]

On January 26, Murphy's depleted Company B, down to eighteen battle-ready men from two hundred at full strength, was assigned to hold the woods "at all cost."

"At about 1400 hours we received a terrific concentration of artillery fire," Lieutenant Walter W. Weispfenning, forward observer, attested. "I saw six heavy tanks emerge from enemy-held woods about 400 yards to our front, firing on us with their 88s as they advanced across snow-covered ground."

Murphy ordered his company to withdraw to prepared positions a hundred yards into the woods behind them. He remained in his command post, a shallow dugout under a pine tree at the edge of the woods, using a wired telephone handset to call in artillery on the enemy. "As we withdrew, hundreds of enemy infantrymen poured out of the woods behind the tanks, firing automatic weapons as they came," said Sergeant Elmer C. Brawley in his sworn statement.

From his command post, Murphy called in artillery fire to within ten yards of his own position. The artillery fire he directed "had a murderous effect on the Kraut infantry," Weispfenning said. "I saw Germans falling or disappearing in clouds of dirt and snow, but others immediately took their place."

A U.S. M18 tank destroyer, sited about ten yards into the clearing, took a direct hit from a German 88. "The crew piled out as fast as they could," said PFC Anthony Abramski, "and withdrew toward our company position in the forest." The tank destroyer was fully fueled and carried dozens of rounds of high-explosive shells. It was slowly burning and threatening to explode at any moment.

Murphy stood bolt upright in his dugout, giving fire directions on the field telephone, observers said. They could see bullets and shell fragments clip the branches of the fir tree he stood under.

By this time the enemy tanks were charging abreast of Murphy's position, just fifty yards away on both sides. "The tanks fired at him as they passed, but apparently wanted to avoid the burning tank destroyer and so didn't come any closer," Brawley said.

As the tanks turned their fire toward the troops in the woods, German infantrymen circled the edges of the open meadow to outflank Murphy, firing with their rifles and machine pistols all the while. Still composed and unhurt, Murphy phoned in more artillery fire using his own position coordinates.

"How close are they to your own position?" an incredulous artillery sergeant asked.

"Just hold the phone and I'll let you talk to one of the bastards," Murphy answered.[21]

Lieutenant Weispfenning then "saw Murphy do the bravest thing that I have ever seen any man do in combat." Murphy sprinted to the slowly burning tank destroyer, climbed atop the turret, and began firing the .50 caliber gun at the approaching Germans. "There he was, completely exposed and silhouetted against the background of trees and snow, with a fire under him that threatened to blow the destroyer to bits if it reached the fuel and ammunition."

Yard by yard the German infantry edged closer to Murphy's position. From his vantage point Abramski could see their white tracers glance off the hull and turret of the disabled tank destroyer.

Damaged by artillery and having lost their infantry support, the German tanks began a slow retreat, firing at Murphy's position as they left. "I could see Lieut. Murphy fire his machine gun at the approaching tanks, forcing them to button up," Abramski said. "Then he turned his fire on the infantry, which was still advancing."

The Germans advanced to within ten yards of Murphy's one-man stronghold, Brawley said, "but he killed them in the draws, in the meadows, in the woods—wherever he saw them."

After almost an hour the Germans halted their advance and began a retreat to the other side of the meadow. Flames and smoke burst from the destroyer's hatches, and Murphy was running out of live targets.

"When the smoke cleared, I saw that Lieut. Murphy was hit," Abramski said. "His uniform was tattered and spattered with dirt, and blood was seeping through his torn trouser leg."

Murphy slid off the burning destroyer and limped back to the company position. He refused to wait for treatment by the medics and, instead, reorganized his company and led them on a counterattack, driving the Germans from the area.

Only then did he stop for first aid, but he insisted on staying with his company and refused to be evacuated from the field.[22]

Lieutenant Abramski later told a field summary court and the army decorations board: "The fight that Lieut. Murphy put up was the greatest display of guts and courage I have ever seen. There is only one in a million who would be willing to stand up on a burning vehicle, loaded with explosives and hold off around 250 raging Krauts for an hour, and do all that when he was wounded."

In his recommendation to the army decorations board, Lieutenant Colonel Keith Ware, commanding officer, said that Murphy "shattered the enemy attack, saving his Company from possible encirclement and destruction and enabling his regiment to hold the woods which had been won with such difficulty."

The recommendation and statements went up the chain of command to the commanding general of the Third Infantry Division, to the commander of the U.S. Seventh Army, to the U.S. Army adjutant general in Washington, and, finally, to the desk of the secretary of war. Approval didn't take long. By mid-February, orders that Second Lieutenant Audie Leon Murphy was to receive the Congressional Medal of Honor took the same path down the chain of command. Details were still pending as to when the presentation ceremony would occur.

Shortly after news of the award reached France, Audie was pulled from front-line combat duty and assigned a division liaison job. "The Army's reasoning was simple," one writer explains. "It didn't want a dead Congressional Medal of Honor winner on its hands. Awards to live soldiers were much preferable to posthumous ones."[23]

Germany was collapsing through March and April. May 8 was declared V-E Day, and Allies everywhere—military and civilian alike—celebrated the end of hostilities in Europe.

Audie was on leave in Lyon when his war ended, but he found it hard to celebrate. He felt only a bone-deep weariness. He tried to sleep but, "like a horror film run backwards, images of the war flicker through my brain."

Those images would haunt Audie's sleep for the rest of his life.[24]

On June 2, 1945, on an airfield just outside Salzburg, troops with crisp new uniforms stood in precise rows and columns at parade rest before a platform on which were seated nine U.S. senators and more army brass than the GIs had ever seen in one place. After some opening remarks and the awarding of some lesser medals, General Alexander Patch, commander of the U.S. Seventh Army, picked up a printed certificate and a plain red box that held the Medal of Honor. He ordered Lieutenant Audie Leon Murphy to stand before him.

"For conspicuous gallantry and intrepidity involving risk of life above and beyond the call of duty in action with the enemy . . . ," General Patch read from the printed citation describing events in the Holtzwihr forest on January 26. The reading complete, General Patch placed the blue ribbon around Audie's neck and saluted him. The Texas sharecropper's son answered the salute with tears in his eyes.[25]

Even before the award ceremony, the army saw that, with the French and Belgian awards for valor, an overdue Good Conduct medal, and the Medal of Honor, Lieutenant Murphy was the most-decorated soldier in U.S. history. The army's publicity machine wanted him back in the United States as soon as possible.

The final push to defeat Japan had turned into a particularly bloody grind that would become even deadlier once troops invaded the Japanese mainland as planned. Some feared that the butcher's bill could continue to mount for another year. America needed a live returning hero, someone to epitomize the gallantry of the country's fighting men, a reminder that the sons, husbands, brothers, and fathers in uniform would eventually return with honor to a proud, civilian nation.

Audie Murphy was exactly what the nation (and the army publicity people) were looking for.

After four hundred days in an active theater of war, Audie flew home from Salzburg on June 10. He was still ten days shy of his twentieth birthday. He slept little as the air transport hopped from Paris to the Azores, to a military base in Maine, and then to Houston. The final hop was a flight to San Antonio, and he may have gotten an inkling of the celebrity that was about to land on him when an escort of eighty fighters and bombers met his transport in the air.

Audie limped down the ramp of the C-24 transport plane onto the San Antonio airfield's tarmac. A crowd of newsmen and civilians waited to greet him, but they had trouble picking him out from among the twenty other GIs on the plane. "He could have been their mascot," a reporter said later. "He looked about seventeen years old."[26]

Military handlers ushered him through a receiving line of civic leaders and then to a waiting convertible automobile. With Audie in the back seat, the car lined up with others for a parade through San Antonio. More than 300,000 people waved to Audie, blew kisses, and showered him with flower petals as the motorcade made its way to a reception in downtown San Antonio.

The city had planned this celebration for thirteen generals who flew from Paris on the same air transport Audie hitched a ride on. It was pure coincidence that Audie arrived with the generals, and Mayor Mauermann quickly made Audie the star of the show. Asked to say a few words, Audie spoke the words he would repeat time after time during his homecoming: "There are fellows I served with who will stay over there forever. They are the fellows I want the honors to go to, not me." The mayor presented him with an airline ticket home.[27]

Audie had had enough of flying; he wanted to see Texas at ground level. He was offered a ride to Dallas by a group of reporters, and he took them up on it. As the car drove over the hill country, through Austin, and into the black land of North Central Texas, the nineteen-year-old veteran told his story to the reporters. He was softspoken, not a braggart, and deeply patriotic. The reporters wrote glowing stories about the boy hero and his modest upbringing.

Papers across the country couldn't seem to get enough news about Audie Murphy.

Reporters, well-wishers, and old friends surrounded Audie during the months that followed. Audie stayed with his sister and brother-in-law in their small, white frame house in Farmersville, and people dropped in day and night to welcome him home. Photographers followed him to the barbershop for his weekly trim. Reporters accompanied him to Dallas as he shopped for new civilian clothes. *Life* magazine descended on Hunt County for a multipage photo spread on the young hero. He drew crowds when he went on a date with an old girlfriend. Area Rotary clubs, chambers of commerce, fraternal organizations, and veterans' groups invited him to "say a few words" at their meetings, and those words appeared the next day in newspapers throughout America.

Through it all, Audie remained the same polite, softspoken young man with the boyish smile who picked cotton and shot squirrels to feed his orphaned family. In the few minutes he could get away from crowds, he would drive the backroads of Hunt County, just enjoying the green rows of corn, the gentle hills, herds of dairy cattle, and white cottony fields ready for picking.

"This is what I came home to see," he said. "You can't realize how swell this is until you've been away."

The Audie Murphy who returned home to Texas didn't look like a hero—at least, not like the hero most people expect to see. Instead, this youngish-looking man with the infectious grin looked like all the sons, husbands, brothers, and fathers who, at the call of their nation, left homes and farms and jobs to put on uniforms, take up arms, and go to faraway places.

That face on the cover of *Life* was the face of any of twelve million American fighting men who returned from Europe or the Pacific, or those who remained a framed picture on the mantel.

Texan Audie Murphy, a sharecropper's son, became emblematic of them all.

CHAPTER 9

GLENN MCCARTHY

A TEXAS WILDCATTER BUILDS A SHAMROCK

TWO LONGTIME OILMEN WERE DISCUSSING HOUSTON WILDCATTER Glenn McCarthy.

"What's he worth?" one asked.

"He's got fifty million dollars," the other answered, "but he ain't worth a damn."

No man more fit the mid-twentieth-century stereotype of the loud-talking, big-spending, whiskey-swilling, risk-chasing Texas oil millionaire than Glenn McCarthy. In a state increasingly identified with oil wealth, McCarthy epitomized the oil richest in a land of the big rich.

Glenn Herbert McCarthy was born poor as a sawmill rat on Christmas Day 1907. His family was living near Beaumont, within earshot of the creaky pump arms of the dwindling Spindletop oil field. Glenn McCarthy's father was an itinerant oil-field worker and sometime plumber who picked up work wherever it was available. From time to time, when the family managed to get a few dollars ahead, Glenn's father would invest the money in a long-shot wildcat oil well. Those wildcat wells, located based on hunches in unproven ground, never seemed to pay out for the McCarthys.[1]

Whether due to his father's hardworking example, the family's need for additional income, or some engine already churning in his chest, Glenn pursued paying jobs almost from the time he could walk. He was a water boy, pulling a tiny wagon with buckets of water and a tin dipper to workers on the derricks; he was a pipe hauler, harnessed and dragging hundred-pound lengths of drill pipe from the pipe stacks to the well head. He learned carpentry and joinery, shinnying up the tall derricks to affix heavy wood beams to the drilling structure. Glenn worked whenever he could find the jobs while (sometimes) attending school, fighting as an amateur boxer, and earning a reputation as a better-than-average football player on his school teams.

"Success doesn't come to lazy people," he said later about those early years. "It comes to those willing to work from early morning till late at night." His hard work and athletic abilities succeeded in earning him a football scholarship to Texas A&M.[2]

McCarthy's A&M scholarship covered only tuition, so he found a campus job serving meals in the mess hall. He served three meals a day, six days a week, attended classes, and played on the freshman football team. Texas A&M was an all-male military school, and school officials turned a blind eye to the hazing of underclassmen. The upperclassman learned soon enough that Glenn McCarthy's Irish temper and experience in the boxing ring led him to return every poke, slap, punch, and kick the minute he received them. That wasn't how the game was played; college officials expelled him.

Good timing, fast talking, and some remedial academics allowed Glenn to enter Rice Institute in Houston the following year. He settled in to study business administration and earned a starting spot on the Rice football squad. It didn't take long for McCarthy to become the big man on campus. He had an athletic build, muscular but slim and tall. Glenn had an Irishman's full and curly head of hair, dark, and often a little curl hung down over his forehead. His eyes were dark, he wore a thin Clark Gable mustache, and he sported a winner's grin, especially around the coeds. To use a word of the day, he was catnip.

The following September, when it came time to register for his second year at Rice, however, Glenn was a no-show. The Rice student newspaper, *The Thresher*, explained why: "An early marriage of the summer was that of Glenn McCarthy, freshman football star, to Miss Faustine Lee."[3]

Faustine Lee may have been the greatest deal in Glenn McCarthy's deal-making career. He was working as a pump jockey at a filling station near the Rice campus when a beautiful young woman drove up to the pump. She was dressed for a party and driving her family's new top-of-the-line convertible automobile; he was wearing greasy shop overalls, and his hands were black with motor oil. It was love at first sight. Seven weeks later, on May 18, 1930, Glenn and Faustine eloped and were married at a tiny courthouse in Hemphill. She was one day short of her seventeenth birthday, he was twenty-two. With borrowed money, Glenn took them on a two-day honeymoon to Austin.[4]

Faustine's parents were furious. Her father was a wealthy oil man in his own right, co-owner of the Yount-Lee Oil Company in Beaumont. This no-account shanty-Irish grease monkey had stolen his daughter and, worse yet, the boy worked at a filling station owned by Yount-Lee Oil Company. Glenn called on his new father-in-law, who was threatening to have the marriage annulled then and there. Glenn described to the irate man his plans and ambitions, the conversation ending with two promises. Glenn promised the father that he would never—*ever*—ask for a penny from Faustine's family. He vowed that, though there might be some rough roads to travel while he was getting there, he would eventually be able to provide Faustine with everything—and more—that her family could provide her.

Glenn and Faustine would remain happily married for the rest of their lives. And McCarthy kept both promises to her family.

Those rough roads stretched out in every direction for Glenn in 1930, as the Depression was beginning to settle in on Texas. He was able to pay for groceries and the twenty-dollar-a-month rent on their one-bedroom apartment, but after a few false job starts, Glenn decided to go back to what he knew—the filling station business. He pestered Sinclair Oil to let him open a station on Main Street south of downtown.

Sinclair kept most of the gasoline profits, so Glenn began adding other services: tire repair, oil changes, lubing joints, tune-ups, glass replacement. He taught himself to repair, rebuild, and replace major mechanical items. He was willing to work from early morning to late at night, expanding the station's hours until he was open twenty-four hours a day. (He paid his father to relieve him while he caught naps on a cot in the back room.) Soon, he was taking in more money than any

Sinclair station in the area, and the company allowed him to open a second location.

By 1933 he was bringing home more than $1,500 a month—the equivalent of $32,500 today—in the middle of a depression. With two children added to the family, the money came in handy. But McCarthy was convinced that the big money came from the oil still in the earth, not the oil in Sinclair cans. He sold both stations for a profit and began his search for oil.

McCarthy bought drilling equipment—most of it secondhand or out of date—and played a hunch on a lease in Hardin County. He recruited his father and brother as helpers, and the three drilled down to six thousand feet before admitting that it was a dry hole. His luck proved no better in Conroe, and he left town just steps ahead of a sheriff who had orders to repossess the equipment.

With his last thousand dollars he invested in a friend's well. It was a moderate producer, and McCarthy walked away with an $8,000 profit that he spent to wildcat another well on his own in Chambers County. Finally, a McCarthy well hit in Anahuac, and Humble Oil Company handed over a check for $700,000 in 1936. Convinced that he was on his way, Glenn ordered a Houston mansion built for Faustine and his growing family—seven thousand square feet with tall white columns. For himself, he bought a ring with a diamond as big as a dime. And he kept on plunging.

Experienced oil men and trained experts will tell you there's no such thing, but McCarthy seemed to have a nose for oil. Though he used geologists and seismic surveys when he could afford them, he ignored their findings as often as he accepted them. The wildcatter uses some other method—a Sherlock Holmes level of observation, super hearing, tasting the dirt, or some type of bibbidi-bobbidi-boo wand waving—to confidently invest hundreds of thousands of dollars to drill into unproven land. As a young attorney, Watergate Special Prosecutor Leon Jaworski represented McCarthy and some lesser wildcatters. "The wildcatter had to be a gambler, a trader, and an entrepreneur," Jaworski said. "He exists for the sole purpose of finding new deposits of oil, or digging deeper in fields the major companies had abandoned."[5]

McCarthy couldn't miss. Five straight gushers—a quintuple par-ley—made him a millionaire several times over before he was thirty. He put all his chips on a sixth well and lost it all. A collapsed derrick and an unstoppable fire cost him $700,000 in leases and $1 million in equip-ment. Before he could move into his mansion, the wildcatter was $1.5 million in debt.[6]

In the same circumstance, a major oil company wouldn't have lost a step; it could weather a dozen dry holes. For wildcatters, however, every well meant playing cards with the devil in a no-limit game. McCarthy lost; he had no money and no credit to acquire new leases or replace his equipment. The best McCarthy could do was hire out to other wildcatters as a contract driller.

A contract driller is like a general contractor, given a fixed budget for equipment and a strict time limit with the expectation that he would meet the budget and the schedule. Glenn's expectation was that he would spend less than what was budgeted and take less time than expected. His contract allowed him to keep a portion of the savings; the quicker he completed the current contract, the sooner he could begin the next. McCarthy pressed his crews as hard as he drove himself, working from early morning into the night. "Anyone leaves this rig I'll beat the hell out of him," was his regular warning to keep up the pace.[7]

According to one observer, he "lives like a burning roman candle," shooting off sparks and balls of fire, ready to settle any dispute with fists. He would go for long periods without sleep or food, "drinking steadily for days on end without a tremor of unsteadiness." "Even during normal times, he often awakens, apparently fresh, after only a few hours' sleep, reading leases, studying maps, and impatiently awaiting the new dawn."[8]

There's a story that Glenn was in a Galveston gambling joint when he spotted the salesman for a favorite tool manufacturer standing at a dice table. The salesman had had a bad run with the dice, his wallet was empty, and he was turning to go. Someone tapped him on the shoulder, saying, "Keep shooting," and laid out thirty $100 chips. The loser stayed in the game, won back his losses and then some, and returned the $3,000 to his benefactor. "See there," said McCarthy. "You'll never get anywhere by quitting."[9]

At thirty years old, Glenn McCarthy had fallen from multimillion-aire to hired hand, a fall that would have left a lesser man shattered on the rocks. McCarthy never hit bottom. He never quit.

McCarthy recovered. He acquired new leases, bought new equipment, and got back in the game. Determined to stick to coastal areas around Houston, McCarthy's magic sense guided him to unproven swamps, barren bogs, and properties that had been sucked dry years before. And every well was a winner. An unbroken string of productive wells earned the thirty-four-year-old oilman the headline name of King of the Wildcatters.

In 1940, war was breaking out in Europe, and the Japanese were more challenging every day. When—not *if*—America went to war, it would be fought with heavy machines on land and fast ships at sea. Petroleum products from Texas would be vital to the war effort, and McCarthy did his patriotic duty by finding as much as he could. By the end of the war, his wealth was estimated to be somewhere between $150 million and $300 million.

It wasn't money that kept him going anymore, he told an interviewer. "It's more the achievement or the challenge of being able to make a successful venture out of the thing you attempt to do." But it was the money that spurred a *Life* reporter and photographer to track down the King of the Wildcatters when they came to Houston in October 1946. The resulting photo feature was "Booming Houston: Texas's Biggest City Is Suddenly Growing Bigger and Wealthier," centered around how the city's industrial and population growth resulted from the oil riches flowing through it.[10]

An accompanying feature article was "Wildcatter: Brawny Glenn McCarthy Embodies the City's Success." The article charted the million-aire's investments and excesses—purchase of the twenty-two-story Shell office building, bank ownership, family mansion, 55,000-acre West Texas ranch, private DC-3 aircraft—and personal charities such as March of Dimes, 4-H Clubs, and the Houston Livestock Show. Almost as an afterthought, the article mentions an $18 million multiuse real estate development he was planning southwest of downtown: the McCarthy

Center. He's not so sure the project will make any money, McCarthy admits in the article, but he feels Houston needs it.

"Success doesn't come to lazy people" was Glenn's reply to anyone who asked for the secret of his success. "It comes to those willing to work from early morning till late at night." Glenn put in those dawn-to-dark hours for most of his life, but by the time he neared forty, he felt he could ease back on the throttle.

Of his five children, the oldest was well into her teen years; his youngest, a son, was ready to join Cub Scouts. Glenn was a good father, playing with the youngsters when he wasn't away on a business trip or at a well site. Though he wasn't always a faithful husband, he still loved Faustine deeply and enjoyed being with her. He treasured the time the seven of them spent at the West Texas ranch, where he taught Faustine and the kids to hunt, fish, hike, catch horned frogs, and stay away from rattlers. He still lapped up liquor like a fired cowboy but never at any time or place that might embarrass his children.

Glenn had other interests, too, interests that some men might call hobbies but Glenn called business opportunities. Howard Hughes introduced him to air racing, a popular rich-man's sport, especially in California. To test it out, McCarthy spent $200,000 on a racing plane, pilot, and crew, and a maintenance hangar to win a $25,000 prize. The air racing and Hughes connections (of Houston and oil wealth) drew the Hollywood set to Glenn's money. He heeded Howard's advice about never spending his own money and never putting starlets under long-term personal contact. To earn more publicity, he gave Texas actress Dorothy Malone ten-year mineral lease rights to fifteen thousand acres in West Texas to celebrate her starring role in Warner Bros.' *Two Guys from Texas*.[11]

McCarthy's involvement in Houston civic affairs was limited to his chamber of commerce membership (and he occasionally forgot to mail a check for his annual renewal). But he was proud of his city. Houston was where he got his start, and it was Houston people who supported him when he was gassing cars and wiping windshields. When he saw something that his city needed, he tried to provide it. If a profit should result from his gift, all the better.

Though not a pilot, McCarthy flew in and out of the Houston municipal airport enough to know that Houston needed a new facility. The terminal building, just six years old, was already crumbling; it didn't have enough gate space for the increasing number of flights; the runways were too short to accommodate soon-to-arrive jet aircraft; thick fog creeping up from the marshy areas south of the airport delayed or endangered flights. McCarthy corralled Captain Eddie Rickenbacker's endorsement, and the pair made speeches at clubs across the city promoting a new airport on four thousand acres McCarthy acquired for that purpose out Richmond Avenue near Bellaire. Public pressure forced Mayor Holcombe to put the issue to a citywide vote, but the measure failed.[12]

The appeal of professional football had grown considerably during the previous two decades, but Houston had no local team. McCarthy reached out to the National Football League (NFL) and the fledgling All-American Football conference (AAFU), offering up $125,000 in prize money for a world title game played in Houston for charity. The AAFU accepted right away, knowing that, win or lose, such a game would enhance the league's credibility. The NFL refused out of hand for the same reason. It wanted nothing to do with a matchup that might benefit its puny competitor. This proto–Super Bowl never happened, but McCarthy was able to bring an AAFU All-Star game to the stadium at Rice Institute, the final game the AAFU played before the league disbanded.[13]

But McCarthy wasn't through with football. He negotiated to buy the Cleveland Browns and bring them to Houston. As a sweetener, he promised to build a 180,000-seat stadium on acreage he bought south of Houston for that purpose. The deal never went past the talking stage, but after changing hands several times, the property became the site of the Astrodome sixteen years later.[14]

Despite his seeming nonchalance in the October 1946 *Life* article, McCarthy was well into development of the $18 million McCarthy Center project. Sometime in the past he had acquired an awkward, wedge-shaped property at the intersection of Main Street and Bellaire. He had plans to build a shopping center, medical center, supermarket, and hotel on the property. The general consensus was that McCarthy had taken one too many punches to the head. The location was miles from the city center where people most often shopped and lacked the highway access that most overnight visitors would require.

McCarthy had been told that he was wrong by too many experts. He had an answer for the critics and naysayers: "I went into the oil business in 1933 when everybody said I was a damn fool. Now they're saying it again about my hotel."[15]

Time for palaver was over; it was time to turn dirt. He invited the city to his groundbreaking ceremony.[16]

The groundbreaking drew a large crowd when it was announced that McCarthy's Hollywood actor friend Pat O'Brien would join Glenn in turning the first spade of earth. All he lacked was a name. Unlike Conrad Hilton, William Marsh Rice, and others, McCarthy chose not to name the hotel for himself. Instead, he announced a contest.[17]

"Name the McCarthy Center Hotel and Win $1,500." In an ad for entries, he promised to judge the contest himself. Thousands of entries poured in. Half of Texas, it seemed, suggested naming it "The Wildcat." The other half thought "The Shamrock" fit McCarthy's Irish heritage and reputation for luck. The thirty-nine people who submitted "The Shamrock" each received McCarthy checks for $38.46, an equal share of the prize money. Thinking the amount was a little niggardly, McCarthy threw in a set of corporate cufflinks for the men and a gold bracelet for the women.

When he first described the McCarthy Center, it was a $16 million multiuse retail project. After construction began, it was an $18 million project. With the opening near, McCarthy cited a cost of $20 million *for the hotel alone.* (He abandoned all retail and medical construction in order to complete the hotel.)

As the hotel took shape, McCarthy set out to prepare for the grand opening. The only thing big enough, he thought, would be something like a Hollywood premier, with searchlights, stars in tuxes and furs stepping out of limousines, a coast-to-coast radio hookup, and fans on hand to wave and scream. Where better to plan a Hollywood premiere than Holly-wood? He packed a bag, called his pilot, and was on his way.

Pat O'Brien introduced McCarthy around the movie town, introduced him to friends, arranged dinners with stars—Myrna, Bing, Dorothy, Bob, Natalie, Gene, and others. Reporters followed him and wrote stories about the Texas oil millionaire in Hollywood planning to go into the movie business. It turned out that making a movie was easier than drilling for oil. He found a director, bought a script, and wrote checks.[18]

Back in Houston he plunged into final details. The Shamrock Hotel would be the nation's finest, the largest hotel in the country, and a suitable tribute to Glenn's hometown of Houston. For the opening he'd bring glamor, a wagonload of celebrities, and the world premiere of the first Glenn McCarthy Productions movie.

The day before the opening, the Shamrock looked beautiful (if you could ignore the workmen scurrying around to deal with last-minute emergencies). The hotel was the tallest building on the horizon—eighteen floors in the arte moderne style. It boasted fifteen hundred guest rooms and suites, each different, each decorated with original oil paintings. Every room was air-conditioned, wired with radio, Muzak, and a television. One edge of the swimming pool was surrounded by an arc of private cabanas connected by a long lanai suited for strolling or drinking. The sparkling green pool was 165 feet by 143 feet and fed by the hotel's own well; water-skiing demonstrations and lessons were available in the oversized pool on Saturday and Sunday afternoons.[19]

Above the reception desk and lobby were thirty-foot arched ceilings; the walls appeared to be gold plate. Eight noiseless elevators waited to whisk guests up their rooms. At the end of the elevator corridor was a twice life-size portrait of Glenn McCarthy, staring like a house detective hoping to catch an unmarried couple trying to sneak upstairs.

The Emerald Room was a combination dining room lounge that could seat a thousand diners with room left for a large dance floor and a thirty-piece dance band complete with music stands and chairs. The hotel had nine other dining areas scattered about. Down the hall from the Emerald Room was the Cork Club, a darkish bar for meeting, drinking, and late-night private high-stakes card games.[20]

The lobby and basement arcade had a collection of tastefully expensive stores and businesses—a jeweler, a barber, a furrier, a drugstore, and a menswear store. Hidden away were a 100,000-pound-a-week laundry and a refrigerated garbage room.

Altogether, it looked like every penny of its $21 million cost. The only thing the Shamrock had in common with any other hotel were the Gideon Bibles in the rooms.

Thursday, March 17, 1949, was St. Patrick's Day, opening day for Glenn McCarthy's Shamrock Hotel. He'd barely slept, if at all, the previous night, inspecting, bossing, and solving tiny emergencies on almost every floor. A worker rolled some scrap into a wall, requiring repair and repaint. Some stage lights had been installed improperly. The florist was still unloading 2,500 shamrocks flown in from Ireland that morning and destined to fill small planter boxes throughout the hotel. Just one problem after another for Texas's best-known oil millionaire.

Shaved and dressed in his Hollywood clothes and wearing gold-framed sunglasses, he drove to Union Station. Police estimated that five thousand people were at the station awaiting the arrival of the "Shamrock Special," a sixteen-car streamliner McCarthy leased to bring 150 of his Hollywood guests to Houston. One at a time Robert Ryan, Joan Davis, Andy Devine, Ruth Warwick, J. Carroll Nash, Ellen Drew, Van Heflin, and others stepped down from the train to McCarthy's greeting. The encircling crowd oohed, aahed, screamed, and thrust out autograph books as the stars walked down a receiving line of city officials and selected Texas society bigwigs.[21]

McCarthy couldn't linger. He was to meet his new four-engine Boeing Stratocruiser (with shamrocks painted on the tail fins) arriving soon with more celebrities. Fans crowded around to watch McCarthy greet Walter Brennan, Gale Storm, Kirk Douglas, Edgar Bergen, Charlie McCarthy (who said he was Glenn's heir), Leo Carrillo, and other notables as they descended the stairs onto the tarmac.

McCarthy hustled through the rest of the day, meeting other trains and planes arriving with celebrities, writers, producers, politicians, and other leaders of the business and financial world.

At one o'clock that afternoon, Glenn, Faustine, and their five children stood under the entry awning in front of a wide green ribbon stretched from stanchion to stanchion. McCarthy expressed the conviction—which some said sounded more like a prayer—that the venture would pay a profit. Then, each family member simultaneously cut the ribbon, officially opening the Shamrock Hotel.

The ribbon cutting was, perhaps, the last thing to go according to plan for the rest of the day.

The first official event of the evening was a 6 p.m. champagne reception mainly for the special invitees, celebrities, and VIPs. A group of fifteen hundred or so others had paid a premium price for dinner and an opportunity to mingle with the stars. They would begin arriving around 7. A nationwide radio hookup would begin at 7:30.

As the sun set and searchlights beamed across the sky, fans and others with no tickets at all gathered outside the building. As many as five thousand of these "have-nots" may have been milling near the entrances at 7 when the premium ticketed guests arrived. Many of the have-nots attached themselves to the ticketed guests and walked with them into the dining room around the same time the celebrities and VIPs arrived.

Other have-nots simply forced the doors and crashed the party. Chaos erupted. Recognizing that there were far more people in the room than place settings, a vicious game of musical chairs broke out. Many ticket holders found there was no place at the tables for them; or if they could find a place at a table, there was no chair to sit in. Security people were either too inexperienced or too intimidated to be of much help.

Some celebrities, having had little experience in Texas bar fights, hid behind the stage curtains. Others ran from crowds like possums looking for a tree. Actors Dorothy Lamour and Van Heflin tried to begin the 7:30 radio network program. Two guests seized the microphone and shouted into it enthusiastically. The control board in Chicago thought they heard some words not meant for radio and pulled the plug on the broadcast. Servers and stewards continued to serve dinner and liquor, as if this were a regular occurrence at the Shamrock. Later in the evening, the public address system and some of the lights went out.

There were no major injuries, and none of the guests or celebrities seemed particularly upset. A Los Angeles society columnist who was present minimized the event to her readers. "What matter if their thoroughly laid plans forgot to take in the human element," she asked, "and, on execution, failed somewhat of perfection?" For Texas-born actress Gale Storm, it was a county fair in ermine.[22]

Altogether, it was the sort of gloriously out-of-control gesture that Texans love and that others love about Texans.

As a result of McCarthy's success as a wildcatter and his public profile, he emerged as the flesh-and-blood symbol of the oil industry. He was extravagant, hard drinking, and too willing to settle disputes with his fists. Glenn McCarthy lives on today in the persona of Jett Rink in Edna Ferber's book and George Stevens's movie version of *Giant* (1956). Though the author and director swore that the resemblance is purely coincidental, it's impossible to see a silver-haired Jett Rink stagger into the dining room in front of his oil friends at the grand opening of his luxury Houston hotel and *not* think of McCarthy.

They weren't particularly vocal about it, but one group was upset about McCarthy's visibility and excesses. Just like the characters in *Giant*, the oil industry was dancing a delicate minuet with regulators over proration and the oil depletion allowance, and there was a risk McCarthy could take a good thing and turn it into a sow's ear.

Proration and the depletion allowance are long gone today. So is the Shamrock. But the association of the upstart wildcatter drenched in oil and Texas is permanent, and it comes from Glenn Herbert McCarthy and his Shamrock Hotel.

NOTES

INTRODUCTION

1. The story and quotes come from Marcus, *Minding the Store*, 32; and Ragsdale, *The Year America Discovered Texas*, xiii.

2. "Books of Special Interest," *Saturday Review of Literature*, May 16, 1925.

3. Steinbeck, *Travels with Charley* (New York: Viking, 1962), 202.

4. A half dozen dissertations and a handful of history fellowships could be sewn from the slight fabric in this paragraph alone. In Texas history circles, the arguments over myth history ("traditionalism") and history history ("revisionism") are threatening to burn up the pages of academic journals and are far beyond the scope of this book. For a good read on the subject with no academic jargon, read Bryan Burrough, Chris Tomlinson, and Jason Stanford, *Forget the Alamo: The Rise and Fall of an American Myth* (New York: Penguin, 2021).

5. Jesús "Frank" de la Teja, "Coahuila and Texas," *Handbook of Texas Online*, https://www.tshaonline.org/handbook/entries/coahuila-and-texas.

6. As an independent republic and state, Texas remained unswervingly pro-slavery. For a full text of the "Declaration of Causes" passed by the state legislature in 1861, see https://www.tsl.texas.gov/ref/abouttx/secession/2feb1861.html.

7. John Henry Brown, *History of Texas from 1685 to 1892* (Austin, TX: Jenkins, 1970), 2, 4.

8. "Texas Past and Present," *The Forum*, August 1900.

9. "The Great Southwest," *Munsey's Magazine*, March 1905; and "The Causes of Race Superiority," *Annals of the American Academy of Political and Social Science*, July 1901.

10. "Texas Types and Contrasts," *Harpers Monthly*, July 1890.

11. From Hynes's introduction of O. Henry, *Heart of the West*.

12. Moviemakers released a silent version of *The Texas Steer* in 1915, the first of at least four versions of the play to make its way onscreen before 1950. For the origins of "Home on the Range," see Stephen Harrigan, *Big Beautiful Thing: A History of Texas* (Austin: University of Texas Press, 2019), 355. Sheet music and lyrics for "My Heart's Tonight in Texas" (words and music by Roden and Witt) are available from the Library of Congress, https://www.loc.gov/collections/historic-sheet-music/about-this-collection/, along with dozens more Texas-related song sheets.

13. Don Graham, *Cowboys and Cadillacs: How Hollywood Looks at Texas* (Austin: Texas Monthly Press, 1983), 2.

14. Mike Cox, *Texas Ranger Tales: Hard-Riding Stories from the Lone Star State* (New York: Lone Star Books, 2016). "Hollywood adored Texas," writes journalist Lawrence Wright in *God Save Texas: A Journey into the Soul of the Lone Star State* (New York: Knopf, 2019). "On the silver screen, 'Texas' was not a real place, it was a symbol for the unbridled West, a playground for the frontier legend." Also see "Unreality Bites," *Texas Monthly*, May 1998.

15. To many historians today, the subject of Texas exceptionalism is a fraught one. Critics argue that "Texceptionalism," as some refer to it, ignores the roles of all but white Anglo men: martial men who plotted the overthrow of a legitimate national government and attributed their success to divine providence. Mexicans and Hispanic Texans, they say, are painted as a flawed and defeated people; the roles of enslaved and free Black people, the indigenous peoples who accommodated some early settlers, and ethnic Europeans, are barely mentioned at all. Twenty-first century historians are increasingly dissecting the myth of Texceptionalism with narratives that include gender, ethnic, cultural, economic, political, and urban studies.

16. "A Letter from the Southwest," *Saturday Review of Literature*, December 6, 1930.

CHAPTER 1

1. Mody C. Boatright, ed., "More About 'Hell in Texas,'" *From Hell to Breakfast* (Dallas, TX: Southern Methodist University, 1943). The entire poem is still to be found reprinted on postcards sold at souvenir shops across Texas. For examples of how newspaper editors treated the news of Old Rip, see the front pages of these newspapers on February 20, 1928: *Imperial Valley* (CA) *Press, Alaska Daily Empire, Douglas* (AZ) *Daily Dispatch, Sioux City* (IA) *Journal, Frederick* (MD) *News, Anniston* (AL) *Star, Berkeley* (CA) *Gazette*, and others.

2. Boyce House, "Memphis Memories of 50 Years Ago," *West Tennessee Historical Society Papers* 14 (1960): 103–12.

3. Boyce House, *Cowtown Columnist* (San Antonio, TX: Naylor, 1946), 155.

4. House, *Cowtown Columnist*, 157.

5. As an adult, Boyce often wrote about his father's frail condition and decline, but he never specified the cause of the debility. The symptoms Boyce mentions (coupled with his father's early health but inability to keep a job) raise the possibility that he was a functioning chronic alcoholic. Though it can never be known for sure, the father's condition during his final months is consistent with cardiomyopathy, common among end-stage alcoholics.

6. House, "Memphis Memories." The stories related to Boyce's time with the *Commercial Appeal* come from House, *Cub Reporter*.

7. Sometimes Boyce was *too* prolific. Once an editor had to remind him that the creation of the world and the making of man was told in Genesis in six hundred words; House didn't need two thousand words to describe the results of a pie-baking contest.

8. "Mud, Blood at the Ranger Museum," *Abilene Reporter-News*, October 23, 2017; "Ranger, Desdemona, and Breckinridge," *Handbook of Texas Online*; Boyce House, *As I*

Was Saying (San Antonio, TX: Naylor, 1957), 72; and Boyce House, *Roaring Ranger* (San Antonio, TX: Naylor, 1951), 1–15.

9. "I Give You Texas," *Taft Tribune*, September 21, 1939.

10. "Metro Signs Boyce House as Technical Advisor," *Boxoffice*, November 11, 1939; and "Lucky Newsman: Two Dreams Come True," *Llano News*, March 21, 1940. Boyce's MGM script and technical notes can be found in Outline by Boyce House (372.f-B-1717), November 1, 1939, Turner/MGM Scripts; Margaret Herrick Library, Fairbanks Center for Motion Picture Study, Beverly Hills, CA.

11. House, *Roaring Ranger*, 6–7.

12. House, *Roaring Ranger*, 8.

13. There are numerous accounts of the events of that day; some details vary slightly. I've relied primarily on House's *Cowtown Columnist*, 209–24, and his contemporaneous coverage in *the Eastland Daily Telegram*, December 23–30, 1927.

14. Fourteen-year-old Woodrow Harris, the quick-thinking boy who foiled the robbers by taking his car key, didn't run far. He hid behind a barn watching the frantic transfers. When the bandits had driven away, Harris returned to his car and found the dying robber and the loot. He disarmed the robber and drove him to the hospital in Cisco. He then returned the stolen money to the bank. Later that year he was presented with a twenty-one-jewel gold Hamilton watch with the inscription, "Presented to W. W. Harris by The Fidelity Casualty Insurance Company of New York for his foresight and courage in frustrating the robbery of the First National Bank of Cisco, Texas, December 23, 1927." See "Student Played Part in the Famous Santa Claus Bank Robbery," *The* (Brownwood) *Collegian*, September 16, 1933.

15. The robber who wore the Santa Claus suit had local connections, and he feared that he might be recognized in Cisco. He had the bright idea of disguising himself in an old Santa outfit two days before Christmas, thinking that no one would notice him.

16. The bluegrass/gospel musical played for four weeks in Cisco: "Santa Claus Robbery a Must See," *Dublin Citizen*, June 14, 2007. A. C. Greene's *The Santa Claus Bank Robbery* is a delightful book-length retelling of the robbery, the search, and the legal aftermath.

17. House, *Cowtown Columnist*, 3.

18. Mody C. Boatright, *And Horns on Toads* (Dallas, TX: Southern Methodist University Press, 1959), 3–5.

19. "Find Live Horned Toad in Cornerstone," *Ranger Times*, February 19, 1928.

20. "Froggery," *Dallas Morning News*, January 22, 1928; and "Skeptical Scientists Renew Attack on Claim That Reptile Lived through 31 Years of Continuous Hibernation," *Washington* (DC) *Evening Star*, February 22, 1928.

21. House, *Cowtown Columnist*, 4.

22. House, *Cowtown Columnist*, 5.

23. Boyce's most complete retelling of the events of the day can be found in *Cowtown Columnist*. Other accounts by other parties differ in some significant details.

24. *New York Times*, February 20, 1928; *Chicago Defender*, February 25, 1928; and *Los Angeles Times*, February 22, 1928.

25. "Twenty-Four Nice Toads," *Washington* (DC) *Evening Star*, February 27, 1928.

26. Sandera's Red & White Grocery advertisement, *Flatonia Argus*, February 21, 1935; "Sweet Caporels and Wings Stir Smokers' Nostalgia and Still Sell Well," *New York Times*, October 19, 1962; Abilene Candy Mfg. Company advertisement, *Simmons Brand*, October 27, 1928; "Coleman Claims First Horned Frog Raiser as Citizen," *Coleman Democrat-Voice*, March 1, 1929.

27. "Volstead Praises Frog That Ignored Drink for 31 Years," *Washington* (DC) *Evening Star*, February 22, 1928.

28. "Would Insure 'Old Rip's' Life for $100,000," *Ranger Times*, March 30, 1928. The Ranger insurance agent who accepted the application was unable to find a company to insure the celebrity horned toad's life.

29. House, *Cowtown Columnist*, 10.

30. "President Views Toad Which Caused Debate," *Washington* (DC) *Evening Star*, May 4, 1928; and "I Give You Texas," *Coleman County Chronicle*, July 13, 1939.

31. "Old Rip to Lie in State Here," *Eastland Telegram*, January 21, 1929.

32. "Cornerstone Toad Lured to His Death," *Washington Post*, January 20, 1929.

33. "Old Rip to Rest on Bed of Fame," *Los Angeles Times*, January 21, 1929; and "In Death Rip's Body Cuts a Figure," *Borger Daily Herald*, January 21, 1929.

34. No Headline, *El Dorado Success*, March 1, 1929.

Chapter 2

1. "State Items," *Dallas Herald*, November 30, 1872.

2. See *Congressional Record*, 43rd Cong., 1st sess., vol. 2, for the full text of the bill.

3. "Denison 62–50–35 Years Ago," *Denison Press*, August 28, 1937, reprinting an article that originally appeared August 28, 1875. Corporate officers and major shareholders of the Red River Bridge Company are listed in a Denison news wrap-up, "Held Up by Highwaymen," *Dallas Morning News*, May 10, 1893. They include a railroad executive, a surgeon, a factory president, and a bank owner, as well as Frank Colbert and his son.

4. "Big Bridge Completed," *Dallas Morning News*, October 31, 1891; and "Denison Doings," *Dallas Morning News*, November 17, 1891.

5. "Contract for $50,000 Bridge," *Dallas Morning News*, January 26, 1913.

6. From advertising appearing in the *Denison Daily Herald*, June 16, 1931.

7. "No Effort to Conceal, Say Road Officials," *Fort Worth Star-Telegram*, June 14, 1931.

8. *J. R. Handy vs. Johnson*, et al. (#348), order, July 10, 1931, Litigation Files, Records, Attorney General's Office, Texas State Library and Archives.

9. This account of the confrontation between Davis and the Oklahoma highway crew is from "Hickman and Sterling on Job at Span," *Denison Herald*, July 17, 1931.

10. "Motorists Have Inning as Free Span Is Temporarily Opened," *Denison Herald*, July 17, 1931.

11. "The State Press," *Dallas Morning News*, May 18, 1887; and Alexander and Brice, *Texas Rangers—Lives, Legends, and Legacy* {Denton: University of North Texas Press, 2022).

12. "Jack Hays and His Men," *Martinsburg* (WV) *Gazette*, November 19, 1846.

13. Ironically, Quanah Parker—often referred to as "Chief" of the Comanche—was the son of a white woman captured during a raid on a Texas settlement in 1836. Cynthia

Ann Parker was recaptured from the Comanche twenty-five years later and returned to her family. Natalie Wood portrayed a character much like Cynthia Ann, and John Wayne was her rescuer in the John Ford movie *The Searchers* (1956).

14. Leaving the dead in the underbrush to be eaten by predators was, apparently, not uncommon among Rangers at the time. A Ranger of a later generation tells the story of the time an official came across a pair of old-time Texas Rangers surrounded by the bodies of dead bandits. Asked what happened, one of the Rangers drawled, "We had a little shootin' match—and they lost." From Rigler, *In the Line of Duty, Reflections of a Texas Ranger.*

15. Quoted in Patrick Cox, *Texas Ranger Tales, Hard-Riding Stories from the Lone Star State* (Austin, TX: Lone Star Books, 2016). Cox devotes an all-too-brief chapter to Hickman, and other Hickman stories are scattered throughout the book.

16. Rigler and Rigler, *In the Line of Duty: Reflections of a Texas Ranger.*

17. Cox, *Texas Ranger Tales: Hard-Riding Stories from the Lone Star State*; and Robert M. Utley, *Lone Star Lawmen: The Second Century of the Texas Rangers* (New York: Berkley, 2007).

18. "Press Group Kept on Jump Investigating Many Rumors Regarding Bridge Squabble," *Denison Herald*, July 21, 1931.

19. "Guardsmen To Be Used, Says Gov. Murray," *Denison Herald*, July 17, 1931.

20. "Executive Sends Crew to Tear All Barriers," *Sherman Democrat*, July 17, 1931.

21. "Gov. Murray Tells Statesman He'll Defend His Half of Span," *Austin Statesman*, July 17, 1931.

22. "Victory Near for Murray in Toll War," *Daily Oklahoman*; and "Murray Leads in Governors' Bridge Battle," *Dallas Morning News*, both July 19, 1931.

23. "Hundreds of Persons See Span Sunday," and "Press Group Kept on Jump Investigating Many Rumors Regarding Bridge Squabble," both *Denison Herald*, July 21, 1931.

24. A competitive shooter agreed such shooting was almost impossible. "There are 10,000 shooters in the United States who would pay good money to see that," he said. (See "Expert Pistol Shot Ready to Pay Cash to See Such Shooting," *Daily Oklahoman*, July 23, 1931.)

25. "Comment and Censure by the Editor," *Durant Weekly*, July 24, 1931.

26. Williams, *Red River Bridge War*, 143.

27. A description of the Denison meeting (including most speeches) is at "Citizens at Mass Meeting, Demand Immediate Opening of Barricaded 'Free' Span," *Denison Herald*, July 22, 1931.

28. "'Alfalfa Bill' Calls Women to Bring Peace by Sewing Bees at Troop-Guarded Bridges," *New York Times*, July 22, 1931; "Women Asked to Join Battle over Bridges," *Binghamton* (NY) *Press*, July 22, 1931; "Oklahoma Women May Force Bridge," *Washington Post*, July 22, 1931; "Murray War Tactics Scored," *Los Angeles Times*, July 22, 1931; and "Jurisdiction over Texas Bank Claimed by Spanish Treaty," *Dallas Morning News*, July 22, 1931.

29. The full text of the order appears at "Martial Law Order," *Daily Oklahoman*, July 24, 1931.

30. "Armed Forces of Two States Guarding Red River Bridges," *Dallas Morning News*, July 25, 1931.

31. "Hundreds Watch as Rangers Order Bridge Barriers Torn Away," *Sherman Democrat*, July 26, 1931

32. For photos of Tom Hickman posing with some of the earliest bridge crossers and of the Texas Rangers breaking camp, see "Barriers Removed on Free Bridge," *Dallas Morning News*, July 26, 1931.

CHAPTER 3

1. Throughout her career, Babe misrepresented her age. To reporters covering her departure for Chicago she was eighteen (born 1914), on her AAU entry application she wrote nineteen (1913) as her age, on a visa application later in life she claimed to be born in 1919, and Babe's sister located a christening record showing 1911 as her birth year. Due to the uncertainty, I've used her self-reported age in this chapter. See the chapter 1 notes in Don Van Natta, *Wonder Girl: The Magnificent Sporting Life of Babe Didrikson Zaharias* (New York: Back Bay Books/Little, Brown, 2013). "Ants in her pants" is from a letter to Tiny Spurlock, June 30, 1930, cited in *Wonder Girl*, 62.

2. "Babe Didrikson Shows Golf Swing of Champ Eleventh Time on Course," *Minneapolis Star-Tribune*, August 9, 1932.

3. This quote about her childhood and the others that follow come from her autobiography: Babe Didrikson Zaharias, *This Life I've Led: My Autobiography* (New York: A. S. Barnes, 1955).

4. "It's Time to Stop Calling Her a Tomboy," says the developmental psychologist of the Girl Scouts of America. In a section of the organization's website titled "Raising Girls," Dr. Andrea Bastiani Archibald writes, "When we label sporty, adventurous girls as boyish, we're reinforcing the idea that certain behaviors or interests are better suited to boys and men, while the rest are for girls. That's limiting to children of both genders and not good for anyone." https://www.girlscouts.org/en/raising-girls/happy-and-healthy/happy/what-is-a-tomboy.html.

5. Authors William Johnson and Nancy P. Williamson, *Whatta-Gal: The Babe Didrikson Story* [Little, Brown, 1975]) and Van Natta both located and interviewed some of Babe's classmates and teachers for their respective biographies.

6. Johnson and Williamson, *Whatta-Gal*, 55. The photos appear in Russell Freedman, *Babe Didrikson Zaharias* (Boston: Houghton Mifflin Harcourt, 1999), 29–32.

7. Johnson and Williamson, *Whatta-Gal*, 60.

8. Freedman, *Babe Didrikson Zaharias*, 32.

9. Van Atta, *Wonder Girl*, 47–49.

10. Van Atta, *Wonder Girl*, 49.

11. Johnson and Williamson, *Whatta-Gal*, 64.

12. "Texas Flash," *Collier's*, August 6, 1932, 26.

13. Freedman, *Babe Didrikson Zaharias*, 41.

14. Van Atta, *Wonder Girl*, 56.

15. "Texas Flash," *Collier's*, August 6, 1932, 26.

16. "Dallas Girls Sweep Honors in AAU Go," *Dallas Morning News*, June 8, 1931.

17. Zaharias, *This Life I've Led.*

18. "Persuaded Wearing Hat Does Not Make Her a Sissy," *Dallas Morning News,* July 10, 1932.

19. Babe quotes the doctor in Zaharias, *This Life I've Led,* 47.

20. Newsreel, "Movie Trails 'Traveling Husbands,'" *Fort Worth Star-Telegram,* August 23, 1931. For a sample of the James Roach columns, see "Women in Sports," *New York Times,* August 2 and 9, November 20, December 6, 1931.

21. "An Olympian's Oral History: Evelyne Hall Adams, 1932 Olympic Games," LA84 Foundation, Digital Library Collections.

22. "The Unbeatable Babe," *Coronet,* January 1948, 156.

23. "Babe to Leave with American Squad," *Dallas Morning News,* July 17, 1932.

24. Zaharias, *This Life I've Led,* 52.

25. "An Olympian's Oral History."

26. Throughout her life Babe never responded directly to questions about her femininity or sexual orientation. The issue seemed to burn itself out by 1936, when she married pro wrestler George Zaharias and began adopting more stereotypically feminine activities and manner of dress. For a thorough discussion of twentieth-century attitudes toward women in sports, see Cecile Houry, *American Women and the Modern Summer Olympic Games: A Story of Obstacles and Struggles for Participation and Equality*; and Epstein, "Social Perceptions of Four Prominent Female Athletes during the 20th Century in the United States" (East Stroudsburg State College, 1982).

27. "The Unbeatable Babe," *Coronet,* January 1948, 158.

28. "Texas Flash," *Collier's,* August 6, 1932, 49.

29. These official results come from *The Official Report of the Games of the Xth Olympiad, Los Angeles,* published by the Los Angeles Olympic Committee.

30. The Evelyne Hall quotes come from "An Olympian's Oral History."

31. This story was reported in "The Unbeatable Babe," *Coronet,* 159.

32. The Jean Shiley quotes come from "An Olympian's Oral History: Jean Shiley Newhouse, 1932 Olympic Games," LA84 Foundation, Digital Library Collections.

33. From *The Official Report of the Games of the Xth Olympiad, Los Angeles,* published by the Los Angeles Olympic Committee. Some have speculated that the difference in the men's and women's rules for the high jump was the result of an unnoticed typo. The "western roll" allowed for higher jumps and decreased injuries among runners. The "conventional" technique is nowhere to be seen today.

34. "The World-Beating Viking of Texas," *Literary Digest,* August 27, 1932.

CHAPTER 4

1. Kenneth Baxter Ragsdale, *The Year America Discovered Texas: Centennial '36* (College Station: Texas A&M University Press, 1987), 10.

2. (No Headline: "If it's a centennial county fair . . ."), *Houston Post,* February 15, 1924; "Think—And Then Vote 'No'!" *Lubbock Avalanche,* November 3, 1932; "Need Money to Celebrate," *New York Times,* April 26, 1931; "Vote for the Centennial Amendment," *San Antonio Express,* November 4, 1932.

3. Margie Neal had been a determined suffragist, and she was the first woman to win a seat in the Texas Senate. In addition to her work on the Texas Centennial, she helped establish the State Board of Education. Neal resigned her senate seat to direct the women's division of the New Deal's National Recovery Administration before returning to Texas in 1945. For more information and directions to other sources, visit the Texas Legislative Reference Library, https://lrl.texas.gov/index.cfm.

4. "Report of Secretary of Texas Centennial Commission," *Journal of the Senate of Texas, Regular Session of the Forty-Fourth Legislature*, 2142.

5. *Legacies: A History Journal for Dallas and North Central Texas* 24, no. 1 (Spring 2012): 18.

6. Ragsdale, *The Year America Discovered Texas*, 85.

7. "Thornton's Sale Pitch Landed Texas Centennial for Dallas," *Dallas Morning News*, February 16, 1964.

8. Commission visits to the three candidate cities are described in detail in "Report of Secretary of Texas Centennial Commission," 2143–5.

9. "Dallasites Gear Up for Texas's Birthday Bash," *Dallas Morning News*, March 1, 1985.

10. Jerry Flemmons, *Amon: The Life of Amon Carter, Sr., of Texas* (Austin, TX: Jenkins, 1978), 299.

11. Ragsdale, *The Year America Discovered Texas*, 58.

12. Flemmons, *Amon*, 300.

13. Flemmons, *Amon*, 43–44.

14. Flemmons, *Amon*, 35–36.

15. Brian Cervantez, *Amon Carter: A Lone Star Life* (Norman: University of Oklahoma Press, 2019), 10.

16. Cervantez, *Amon Carter*, 11.

17. Flemmons, *Amon*, 53–58.

18. Flemmons, *Amon*, 57.

19. Flemmons, *Amon*, 66.

20. Cervantez, *Amon Carter*, 109; and Jan Jones, *Billy Rose Presents . . . Casa Mañana* (Fort Worth: Texas Christian University Press, 1999), 5–7.

21. Ragsdale, *The Year America Discovered Texas*, 224–25; and "The Lone Star Rises and Shines," *Business Week*, June 6, 1936.

22. Ragsdale, *The Year America Discovered Texas*, 135 and 149.

23. "Elm Street and the Centennial," *Dallas Morning News*, November 25, 1935.

24. Flemmons, *Amon*, 301.

25. Stories of Billy Rose's arrival in Fort Worth are numerous. See Ragsdale, *The Year America Discovered Texas*, 210–15; Jones, *Billy Rose Presents . . . Casa Mañana*, 17–25; Flemmons, *Amon*, 302–6.

26. "Producer of 'Jumbo' Will Run Frontier," *Fort Worth Star-Telegram*, March 10, 1936.

27. Quoted in Jones, *Billy Rose Presents . . . Casa Mañana*, 24; and "Musical Rodeo is the Show Plan," *Fort Worth Star-Telegram*, March 17, 1936.

28. "Show Salvo Is Fired by Billy Rose," *Fort Worth Star-Telegram*, March 11, 1936; "Musical Rodeo Is Show Plan," *Fort Worth Star-Telegram*, March 17, 1936; "Giant Painting May Be in Show," *Fort Worth Star-Telegram*, April 9, 1936.

29. Quote appears in Stephen Harrigan, *Big Wonderful Thing: A History of Texas* (Austin: University of Texas Press, 2019), 573.

30. "350,000 View 3-Mile Parade to Exposition," *Dallas Morning News*, June 7, 1936.

31. Labor issues and design squabbles delayed completion of the Hall of State until after the opening. In later years, a bigger-than-life-sized bronze statue of R. L. "Bob" Thornton was placed on a landing in front of the Hall of State. Thornton's statue seems to wear a satisfied grin as it looks down the length of "his" esplanade toward the admission gates. "Finish State Building," *Dallas Morning News*, June 2 and June 14, 1936.

32. "Great Exposition Opened in Texas," *New York Times*, June 7, 1936. Whereas most accounts of the overall design and decoration of the buildings described it as derivative of Spanish or Mexican cultures, few commented on the irony that the Texas Centennial celebrated the state's violent separation from Mexico and its earlier role (as a Mexican state) in ridding itself of Spanish colonialism. Many of the exposition buildings still stand and are in use today. The restored buildings comprise the largest collection of Art Deco art and architecture from the golden age of world's fairs.

33. "Texas Roundup," *Collier's*, May 30, 1936. The Dallas team tapped into Texas's industrial strengths when signing up sponsors. For instance, Texas auto agencies accounted for one of every six autos sold in the forty-eight United States in 1935, according to the article.

34. Harrigan, *Big Wonderful Thing*, 573.

35. House, *As I Was Saying*, 21–43; and "Texas: Bluebonnet Boldness," *Time*, June 8, 1936.

36. "The Lone Star Rises and Shines," *Business Week*, June 6, 1936; and "On the Rise of the Lone Star in Texas," *New York Times*, May 24, 1936.

37. The description of Frontier Centennial grounds and attractions comes primarily from Jones, *Billy Rose Presents . . . Casa Mañana*, and aerial photos of the grounds in the Fort Worth Star-Telegram Collection, University of Texas at Arlington Libraries. Aerial view of Casa Mañana's open-air outdoor stage, 1936, https://library.uta.edu/digitalgallery/img/10000218.

38. House, *As I Was Saying*, 27.

39. "Frontier Show Amazing, Asserts Damon Runyon," *Fort Worth Star-Telegram*, July 22, 1936.

40. Some visitors to Fort Worth today mistake the smaller, aluminum dome of the modern Casa Mañana for the Centennial-era Casa Mañana. After the Centennial, the original presented splendid theatrical productions for three more seasons. It was dismantled in 1942, its materials salvaged for wartime use. A reborn Casa Mañana opened near the site of its namesake in 1958, a shiny geodesic dome representing the theatrical spirit (if not the extravagance) of the original.

41. Jones, *Billy Rose Presents . . . Casa Mañana*, 103.

42. Ragsdale, *The Year America Discovered Texas*, 300–301.

NOTES

CHAPTER 5

1. Murray Goodman and Leonard Lewin, *My Greatest Day in Football* (New York: Bantam Books, 1949), 17.

2. National Football League Properties, Inc., *The First Fifty Years: A Celebration of the National Football League in its Fiftieth Season* (New York: Simon & Schuster, 1969).

3. Joe Holley has done some excellent research into Sammy Baugh's family, particularly during the period of Sam's childhood and young adulthood. See Holley, *Slingin' Sam: The Life and Times of the Greatest Quarterback Ever to Play the Game.* (Austin: University of Texas Press, 2012). Martin Donell Kohut's entry in the *Handbook of Texas Online* is useful but gives Sam's pre-TCU days short shrift.

4. Quoted in Holley, *Slingin' Sam*, 17.

5. This encounter and Meyer's effort to find a place for Baugh at TCU is described in detail by Joe Holley, *Slingin' Sam*, 10–23.

6. "The Early History of Football's Forward Pass," *Smithsonian Magazine*, December 2010, https://www.smithsonianmag.com/history/the-early-history-of-footballs-forward-pass-78015237/.

7. "Unfathomable," *Washington Times*, December 19, 2008.

8. This quote from the *New Orleans Item* is included in Holley, *Slingin' Sam*.

9. "Noted Figures in Denver Play," *Brownsville Herald*, July 29, 1937; and "Sam Baugh Signs St. Louis Cardinal Contract," *Dallas Morning News*, August 9, 1937.

10. Joe Holley, author of *Slingin' Sam*, does a master detective's job of tracking down and explaining all the threads of this negotiation.

11. Corinne Griffith, George Marshall's wife, says in her memoir that George didn't hire Sam as much as Sam hired George. Griffith, *My Life with the Redskins* (New York: Barnes, 1947).

12. "This Morning," *Washington Post*, December 13, 1937.

13. Footballs were bigger then, fatter around the middle and harder to grasp. Recessed stitches in the ball made a good spiral throw unlikely in the best of circumstances, and frozen-fingered receivers would find it hard to hold onto a flying football.

14. This description of the play-by-play comes from "Redskin-Bear Detail," *Washington Post*, December 13, 1937.

15. "This Morning: Slingin' Sammy Baugh a Real Hero," *Washington Post*, December 13, 1937.

16. The stories of Marshall's early career come from Holley, *Slingin' Sam*.

17. Plasman, who spent eight seasons with the Chicago Bears and Cardinals, is noted in NFL history as the last pro player to play without a helmet. Helmets were optional for players, and Plasman hated hats of any kind. His 1939 season ended early when he ran head-first into a concrete end-zone wall at Wrigley Field. The collision left him with a depressed skull fracture and led to his decision to wear a helmet during the 1940 season. See a profile of Plasman during his later years: "Last Man to Play Without a Helmet Has Hole in His Head," *Southeast Missourian*, October 31, 1974.

18. "Sammy Baugh Idol of Fans; Team Mobbed," *Washington Post*, December 13, 1937.

19. David Boss, *The First Fifty Years: A Celebration of the National Football League in Its Fiftieth Season* (New York: Simon & Schuster, 1974).

CHAPTER 6

1. From the author's conversation with Mrs. Jerrie Marcus Smith, March 12, 2022.
2. John William Rogers, *The Lusty Texans of Dallas* (Whitefish, MT: Kessinger Publishing, 2011), 318; and *Handbook of Texas Online*, https://www.tshaonline.org/handbook/entries/marcus-herbert.
3. This version of the Coca-Cola story appears in Frank X. Tolbert's 1953 *Neiman-Marcus, Texas: The Story of the Proud Dallas Store* (New York: Holt, 1953). (Stanley Marcus admits that the story may be apocryphal but used it in his 1974 memoir and numerous speeches. There is no contemporaneous record in Texas or Georgia to verify the choice Marcus describes.)
4. These early family remembrances come largely from Stanley Marcus, *Minding the Store* (Denton: University of North Texas Press, 2001).
5. "Building Occupied by Neiman Marcus Is Practically Destroyed," *Dallas Morning News*, May 12, 1913.
6. "Big Crowds at Fire Sale," *Dallas Morning News*, May 29, 1913.
7. Tolbert, *Neiman-Marcus, Texas*, 75.
8. Marcus, *Minding the Store*, 27. Stanley sold *Saturday Evening Post* subscriptions as a youngster. Years later, when speaking before a group of publishing executives, he told of his early job and presented the publisher of the *Post* with a fur-framed issue of the magazine.
9. Marcus, *Minding the Store*, 32.
10. *Handbook of Texas Online*, https://www.tshaonline.org/handbook/entries/marcus-harold-stanley.
11. Marcus, *Minding the Store*, 47.
12. James Howard, *Big D Is for Dallas: Chapters in the Twentieth-Century History of Dallas* (Austin, TX: University Cooperative Society, 1957), 46.
13. Tolbert, *Neiman-Marcus, Texas*, 81.
14. Marcus, *Minding the Store*, 56–58.
15. Boyce House, *Oil Field Fury* (San Antonio, TX: Naylor 1954) and *Roaring Ranger: The World's Biggest Boom* (San Antonio, TX: Naylor, 1951).
16. Marcus, *Minding the Store*, 71.
17. James Ward Lee, *Adventures with a Texas Humanist* (Fort Worth: Texas Christian University Press, 2004).
18. Marcus, *Minding the Store*, 73–74.
19. Marcus, *Minding the Store*, 75.
20. "Dallas in Wonderland," *Fortune*, November 1937; and Howard, *Big D Is for Dallas*, 45.
21. The quote is from Green Peyton, *The Face of Texas* (New York: Bonanza Books, 1966). James Howard repeats the quote in *Big D Is for Dallas*, expanding on the role show business played in Marcus's success.
22. Marcus, *Minding the Store*, 100.
23. "Dallas Store to Give Award to Designers," *Dallas Morning News*, September 4, 1938.
24. Tolbert, *Neiman-Marcus, Texas*, 101.

25. Rogers, *The Lusty Texans of Dallas*, 315.

26. "Two Fashion Events Added to Store's Monday Program," *Dallas Morning News*, September 11, 1938. For photos, see "New Mannequin Completed for Dallas Store," *Dallas Morning News*, September 14, 1938.

27. Tolbert, *Neiman-Marcus, Texas*, 104.

28. "Fashion Leaders Arrive for Presentations," *Dallas Morning News*, September 12, 1938

29. "Two Fashion Events Added to Store's Monday Program," *Dallas Morning News*, September 11, 1938.

30. "Dallas Store to Give Award to Designers," *Dallas Morning News*, September 4, 1938.

31. "On and Off Elevators," *Dallas Morning News*, September 12, 1938.

32. Marcus, *Minding the Store*, 100.

33. "Designers See Own Creations," *Dallas Morning News*, September 13, 1938.

34. "Brilliant Fashion Evening," *Dallas Morning News*, September 13, 1938.

35. Marcus, *Minding the Store*, 100.

36. "On and Off Elevators"; and "Texas Tells 'Em," *Collier's*, September 16, 1939.

37. "Texas Tells 'Em."

CHAPTER 7

1. "Nocona's Pony Express Race to Coast Started," *Fort Worth Star-Telegram*, March 2, 1939.

2. "Miss Enid" (as friends called her) is a beloved figure in the history of Nocona. Examples of her generosity abound throughout the town. Privately, however, many who knew her (or heard stories from parents who knew her) admit that she could be dismissive, harsh, callous, or even cruel to anyone who crossed her or threatened her business. She was loyal to her employees and learned the names of their children. But she could be strict, too. "Step on Miss Enid's toes," one former employee told me, "and you could expect to pay the price."

3. This account of the origins of the Justin and Nocona boot companies and the Justin family comes mainly from the "Herman Joseph Justin," "Justin Industries," "Nocona Boot Company," and "Nocona" entries in the *Handbook of Texas Online*, https://www.tshaonline.org/handbook.

4. Sharon DeLano, *Texas Boots* (New York: Viking, 1981), 94.

5. *Probate Minutes, 1873–1935*, county court, Montague County, Montague, Texas.

6. Tyler Beard, *The Cowboy Boot Book* (Layton, UT: Peregrine Smith Books, 1992), 14.

7. DeLano, *Texas Boots*, 96.

8. Transcribed from an oral history of Enid Justin, "Born into Boots: An Interview with Enid Justin," *Humanities Texas*, March 2014. Her direct quotes come from this lengthy interview.

9. While she was married, Enid, by custom, took on her husband's last name. After the divorce (and for the rest of her life) she went by "Enid Justin." Every ad for Nocona Boot Company thereafter included the line, "Miss Enid Justin, President."

10. Newspaper: "Cage Founded First Pharr Paper in 1912," *Pharr Press*, February 13, 1959; Park: "Hancock Park Leased by L. A. Parton," *Lampasas Daily Leader*, April 24, 1935; and "City Business," *Lampasas Daily Leader*, October 30, 1935.

11. "L. A. Parton, Editor of the Evant News, Enters Co. Judge Race," *Coryell County News*, March 6, 1936; "$1,000 Prize to Winner of Lampasas-Dallas Horse Race," *Lampasas Leader*, May 29, 1936; "Staging 180-Mile Free-for-All Horse Race June 5 and 6," *Fairfield Recorder*, June 4, 1936; "Marathon Racers Leave Promptly at 8 a.m., 15 Riders off on 184-Mile Jaunt," *Lampasas Daily Leader*, June 5, 1936. The local newspaper published a letter from the winner regarding his prize money: "Winner of Race Tells about Things and Horse," *Lampasas Record*, June 11, 1936.

12. "Ankle Express from Marlin to Fort Worth," *Lampasas Daily Leader*, July 16, 1936.

13. See Parton's promotions in "Race Meet Drawing Crowds Here Daily," *Goldthwaite Eagle*, August 14, 1936; "Pony Ready for Express Route," *El Reno* (OK) *Daily Tribune*, March 30, 1937; "'Lobo Jim' Is on Time Now," *Daily News Telegram* (Sulphur Springs), April 8, 1937; No Headline, *Harlow's Weekly* (Oklahoma City), January 29, 1938; "Pony Express Right on Time," *Fort Worth Star-Telegram*, March 12, 1938.

14. "Pony Express to Run from Nocona to San Francisco," *Nocona News*, February 3, 1939.

15. "Miss Justin Attends Shoe Convention in San Antonio," *Nocona News*, January 27, 1939.

16. "Pony Express to Run from Nocona to San Francisco"; and "Forty-Two Applications to Enter Pony Express Race," *Nocona News*, February 10, 1939.

17. "Pony Express Riders Will Ride from Texas to Fair," *Fort Worth Star-Telegram*, February 5, 1939; and "And We'll Ride, Ride, Ride," *Electra Star*, February 16, 1939.

18. "Pony Express Race Planned," *Reno* (NV) *Evening Gazette*, February 19, 1939; "Special Stamps Are to be Used in Pony Express Stunt," *Big Spring Daily Herald*, February 20, 1939; (No Headline), *Lubbock Morning Avalanche*, February 21, 1939.

19. "Deep Producer West of Nocona," *Bowie News*, January 6, 1939; "Oil Excitement Runs Wild!" *Nocona News*, January 13, 1939; "Mist Envelops Area after Showers," *Abilene Reporter News*, February 6, 1939.

20. My description of the start of the race comes from two newspapers, both of which had a reporter and photographer on the scene: "Nocona's Pony Express Race to Coast Started" and "Pony Express Thunders toward Setting Sun," *Nocona News*, March 3, 1939.

21. "Pony Express Riders End First Lap," *Dallas Morning News*, March 2, 1939.

22. "Sykes Leads Pony Express Riders Here," *Olney Enterprise*, March 3, 1939.

23. In Nocona, a small town where a reputation can mark a person for decades, when people speak of Bennie Greenwood (if they speak of her at all) it's as a naive schoolgirl who was sweettalked into an unfortunate situation.

24. "Pony Riders Reach Abilene," *Dallas Morning News*, and "Pony Express Lead Changes," *Fort Worth Star-Telegram*, both March 4, 1939.

25. "3 Riders Pass through Pecos," *Fort Worth Star-Telegram*, March 7, 1939.

26. "Riders Carry Electra Mail for 48 States," *Fort Worth Star-Telegram*, March 6, 1939.

27. "Texas Leads Derby; Riders Near El Paso," March 9, 1939, and "Pony Express Riders Cover Third of Way," March 10, 1939, both *Dallas Morning News*.

NOTES

28. "Sykes out of Pony Express," *Fort Worth Star-Telegram*, March 12, 1939.

29. "Davidson Leads Express Riders," *Oakland* (CA) *Tribune*, March 15, 1939.

30. "Pace-Setter Maintains Big Lead in Pony Race," *Dallas Morning News*, March 15, 1939.

31. "Pony Derby Leader Reaches California; Has 87-Mile Lead," *Dallas Morning News*, March 17, 1939.

32. "Saddle-Gall Derby," *Time*, April 17, 1939.

33. "Miss Justin to Assist in Celebration," *Nocona News*, March 17, 1939.

34. "Pony Express Leader Reaches Indio," *Oakland* (CA) *Tribune*, March 18, 1939; (No Headline), *Palm Springs* (CA) *Desert Sun*, March 20, 1939; "Pony Express Rider," *Madera* (CA) *Tribune*, March 24, 1939.

35. "Pony Express Riders Gallop through Arcadia," *Arcadia* (CA) *Tribune*, March 23, 1939.

36. Associated Press photo and Cates, "Rider Is in 24 Hours of His Goal," *Fort Worth Star-Telegram*, March 23, 1939; Reed, "End of Long Ride for Pony Express," *Electra Star*, March 23, 1939.

37. "Oakland Prepares Welcome for Matador Cowboy," *Big Spring Herald*, and "Father of Famed Mission Blesses Rider," *Fort Worth Star-Telegram*, both March 24, 1939.

38. My account of Davidson's arrival in Oakland and the Golden Gate Exposition is drawn from "Pony Express Winner Gets Riproarin' Welcome Here," March 24, 1939, and "Two More Pony Express Riders Arrive; Winner Gets Prize and Kisses," March 25, 1939, both *Oakland Tribune*. Also, the Associated Press and United Press accounts published in full or part in newspapers across the country on March 25, 1939.

39. "Pony Express Accuses Fair of Runaround," *Oakland Tribune*, March 28, 1939.

40. "C. of C. Manager Resigns," *Dallas Morning News*, April 15, 1939. Parton went directly to Mineral Wells, where the Mineral Wells Chamber of Commerce announced that Parton had been hired to run a "stagecoach express" from there to the New York World's Fair that summer. Plans included a caravan of stagecoaches (carrying mail and commemorative stamps), accompanied by a thirty-piece band and traveling show. "Chamber Plans 'Stage Express' to New York City," *Fort Worth Star-Telegram*, April 16, 1939.

41. "Pony Express Riders Finally Get to Fair," *Oakland Tribune*, March 29, 1939.

42. "Pony Express Pair Visit Here," *Los Angeles Times*, April 7, 1939.

43. When Enid returned to Texas, she left Shannon Davidson in Hollywood. Gene Autry offered him a small part in his next movie, *Colorado Sunset*. The young cowboy remained in Hollywood as an uncredited bit player and stock wrangler for two more movies before returning to Texas and enlisting in the U.S. Navy in 1942.

CHAPTER 8

1. "*Life* Visits Audie Murphy," *Life*, July 16, 1945

2. "Hunt County" and "Audie Leon Murphy," *Handbook of Texas Online*, https://www.tshaonline.org/handbook. There is some disagreement among sources as to the year of Audie's birth. The primary documents—census records, delayed birth certificate, army enlistment papers, and so forth—disagree on whether he was born in 1923, 1924, or

1925. Richard L. Rodgers, writing in the Audie Murphy Memorial Foundation quarterly newsletter, examines the evidence, interviews living relatives, makes some reasonable assumptions, and settles on 1925 as his birth year. I've adopted that conclusion throughout. See "When Was It? A Discussion of Audie's Birth Year," *AMRF Quarterly Newsletter*, June–September 2020, www.audiemurphy.com.

3. Audie Murphy, *To Hell and Back*, 6.

4. Murphy, *To Hell and Back*, 6; and "Cotton Culture," *Handbook of Texas Online*, https://www.tshaonline.org/handbook.

5. The cotton prices I quote come from auction prices for "middling" grade in Dallas, as published daily in the *Dallas Morning News* through the 1920s and 1930s.

6. Murphy, *To Hell and Back*, 7.

7. Murphy, *To Hell and Back*, 6.

8. In *To Hell and Back*, Audie conflates his uncles into a single character, a grandfather who, despite "a touch of the [poison] gas" during the war, regales Audie with his combat stories while working in the cotton fields. "If you want to fight," the grandpa says, "start fightin' those weeds" (see page 4).

9. Whiting, *American Hero*, 22.

10. Murphy, *To Hell and Back*, 6.

11. Murphy, *To Hell and Back*, 7.

12. Murphy, *To Hell and Back*, 7.

13. I've relied on Colonel Harold B. Simpson in writing about matters military. A decorated veteran and educator, Simpson is the author of *Audie Murphy, American*, but out of print now. Simpson conducted extensive interviews with Murphy family members and acquaintances as well as those who shared foxholes and patrols with Audie. *American Soldier* (and *Simpson Speaks on History* [Hillsboro, TX: Hill College Press, 1986]) comprise the plinth on which every later Audie Murphy biography rests.

14. "He Doesn't Want to Be a Star," *Saturday Evening Post*, April 18, 1953.

15. "A Soldier's Business," *Saturday Review*, March 26, 1949.

16. Murphy, *To Hell and Back*, 204.

17. Murphy, *To Hell and Back*, 220.

18. Simpson, *Simpson Speaks on History*, 4. In the end, Audie earned five of the seven awards for heroism that the United States gave in WWII. He didn't qualify for the Distinguished Flying Cross (no aerial combat) or the Soldier's Medal (given for heroism *not* involving actual conflict). After the liberation of France, he would receive the French Legion of Merit, its highest award for heroism.

19. Don Graham, *No Name on the Bullet: A Biography of Audie Murphy* (New York: Penguin, 1989), 88.

20. The quotations describing Murphy's actions on January 26, 1945, come from individual "Complete Description of Services Rendered" statements and Ware's "Certificate." See ARC Identifiers 299775 (Abramski), 299776 (Brawley), 299785 (Weispfenning), and 299784 (Ware) at U.S. National Archives and Records Administration.

21. Murphy, *To Hell and Back*, 241.

22. I've read and reread the battle action reports and Murphy's account of the events at the Holtzwihr forest, and I feel like I came to a clear understanding of the events of

January 26. But it wasn't until I saw the skirmish depicted on-screen in the movie, *To Hell and Back*, that I fully understood the danger Murphy faced. The distances, the terrain, the proximity of the enemies, and even the weather conditions shown in the movie made Murphey's actions seem more heroic. He played himself in the movie, of course, and reports at the time say he insisted that the movie represent the battle scenes—especially the January 26, 1945, encounter—in exacting, realistic detail.

23. Graham, *No Name on the Bullet*, 98. Audie wasn't entirely happy about the new assignment. In *To Hell and Back*, he describes several unauthorized trips to the front to support his old company.

24. Murphy, *To Hell and Back*, 273.

25. Murphy's original citation is Catalog #1985.0428.04, Armed Forces History, Division of History of Technology.

26. "Looks Like a Scout—But Little Audie Murphy of Texas Was a Holy Terror," *Abilene Reporter-News*, July 8, 1945.

27. "Home Front Support to Hasten Victory over Japs," *Dallas Morning News*, June 14, 1945.

CHAPTER 9

1. The biographical profile of McCarthy's pre–Shamrock Hotel years is compiled from Bryan Burrough, *The Big Rich: The Rise and Fall of the Greatest Texas Oil Fortunes* (Penguin, 2010); Wallace Davis, *Corduroy Road: The Story of Glenn H. McCarthy* (Houston, TX: Anson Jones Press, 1951); and James Presley, *Saga of Wealth: The Rise of Texas Oilmen* (New York: Putnam, 1978).

2. "Rich Texan Gambles against Film Slump," *Los Angeles Times*, August 22, 1948.

3. "Rice Couples Commit Matrimony," *The Thresher*, September 18, 1930.

4. Twenty years after Glenn and Faustine eloped, their eighteen-year-old daughter eloped with a self-described "poor boy," a friend from college. Just like his father-in-law, Glenn was furious. "Oil Man Fumes at Elopement," *Washington Post*, December 28, 1950.

5. Leon Jaworski, *Confession and Avoidance: A Memoir* (New York: Doubleday, 1979).

6. "McCarthy Well Set on Fire Once More with Crew Helpless," *Dallas Morning News*, April 24, 1936; and "King of the Wildcatters," *Time*, February 13, 1950.

7. Kirk Dooley and Eben Price, *Read My Lips: Classic Texas Political Quotes* (Lubbock: Texas Tech University Press, 1995).

8. "King of the Wildcatters," *Time*, February 13, 1950.

9. Davis, *Corduroy Road*.

10. "Interview with Glenn McCarthy," The Mike Wallace Interview Collection, Harry Ransom Center, University of Texas at Austin; and "Booming Houston," *Life*, October 21, 1946.

11. "Bendix Trophy Won by Mantz," *Dallas Morning News*, August 31, 1937; and "McCarthy Gives Oil Lease to Actress," *Daily Sun* (Baytown), September 23, 1948.

12. The referendum failed to pass, so McCarthy subdivided the property and made a bundle when he flipped the property to Frank Sharp, who developed it as Sharpstown. "New \$14,000,000 International Airport Slated to Do Much for Southwestern Area," *Southwestern* (Houston) *Times*, October 24, 1946.

13. "Pro Football 'World Series' Stymied Again; Bicker over Where Game Should Be Played," *Plain Dealer* (Cleveland, OH), July 9, 1949; and "Sixty Years Later, Shamrock Bowl One to Remember," *Houston Chronicle*, December 17, 2009.

14. "McCarthy Wants to Purchase Football Browns for Houston," January 16, 1950, and "That Man McCarthy Plans 180,000-Seat Covered Stadium," January 20, 1950, both *Washington* (DC) *Post*.

15. "Hotels: Luck of the Irish," *Time*, Monday, March 21, 1948.

16. "Public Invited to McCarthy Center Ceremonies Today," *Southwestern* (Houston) *Times*, March 21, 1946.

17. Half-page ad, *Southwestern* (Houston) *Times*, January 24, 1946.

18. "Rich Texan Gambles against Film Slump," *Los Angeles Times*, August 22, 1948.

19. The description of The Shamrock when it opened is mainly from "$21 Million Hotel Opens," *Life*, March 28, 1949; and Burrough, *The Big Rich*.

20. McCarthy never explained whether the club was named for his ancestral County Cork or the cork in a whiskey bottle.

21. "Celebrities Crowd Houston for Shamrock Hotel Opening," *Dallas Morning News*, March 17, 1949.

22. "Carrousel," *Los Angeles Times*, March 22, 1949.

BIBLIOGRAPHY

Alexander, Bob, and Donaly E. Brice. *Texas Rangers: Lives, Legend, and Legacy*. Denton: University of North Texas Press, 2022.

Banks, C. Stanley, and Grace Taylor McMillan. *The New Texas Reader*. San Antonio, TX: Naylor, 1961.

Beard, Tyler. *The Cowboy Boot Book*. Layton, UT: Peregrine Smith Books, 1992.

Benton, Minnie M. "The Portrait of a Boom Town: Burkburnett." North Texas State College, University of North Texas, 1952.

Boatright, Mody C., and Donald Day. *From Hell to Breakfast*. Austin: Texas Folk-Lore Society, 1943.

———. *And Horns on Toads*. Dallas, TX: Southern Methodist University Press, 1959.

Boss, David. *The First Fifty Years: A Celebration of the National Football League in Its Fiftieth Season*. New York: Simon & Schuster, 1974.

Boyce House: Public Speaker, Author, Newspaperman, Collector of Texas Lore. Association of Consumer Finance Companies, 1962.

Braden, G. B. "The Colberts and the Chickasaw Nation." *Tennessee Historical Quarterly*, 222–41.

Brief Biography of Murray (Alfalfa Bill): The Statesman and Sage of Oklahoma. Oklahoma City: McClean, 1929.

Brown, John Henry. *History of Texas from 1685 to 1892*. Austin, TX: Jenkins, 1970.

Brown, Norman D. *Hood, Bonnet, and Little Brown Jug: Texas Politics, 1921–1928*. College Station: Texas A&M University Press, 1984.

Bryant, Keith L. *Alfalfa Bill Murray*. Norman: University of Oklahoma Press, 1968.

Burrough, Bryan. *The Big Rich: The Rise and Fall of the Greatest Texas Oil Fortunes*. New York: Penguin, 2010.

Burrough, Bryan, Chris Tomlinson, and Jason Stanford. *Forget the Alamo: The Rise and Fall of an American Myth*. New York: Penguin, 2021.

"Business: Toll Bridges." *Time*, April 23, 1928.

Campbell, Randolph B. *Gone to Texas: A History of the Lone Star State*. New York: Oxford University Press, 2003.

Cantrell, Gregg, and Elizabeth Hayes Turner, eds. *Lone Star Pasts: Memory and History in Texas*. College Station: Texas A&M University Press, 2007.

Carnes, Mark C., and John A. Garraty. *American Destiny: Narrative of a Nation*. New York: Longman, 2003.

Cayleff, Susan E. *Babe: The Life and Legend of Babe Didrikson Zaharias*. Urbana: University of Illinois Press, 1996.

Cervantez, Brian. *Amon Carter: A Lone Star Life*. Norman: University of Oklahoma Press, 2019.

Cox, Mike. *Gunfights & Sites in Texas Ranger History*. Charleston, SC: History Press, 2015.

———. *Historic Photos of Texas Oil*. Nashville, TN: Turner, 2012.

———. *Texas Ranger Tales: Hard-Riding Stories from the Lone Star State*. Austin, TX: Lone Star Books, 2016.

———. *The Texas Rangers*. New York: Forge, 2008.

———. *Time of the Rangers: Texas Rangers from 1900 to the Present*. New York: Forge, 2009.

Cox, Patrick. *The First Texas News Barons*. Austin: University of Texas Press, 2005.

Cummins, Light Townsend, and Mary L. Scheer, eds. *Texas Identities: Moving beyond Myth, Memory, and Fallacy in Texas History*. Denton: University of North Texas Press, 2016.

Dean, John E. *How Myth Became History: Texas Exceptionalism in the Borderlands*. Tucson: University of Arizona Press, 2016.

DeLano, Sharon. *Texas Boots*. New York: Viking, 1981.

Dobie, J. Frank, et al., eds. *Texas Folklore Society, Coyote Wisdom*, vol. 14, Dallas, TX: Southern Methodist University Press, 1938.

Epstein, Karen V. "Social Perceptions of Four Prominent Female Athletes during the 20th Century in the United States." East Stroudsburg, PA: East Stroudsburg State College, 1982.

Farman, Irvin. *Standard of the West: The Justin Story*. Fort Worth: Texas Christian University Press, 1996.

Flemmons, Jerry. *Amon: The Texan Who Played Cowboy for America*. Lubbock: Texas Tech University Press, 2005.

Foreman, Grant. "The California Overland Mail Route Through Oklahoma." *Chronicles of Oklahoma*, 1931, 300–313.

———. *Down the Texas Road: Historic Places along Highway 69 through Oklahoma*. Norman: University of Oklahoma Press, 1936.

Fossey, W. Richard. "The Red River Bridge Conflict: A Minor Skirmish in the War against Depression." *Red River Valley Historical Review* 1, no. 3 (1974): 233.

Freedman, Russell. *Babe Didrikson Zaharias: The Making of a Champion*. Boston: Houghton Mifflin Harcourt, 1999.

Fuermann, George. *Reluctant Empire: The Mind of Texas*. New York: Doubleday, 1957.

The Games of the Xth Olympiad, Los Angeles 1932: Official Report. Xth Olympiad Committee of the Games of Los Angeles, 1933.

Goodman, Murray, and Leonard Lewin, eds. *My Greatest Day in Football*. New York: Bantam, 1949.

Graham, Don. *Cowboys and Cadillacs: How Hollywood Looks at Texas*. Austin: Texas Monthly Press, 1983.

———. *No Name on the Bullet: A Biography of Audie Murphy*. New York: Penguin, 1989.

———. *State Fare: An Irreverent Guide to Texas Movies*. Fort Worth: Texas Christian University Press, 2008.

Greene, A. C. *900 Miles on the Butterfield Trail*. Denton: University of North Texas Press, 1994.

———. *A Personal Country*. Denton: University of North Texas Press, 1998.

———. *The Santa Claus Bank Robbery*. Denton: University of North Texas Press, 2005.

Haile, Bartee. *Texas Boomtowns: A History of Blood and Oil*. Charleston, SC: History Press, 2015.

Haley, James L. *Texas: From Spindletop through World War II*. New York: St. Martin's, 1993.

———. *The Handy Texas Answer Book*. Detroit, MI: Visible Ink Press, 2018.

The Handbook of Texas Online. Texas State Historical Association, tshaonline.org/handbook/online.

Harrigan, Stephen. *Big Wonderful Thing: A History of Texas*. Austin: University of Texas Press, 2019.

Harris, Charles H., and Louis R. Sadler. *The Texas Rangers in Transition: From Gunfighters to Criminal Investigators, 1921–1935*. Norman: University of Oklahoma Press, 2019.

Hazel, Michael V. *Dallas Reconsidered: Essays in Local History*. Dallas, TX: Three Forks Press, 1995.

Henry, O. *Heart of the West*. New York: Barnes & Noble, 2009.

Himmelberg, Robert F. *The Great Depression and the New Deal*. Westport, CT: Greenwood Press, 2001.

Holley, Joe. *Slingin' Sam: The Life and Times of the Greatest Quarterback Ever to Play the Game*. Austin: University of Texas Press, 2012.

Houry, Cecile. "American Women and the Modern Summer Olympic Games: A Story of Obstacles and Struggles for Participation and Equality," 2011, https://scholarship.miami.edu/esploro/outputs/doctoral/American-Women-and-the-Modern-Summer/991031447096702976.

House, Boyce. *As I Was Saying*. San Antonio, TX: Naylor, 1957.

———. *Cowtown Columnist*. San Antonio, TX: Naylor, 1946.

———. *Cub Reporter: Being Mainly about Mr. Mooney and the Commercial Appeal*. Dallas, TX: Hightower Press, 1947.

———. "In a Little Town, Long Ago." *Arkansas Historical Quarterly* 19, no. 2 (1960): 151–68, doi:10.2307/40025497.

———. "Memphis Memories of 50 Years Ago." *West Tennessee Historical Society Papers* 14 (1960): 103–12.

———. *Oil Boom: The Story of Spindletop, Burkburnett, Mexia, Smackover, Desdemona, and Ranger*. Caldwell, ID: Caxton Printers, 1941.

———. *Oil Field Fury*. San Antonio, TX: Naylor, 1954.

———. "Rip-Roaring Days in the Oil Fields." *Southwest Review* 30, no. 4 (1945): 324–28.

———. *Roaring Ranger: The World's Biggest Boom*. San Antonio, TX: Naylor, 1951.

———. "Santa Claus in Deadly Hold-Up." *Startling Detective Adventures*, March 1930, 14–18.

———. *Were You in Ranger?* Dallas, TX: Tardy, 1935.

Howard, James. *Big D Is for Dallas: Chapters in the Twentieth-Century History of Dallas.* Austin, TX: University Cooperative Society, 1957.

Hunt, Donna. "Judge Jake Loy." *Texoma Living,* June 1, 2007, 3.

Johnson, William, and Nancy P. Williamson. *Whatta-Gal: The Babe Didrikson Story.* New York: Little, Brown, 1975.

Jones, Jan. *Billy Rose Presents . . . Casa Mañana.* Ft. Worth: Texas Christian University Press, 1999.

Kelley, Michael G. "Most Desperate People: The Genesis of Texas Exceptionalism" (PhD diss., Georgia State University, 2011), doi: https://doi.org/10.57709/1768845.

Kramer, Paul. *The Providential History of the State of Texas.* Carrollton, TX: Paul Kramer, 2006.

Lee, James Ward. *Adventures with a Texas Humanist.* Fort Worth: Texas Christian University Press, 2004.

Leighton, Isabel, ed. *The Aspirin Age: 1919 to 1941.* New York: Simon & Schuster, 1949.

Lincecum, Jerry Bryan. *Telling Our Stories: Grayson County Reminiscences: The First 150 Years, 1846–1996.* Sherman, TX: Big Barn Press, 1996.

Lyon, Thomas J. *Updating the Literary West.* Ft. Worth: Texas Christian University Press, 1997.

Marcus, Stanley. *Minding the Store.* Denton: University of North Texas Press, 2001.

McCaslin, Richard B. *Texas Ranger Captain William L. Wright.* Denton: University of North Texas Press, 2021.

McKay, Seth Shepard, and Odie B. Faulk. *Texas after Spindletop, 1901–1965.* Austin, TX: Steck-Vaughn, 1965.

Moore, Hank. *Houston Legends: History and Heritage of Dynamic Global Capitol: Back Stories of Companies, Community Leaders & Innovators in Energy, Medicine, Space, Technology and Entrepreneurship.* Morgan James Publishing, 2015.

Mott, Frank L. *American Journalism: A History, 1690–1960* (New York: Macmillan, 1971.

———. *A History of American Magazines,* vols. 3, 4. UMI, 1994.

Murphy, Audie. *To Hell and Back.* New York: Picador, 2002.

National Football League Properties, Inc. *The First Fifty Years: A Celebration of the National Football League in its Fiftieth Season.* New York: Simon & Schuster, 1969.

Nieman, Robert. "'Twentieth Century Shining Star': William Warren Sterling." *Texas Ranger Dispatch,* 2004, 8–9.

Olien, Roger M., and Diana D. Olien. *Wildcatters: Texas Independent Oilmen.* Austin: Texas Monthly Press, 1984.

Olmstead, Jacob W. "From Old South to Modern West: Fort Worth's Celebration of the Texas State Centennial and the Shaping of an Urban Identity and Image." Provo, UT: Brigham Young University, 2002.

———. *The Frontier Centennial: Fort Worth & the New West.* Lubbock: Texas Tech University Press, 2021.

"An Olympian's Oral History: Evelyne Hall Adams, 1932 Olympic Games, Track & Field." LA84 Foundation Digital Collection, https://digital.la84.org/digital/collection/p17103coll11/id/41/rec/2.

BIBLIOGRAPHY

"An Olympian's Oral History: Jean Shiley Newhouse, 1928 & 1932 Olympic Games, Track & Field." LA84 Foundation Digital Collection, https://digital.la84.org/digital/collection/p17103coll11/id/225/rec/50.

Ormsby, Waterman Lilly, and Lyle Henry Wright. *The Butterfield Overland Mail*. San Marino, CA: Huntington Library Press, 1942.

Peyton, Green. *The Face of Texas: A Survey in Words and Pictures*. New York: Bonanza Books, 1966.

Piacentino, Edward J. *The Enduring Legacy of Old Southwest Humor*. Baton Rouge: Louisiana State University Press, 2006.

Pilkington, Tom. *State of Mind: Texas Literature and Culture*. College Station: Texas A&M University Press, 1998.

Presley, James. *Saga of Wealth: The Rise of Texas Oilmen*. New York: Putnam, 1978.

Procter, Ben H. *Just One Riot: Episodes of Texas Rangers in the 20th Century*. Fort Worth, TX: Eakin Press, 2000.

Ragsdale, Kenneth Baxter. *The Year America Discovered Texas: Centennial '36*. College Station: Texas A&M University Press, 1987.

Ratliff, Harold V. *Towering Texans: Sport Sagas of the Lone Star State*. San Antonio, TX: Naylor, 1950.

Robinson, Charles M. *Texas and the Mexican War: A History and a Guide*. Austin: Texas State Historical Association, 2004.

Rogers, Alfred. *Ranger*. Mt. Pleasant, SC: Arcadia, 2010.

Rogers, John William. *The Lusty Texans of Dallas*. Whitefish, MT: Kessinger Publishing, 2011.

Rosenfield, John, and Jack Patton. *Texas History Movies*. Dallas, TX: Turner, 1943.

Samuels, Peter. "Texas Has a Rich History of Private Toll Concessions." *TollRoadsNews*, April 19, 2007.

Schraff, Anne E., and Barbara Silberdick Feinberg. *The Great Depression and the New Deal: America's Economic Collapse and Recovery*. New York: Watts, 1990.

Simpson, Harold B. *Audie Murphy: American Soldier*. Hillsboro, TX: Alcor, 1982.

———. *Simpson Speaks on History*. Hillsboro, TX: Hill College Press, 1986.

Smith, David A. *Price of Valor: The Life of Audie Murphy, America's Most Decorated Hero of World War II*. Washington, DC: Regnery History, 2016.

Smith, Jerrie Marcus. *A Girl Named Carrie: The Visionary Who Created Neiman Marcus and Set the Standard for Fashion*. Denton: University of North Texas Press, 2021.

Smyth, J. E. *Edna Ferber's Hollywood: American Fictions of Gender, Race, and History*. Austin: University of Texas Press, 2011.

———. *Reconstructing American Historical Cinema from Cimarron to Citizen Kane*. Lexington: University Press of Kentucky, 2009.

Steinbeck, John. *Travels with Charley: In Search of America*. New York: Viking, 1962.

Sterling, Ross S., and Edward W. Kilman. *Ross Sterling, Texan: A Memoir by the Founder of Humble Oil and Refining Company*. Austin: University of Texas Press, 2007.

Sterling, William Warren. *Trails and Trials of a Texas Ranger*. Norman: University of Oklahoma Press, 1959.

Swift, Earl. *The Big Roads: The Untold Story of the Engineers, Visionaries, and Trailblazers Who Created the American Superhighways*. Boston: Houghton Mifflin Harcourt, 2011.

Thompson, Frank T. *The Alamo: A Cultural History*. New York: Taylor Trade, 2001.

Tolbert, Frank X. *An Informal History of Texas: From Cabeza de Vaca to Temple Houston*. New York: Harper & Bros., 1961.

Tolbert, Frank X. *Neiman-Marcus, Texas: The Story of the Proud Dallas Store*. New York: Holt, 1953.

Untiedt, Kenneth L. *Folklore in Motion: Texas Travel Lore*. Denton: University of North Texas Press, 2007.

Utley, Robert M. *Lone Star Lawmen: The Second Century of the Texas Rangers*. New York: Berkley, 2007.

Van Natta, Don. *Wonder Girl: The Magnificent Sporting Life of Babe Didrikson Zaharias*. New York: Back Bay Books/Little, Brown, 2013.

Variety Film Reviews 1907–1980: A Sixteen Volume Set, Including an Index to Titles. Vol. 6, New York: Garland Publishing, 1983.

Watkins, T. H. *The Hungry Years: A Narrative History of the Great Depression in America*. New York: Holt, 1999.

Weaver, Bobby D. *Oilfield Trash: Life and Labor in the Oil Patch*. College Station: Texas A&M University Press, 2013.

Weber, David J. *The Spanish Frontier in North America*. New Haven, CT: Yale University Press, 2009.

Wecter, Dixon. *The Age of the Great Depression, 1929–1941*. New York: MacMillan, 1948.

Welch, June Rayfield. *All Hail the Mighty State!* Waco: Texian Press, 1979.

———. *O Ye Legendary Texas Horned Frog*. Dallas, TX: Yellow Rose, 1993.

Whiting, Charles. *American Hero: The Life and Death of Audie Murphy*. Manchester, UK: Eskdale, 2000.

Williams, Rusty. *The Red River Bridge War: A Texas-Oklahoma Border Battle*. College Station: Texas A&M University Press, 2016.

Wright, Lawrence. *God Save Texas: A Journey into the Soul of the Lone Star State*. New York: Knopf, 2019.

Wright, Muriel H. "The Butterfield Overland Mail One Hundred Years Ago." *Chronicles of Oklahoma*, 1957, 55–71.

———. "Historic Places on The Old Stage Line from Fort Smith to Red River." *Chronicles of Oklahoma*, 1931, 798–814.

Wuthnow, Robert. *Rough Country: How Texas Became America's Most Powerful Bible-Belt State*. Princeton, NJ: Princeton University Press, 2016.

Yearbook of the United States Department of Agriculture, 1901–1919. Washington, DC: U.S. Government Printing Office, 1921.

Zaharias, Babe Didrikson. *This Life I've Led: My Autobiography*. New York: Barnes, 1955.

INDEX

Abilene, TX, 84, 126–27

Abramski, Private First Class Anthony, 144–45

Allred, Gov. James, 69, 72

Amherst College, vii, xiv, 104

Arizona, 118, 122, 128, 129, 130

Barrett, Charles, 30–31

Baugh, Samuel A. "Slingin' Sam," 81–82, 96, 97; background of, 82–84; baseball play by, 82, 84, 89–90; college football play by, 84–88; professional football play by, 90–92, 94–96

Beaumont Miss Royal Purples, 40, 41, 42, 44. *See also* Zaharias, "Babe" Didrikson

Beaumont, TX, 38, 39, 43, 44, 151, 153

Boston Braves/Redskins. *See* Washington Redskins

Brawley, Sergeant Elmer C., 144–45

Brownwood TX, 3, 137

Carter, Amon G., 14, 76, 77, 124–25; background of, 65–67; Centennial planning by, 68, 70–71, 74–75; competition with Dallas by, 64; participation in football by, 86, 88–89

Casa Manana, 74, 77–78, 173n40

Cates, George, 129, 130

Chicago Bears, 90–91; "Ice Bowl" game by, 81–82, 91–92, 94–95

Chicago Century of Progress Exposition, 64, 66

Chicago, IL, 12, 24, 37, 47–48, 101, 162

Cisco, TX, 7, 8, 23, 167nn14–16

Colbert, Benjamin F., 16, 17, 168n3

Comanche Indians, x, 21–22, 168n3

Coolidge, President Calvin "Silent Cal," 2, 12

Dallas TX, xiv, 8, 28, 37, 41, 43, 47, 50, 59–61, 71, 86, 87, 89, 127, 136; benefits of Centennial to, 78–79; Centennial site in, 64, 67, 72–74; comparative size of, vii, ix, xiv, 59; efforts to secure Centennial for, 61–63; Neiman Marcus located in, 99–101, 103–5, 108–11, 114; rivalry with Fort Worth by, 64–65, 68; stylish women of, 101, 107

Davidson, Shannon, 125, 127, 128–29, 130–32, 133–34

Denison TX, 16, 28, 29, 34; effect of bridge war on, 24, 25, 27, 33

Didrikson, Mildrid "Babe." *See* Zaharias, "Babe"

Dobie, J. Frank, viii, xiii

Durant, OK, 16, 31

Durante, Jimmy, 71, 77

Eastland County, TX, viii, 5, 9, 12, 13, 107; Santa Claus bank robbery in, 7–8

Eastland TX, 2, 4, 5–7, 9–13, 14

El Paso, TX, 3, 126, 127, 128

Employers Casualty Insurance Company, 41, 42, 43, 44, 45, 47, 48

Farmersville, TX

Fort Worth Frontier Fiesta, 78, 87

Fort Worth, TX, 14, 20, 28, 61, 71, 88, 90, 121; benefits of Frontier Centennial to, 78–79; comparative size of, xiv, 59; efforts to secure Centennial for, 62; football in, 84, 86, 87; Justin Boots located in, 119–20, 124; newspapers in, 65–67; planning for Frontier Centennial by, 68, 70, 75, 76–77; rivalry with Dallas by, 64, 72, 74

Frontier Centennial Exposition (Fort Worth), 68, 68, 87; attractions at, 75, 76–77; grounds of, 71; publicity for, 71–72, 74. *See also* Casa Manana. *See also* Fort Worth, TX

Galveston, TX, ix, 21, 155

Golden Gate International Exposition, 122, 123, 129, 132, 134

Gonzaulas, "Lone Wolf," 8

Great Depression (1930s), xv, 18, 19, 25, 43, 58, 61, 78, 83, 197, 120, 137, 138, 153

Greenwood, Bonnie, 125, 126, 177n23

Hall, Evelyne, 49, 50, 52

Harris, Woodrow, 167n14

Hollywood (movie capital), xii, xiv, 22, 69, 71, 77, 133–34, 157, 159, 160, 161

Holtzwihr, (Battle of), 143–46

Horned Frog (Toad), viii, 1, 9–10, 11, 12, 157. *See also* Old Rip

House, Boyce, xiii, 2–6, 8–14

Houston, Sam, ix, 74

Houston, TX, 18, 30, 32, 34, 41–42, 147; comparative size of, ix, xiv, 59; efforts to secure Centennial for, 58, 59, 61, 62–63; growth of, 158; Glenn McCarthy's residence in, 151, 152, 154, 156–57, 160; Shamrock Hotel located in, 160, 161, 163

Hudson, Shorty, 126, 129

Humble Oil and Refining, 85, 154

Hunt County TX, 136–37, 139, 141, 148

"Ice Bowl" football game. *See* Chicago Bears

Indian Territory, 15, 16, 60

Jefferson TX, ix, 137

Justin Family, 118–19, 124, 176n3

Justin, Enid, 117–18, 119–22, 124–27, 129, 130, 132, 133–34, 176n2; childhood of, 118–19

Kerley, King, 129, 139, 132

Life Magazine, 2, 115, 135, 136, 148, 149, 156, 158

Loy, Jacob J. "Jake," 27–29, 30–31, 32, 33

Marcus, Edward, 102, 111

Marcus, Harold Stanley, 99–100, 102, 105–15; childhood of, 102, 104; college experiences of, 104–5

Marcus, Herbert, Sr., 100, 102–6, 110, 113

Marshall, George P., 78, 89–90, 92–94, 97

Matador TX, 131, 132

Mathis, Slim, 129, 130

McCarthy, Glenn Herbert, 152, 154, 157; background of, 151–52; civic projects of, 156–57, 158–59; home life of, 152–53, 157; Shamrock Hotel opening by, 159–61, 161–63; wildcatting by, 154–56. *See also* Houston, TX

McCombs, Melvin J., 41–42, 43, 44, 45–47, 49

Mexico, ix, xiii, 21, 22, 57, 58; Mexican War, 21

Meyer, Leo R. "Dutch," 83–88, 90

Murphy, Audie Leon, 140–41, 149; boyhood of, 136–39; Congressional Medal of Honor earned by, 136, 143, 146–47; medals awarded to, 143, 146–47; return home of, 135–36, 148; time in combat of, 142–46; *To Hell and Back,* written by, 138, 142, 143

Murphy, Corinne, 139, 140

Murray, Governor William H. Murray, 19–20, 24, 25, 27–28, 30, 31, 32–33

National Football League (NFL), 81, 82, 90, 93–94, 96, 97, 158

Neal, Margie E., 58–59, 172n3

Neiman Marcus, 102–3, 105–7, 110–13; custom mannequins for, 99, 110, 111, 112, 114; founding of, 100–101; International Fashion Exposition held by, 99, 109–15; national publicity for, 107–8, 114–15; woman typical of, 105, 106, 110, 112–13, 114, 115

Neiman, Abraham "Al," 100, 102–3, 105, 106

Neiman, Carrie Marcus, 100–3, 105, 106

New Mexico, 3, 118, 122, 123, 128

New York, NY, 68, 71, 90, 93, 104; fashion influence of, 107, 109, 111, 113, 114–15

New York Times, 2, 48, 73, 75

Nocona Boot Company, 118, 120, 122, 124–25, 133–34, 176n9

Nocona Chamber of Commerce, 121, 123, 125, 129, 133

Nocona, TX, 119, 121–22, 128, 129, 133, 134, 176n2; race begins in, 117–18, 123–25

Oklahoma, 15, 17, 22, 24–28, 31, 33, 85, 120, 122, 125; bridge war affects, 18, 19, 20

Oklahoma, Hwy. Dept, 17, 19, 20, 25, 32

Oklahoma, Nat. Guard, 30–32

Old Rip, viii, 11, 12, 14

Parton, L. A., 125, 129, 130, 133, 178n40; background of, 120–21; race organized by, 121–23, 126

Ranger TX, 5

Red River, x, 15, 17, 19, 23, 27, 30–32, 34, 118, 126; bridges across, 16, 19, 23, 30, 32, 34–35

Red River Bridge Company, 16–20, 28, 32

Red River Bridge War, 20, 30, 32

Reed, Lige Jr., 125, 127, 128, 129, 130

Republic of Texas, 9, 20–21

Rice Institute (University), 152, 153, 158

Rice Institute (University), football team, 85, 152

Rice, Grantland, 37, 48, 51, 52, 54, 55

Rogers, Will, 22, 124, 125

Rose Bowl, 69, 86

Rose, W. S. "Billy," 70–72, 74–76, 77–78, 89

Salzburg, Germany, 146–47

San Antonio, 1, 21, 64, 109, 147; comparative size of, ix, xiv, 59; efforts to secure Centennial for, 58, 61–63

Santa Claus Bank Robbery, 7–9, 14, 23

Saturday Evening Post, 2, 115, 175n8

Sherman, TX, 27, 34

Shiley, Jean, 53–54

Sinclair Oil Company, 153–54

Southern Methodist University, 10, 69, 86, 87

Southwest Football Conference (SWC), 85, 87, 88

Spindletop, 5, 107, 114

Sterling, Ross S., 17–18, 25, 26, 27, 28, 32, 34; reaction to Gov. Murray by, 24, 25, 28; bridge contract signed by, 18, 26

Sterling, W. W., 20, 24, 28, 30, 31, 32, 34

Sweetwater, TX, 83, 84, 90, 94

"Sweetwater Stringbean," 88, 96

Sykes, T. J. "Tolly," 125, 126, 127, 128

Texas, State of; boots of, 118–20, 133–34; fashion of, 101, 108, 110, 115; independence of, viii, ix, xiii, 57, 58, 75; myth–history surrounding, viii–xiv, 73; New Texas view of, vii–viii, xiv; oil discoveries in, viii, 5, 66, 107, 120, 124, 156, 163; Old Texas view of, vii, xiii, xiv

Texas A&M University, 42, 152

Texas Centennial Exposition, 108, 121; choosing site for, 59–63; description of, 72–74; financing the, 67; legislation establishing, 58–59; publicity for, 69–70, 78

Texas Christian University, 14, 69, 84, 88

Texas Christian University, Horned Frogs, 69, 84, 85, 86–88, 89–90, 96

Texas Highway Dept., 79

Texas Hwy. Commission, 17

Texas Rangers, x, 8, 20–23, 23, 24–26, 28–31, 33–34, 35, 96, 121

Third Infantry Division, Fifth U.S. Army, 141, 143, 146

Thornton, R. L. "Bob," 59; background of, 59–61; Centennial bidding by, 61–63, 67–69, 7; Centennial promotion by, 70

To Hell and Back. See Murphy, Audie Leon

Tom Hickman, 8, 20, 22–35

Uselton, Chris, 127, 128–29, 130–31

Vogue, 107, 108, 114

Ware, Lieutenant Colonel Keith, 143, 145

Washington Redskins, 81–82, 89, 93–96

Weispfenning, Lieutenant Walter W., 143–44

Wichita Falls TX, 125–26

Wood, Ernest, 9

Wood, Mrs. Henry, 47–48, 50

Wood, Will, 12–13

Zaharias, "Babe" Didrikson, 37, 55, 170n1; family life, 38–40; Golden Cyclones team membership of, 43–45; high school basketball participation by, 40–42; Olympic competition by, 50–54 ; track competition by 37, 45–50

ABOUT THE AUTHOR

Writer-historian Rusty Williams is the author of *Red River Bridge War: A Texas-Oklahoma Border Battle* (2016), which won the Oklahoma Book Award and was named the Outstanding Book on Oklahoma History of 2016 by the Oklahoma Historical Society. Williams is also the author of *My Old Confederate Home: A Respectable Place for Civil War Veterans* (2011). He regularly speaks to historical societies, book groups, and cultural gatherings. Williams contributes articles to historical magazines and journals.